Google™ Semantic Search

Search Engine Optimization (SEO) Techniques
That Get Your Company More Traffic, Increase Brand Impact,
and Amplify Your Online Presence

DAVID AMERLAND

que®

800 East 96th Street,
Indianapolis, Indiana 46240 USA

Google™ Semantic Search

ISBN-13: 978-0-7897-5134-8

ISBN-10: 0-7897-5134-8

Library of Congress Control Number: 2013937136

Printed in the United States of America

First Printing: July 2013

Trademarks

Warning and Disclaimer

Bulk Sales

Que Publishing offers excellent discounts on this book when ordered in quantity for bulk purchases or special sales. For more information, please contact

U.S. Corporate and Government Sales

1-800-382-3419

corpsales@pearsontechgroup.com

For sales outside of the U.S., please contact

International Sales

international@pearson.com

CONTENTS AT A GLANCE

TABLE OF CONTENTS

About the Author

David Amerland's involvement with the Web goes back to the days when the number of websites in existence could fit in a printed 80-page directory and SEO consisted of keyword stuffing and pixel-wide hidden text.

Since those less enlightened days he has worked with blue-chip multinationals and individual entrepreneurs alike helping them craft SEO and social media marketing strategies that work with their internal cultures and deliver value to their target audience.

He writes for *Forbes, HP UK, Social Media Today,* and blogs on his own website, HelpmySEO.com. When he is not writing or surfing the Web he spends time giving speeches on how social media is changing everything.

Dedication

This book, like every other, is for N. For me she is meaning enough. But I would also like to add a second N, also female, with pointy ears and a tail. Her company during the small hours of the night, when I write best, made the world feel a lot friendlier. To you both, in different ways, I offer gratitude.

Acknowledgments

No book is ever the work of one man. This one is no exception. The comment on content quality and content management and its impact on semantic search, in Chapter 6, is courtesy of Sergey Adrianov, CEO of www.asmartsolutions.ca, who was brave enough to allow me to use it. The chart on Google Search and its relationship to Google products and services, in the same chapter, is used with the kind permission of Bob Barker of Frontiercoaching (www.frontiercoaching.com) and Thomas Power, both of whom have thoughts and ideas on how the digital domain is evolving that frequently kept me up, thinking.

This is the first book I put to paper since Google+ became part of my life. As a result I owe a huge thanks to all those who I shared snippets of my thoughts with and who were kind enough to provide feedback or add their own ideas. Of a crowd that has now grown way too big to mention fully I need to single out Jeff Jockisch for helping me refine my insights on identity and trust, Gideon Rosenblatt whose Google+ Community provided the forum for some interesting ideas on the impact of Authorship on ranking in search, Mark Traphagen for indefatigably working to keep everyone on the straight and narrow on the subject of Authorship, Bill Slawski who, as an SEO, is the most singularly focused man I know on Google's patents and what they mean, Aaron Bradley whose knowledge of semantic search is exemplary, J.C. Kendall who exemplifies the kind of SEO ethic the industry can use more of, Dan Petrovic whose frequent SEO experiments clarified my own ideas, Lee Smallwood of NOD3X who generously provided data visualizations that drove the point home, and many others I have never met except online who have humbled me with their generosity, help, brilliance, and attention to detail. All of you, collectively, I cannot ever thank enough.

Thanks needs to go to Katherine Bull, senior acquisitions editor extraordinaire, who never pushed even when I knew she had to; to development editor, Amber Avines, whose first reading of this manuscript became invaluable; project editor, Andy Beaster, without whom I am sure files would have gone missing; and to the editing team at Pearson who made sure that my words made sense. Last but not least my thanks goes to AJ Kohn, SEO thinker and doer, for making sure that my flights of fancy when I wrote this book stayed grounded in reality. To him, I owe a very special thanks.

While all these eyes and minds went into creating the attributes of this book, its faults, such as they may be found, lie squarely with me.

We Want to Hear from You!

As the reader of this book, *you* are our most important critic and commentator. We value your opinion and want to know what we're doing right, what we could do better, what areas you'd like to see us publish in, and any other words of wisdom you're willing to pass our way.

We welcome your comments. You can email or write to let me know what you did or didn't like about this book—as well as what we can do to make our books better.

Please note that I cannot help you with technical problems related to the topic of this book.

When you write, please be sure to include this book's title and author as well as your name, email address, and phone number. I will carefully review your comments and share them with the author and editors who worked on the book.

Email: feedback@quepublishing.com

Mail: Que Publishing
           ATTN: Reader Feedback
           800 East 96th Street
           Indianapolis, IN 46240 USA

Reader Services

Visit our website and register this book at quepublishing.com/register for convenient access to any updates, downloads, or errata that might be available for this book.

Introduction

Search is changing. This is not new of course. From a certain perspective it has been on a trajectory of change since day one. But the arc of that trajectory has acquired, now, a steeper angle and a greater velocity to match the Web.

In truth search can no more be considered independent of the Web than the Web can work without search. This symbiotic relationship brings forth all sorts of issues because it becomes part of a traditional push and pull where the Web, represented by those who actively work in it, wants to push all the wrong things, while search wants to pull in everything.

When everything is pulled into the Web the struggle changes from one of indexing information to one of classifying it correctly. Because the Web grows at such a prodigious rate, any kind of classification has to be machine driven and scalable, and there are only two possible ways this can happen: A, with human assistance, and, B, without.

And just like that we go from the realm of Markov chains and Boolean algorithms to the ever-shifting area of ethics and the willingness to do "right" or "wrong." It is a given that the moment something can be deconstructed and the way it works can be understood, people try to optimize its efficiency by gaming it.

This is exactly what happened with search. As search half-enlisted human help in understanding how the data it was indexing should be classified, it created an entire industry based around the techniques necessary to game it.

As search engines fought back with ever more sophisticated ways of countermanding our attempts to game the algorithms and gain greater visibility on the Web, the push and pull between "us" and "them" intensified. Each cycle of search engine updates would bring "pain" in terms of lost visibility that would have to be countermanded by finding fresh ways to game search and so on, and on, and on.

Semantic search holds the premise, and the promise, that this way of carrying on has come to an end. The best way to think of semantic search is like a search light that picks up all the different data nodes of the Web and follows them around creating a picture of how they link up, who they belong to, who created them, what else they created, who they are, who they were, and what they do.

At its most basic level semantic search applies meaning to the connections between the different data nodes of the Web in ways that allow a clearer understanding of them than we have ever had to date. This is a game changer. The Web is made of data. Data is governed by the concepts of volume, velocity, variety, and veracity, and the moment we find a way to deal with these four concepts in an entirely satisfactory way we will have solved the problem of search.

At the moment we haven't. The new dynamic that is growing out of the application of semantic search revolves around these four concepts and the balance between any two of them is far from settled, never mind all four. The moment the question of how to index the massive volume of data that is being generated every minute is solved, the issue of how to classify it in a way that meets requirements of timing becomes critical. When the speed of classification and prioritization (velocity) is addressed, the wealth of variety of content is a problem.

When all three of these are in the bag and the problem of quality in the search results has finally been solved, the question of provenance and trust (veracity) raises its ugly head. And then, just like that, each of the other three concepts becomes problematic again; for how do you verify data that's flooding in at such a prodigious rate, rate it quickly, and successfully deal with all its variations?

The answer lies in incremental gains. Semantic search, unlike anything we had in the past, has ways of caching the attributes it calculates so that data nodes uncovered by its spotlight do not go back in darkness once the spotlight leaves them, waiting to be uncovered again.

This way it learns. Becomes smarter, faster, less fallible, more trustworthy. It also becomes harder to game.

This book is about semantic search—what it is, how it works, and what you can do now to benefit from it. I focused predominantly on Google in writing it for three reasons. First, Google has made significant inroads in semantic indexing in search. Second, the Google+ social network plays a key role in helping a website's online visibility and to discount it is to miss a huge opportunity in search. And third, Google is the world's dominant search engine, with 95% of the global mobile search market and more than 80% of the global desktop search market. Not focusing on it makes no business sense.

In many ways semantic search takes us back to the golden days of the Web when in terms of working online anything was possible as long as you had passion, belief in yourself, and energy to work at it.

That we are there again, I find exciting. I hope this book becomes your guide in your digital journey, but more than that I hope it becomes the springboard you need to make your work leave its mark on the world, digital or otherwise.

David Amerland,

Manchester, 2013

What Is Semantic Search?

Search is the means through which we navigate the Web. If your business is not visible in search it is difficult for it to be found by your customers. Search, above all else, is marketing, and it is undergoing a massive change.

In this chapter we discuss just what is new in Google's search, why the change has happened, and how it will affect your business in just about every way you can imagine. The chapter provides a checklist of everything you need to do to take advantage of the coming changes, and each section of this chapter helps you understand what you need to do to make the best use of Google's semantic search.

The Shift to Semantic Search

These days when I type a search query in Google's box I get the uncanny feeling that there is an intelligence on the other side of the screen giving me the answers. It was not always this way, and the intelligence that I sense today is the result of one of the most ground breaking developments in the field of search technology that has ever been achieved. Of course, like cell phones and 3-D TV, the concept is not new, and it almost did not happen.

It is inevitable that a book about semantic search is going to start with the obvious question of what semantic search really is. The answer can get pretty technical and involved, and it can include mathematical concepts and even some philosophical ones (as they apply to mathematics), but this is not the place for technicalities that simply satisfy the curiosity. The explanations I give about semantic search, throughout the book, are somewhat circumscribed, but they contain everything you need to know that will help you understand it better.

I am a firm believer that knowledge is power but only if it leads to comprehension. So, if at times I gloss over technical details and make semantic search sound a little oversimplified, it's because I am keen to get to the reason you're reading this book: to find out what you need to do to help your business achieve greater visibility on the Web.

To compensate for the simplification I have at the back of the book supplied a full bibliography and academic references, most of which are freely available on the Web and can provide you with many a happy evening reading hour. So, without further ado let's check out what semantic search is and why it is such a big deal in our digital world.

"Semantic" is a Greek word that means "meaning," and the field of Semantics busies itself with the study of the meaning of words and the orthology of logic. In search on the Web, semantic search marks the transition from a "dumb" search of single web pages that have a probabilistic value of containing the information we are looking for to an intelligent search that delivers real answers or leads us to the very answer we are looking for on a web page that has nothing to do with the search query we used and therefore would not have come up in the traditional keyword-activated results of the past.

Semantic search, as a concept, has been around since Tim Berners-Lee, the man who is frequently called the father of the Internet, wrote an article about it in 2001 in *Scientific American*. There he explained that the essence of semantic search is the use of mathematics to get rid of the guesswork and approximation used in search today and introduce a clear understanding of what words mean and how they connect with what we are actually looking for in the search engine box.

Conceptually it cannot get bigger than this. The change allows us to transition from a web of links used to give us a choice of possible answers that we then have to go through manually in search of the information we are looking for, to a web of answers synthesized from the complex association and interaction of massive amounts of data—answers that are served, mostly, right there on the page for us to consume immediately or, at worst, access with a single click.

The pre-semantic web delivered links that were present on search because of the keywords contained in the pages they represented. The semantic web delivers outright answers and pages that are directly associated with the question we have typed in search.

While this may sound simple as a transition, it's not, and evidence of this is found in the fact that more than a dozen years after the concept was first aired we are only just coming to grips with the actuality of semantic search. The reason semantic search has been so hard to implement is found in two factors that are obvious only in retrospect. The first is data. For a search algorithm to make sense of a word typed in its search box and "understand" it, it requires an amount of data associated with it that is considerably higher than anything we have had ready access to until today. More than that it does not just require data, but it also requires a meaningful way of sorting that data and classifying it so that it begins to make sense at a human level.

The second reason is scalability. For semantic search to work across the trillions of pages that make up the Web it has to be able to scale across it in a way that requires no human intervention but still retains quality in the search results. The rub here is that quality in search has been a factor that has always been fine-tuned, a little, by the human operator. When you and I carried out a search and could not find the exact answer to our question even after trawling through five or six pages of links, we huffed and puffed and went back and performed the search again. By refining our own search queries we acted as the controller of accuracy in what we were looking for. Inaccurate results in searches were often the result of insufficiently precise search queries.

"Keywords" as the means through which search served results became part of the vocabulary of businesses trying to rank high on search, individuals trying to get more precise results, faster, and SEO professionals selling a service to, sometimes, the highest bidder.

When we encountered imprecisions in search that arose from misunderstanding in the meaning of the search terms used it was fine because we knew we would be drilling down to the information we were looking for anyway. A pair of eyes attached to a human brain can quickly make sense of the content presented on a web page and decide whether it has the answer it's looking for or not in ways that a computer can't. This inefficient approach also served as a safeguard of sorts against mistakes and misinformation.

To better illustrate the point consider that a traditional search for "Botulinum" for instance would throw up pages describing its effects as one of the most lethal substances known to man and, at the same time, its use in the cosmetic procedure known as Botox. I, as a human operator, would then be able to decide exactly what I was looking for—the means to acutely poison myself or a way to erase time and recapture my youthful looks. In this type of search the person carrying it out is also filtering the results for relevance.

Semantic search takes the ambiguity out of the search results by understanding that the search term refers, predominantly, to the toxin as opposed to Botox and supplies me with the answers I need about it right there on the page. It does this through the calculation of associated data in ways we will see shortly. The point is that mistakes in these kinds of answers are harder to spot, and this makes them potentially more catastrophic.

When the search engine you use to find things changes from being a search engine to being an answer engine, what makes or breaks the entire edifice is the trust we are willing to place in the answers we get. It would take fundamentally few mistakes, for instance, to cause the total destruction of the Google brand in search and the loss of a reputation and presumably a market that has taken over 15 years of sustained effort to build.

One of the reasons semantic search has taken so long to finally arrive lies in the fact that the stakes are high and the margins for error razor thin. The others, of course, have to do with the limiting factors associated with it, and these are defined, first, by the state of the search technology that semantic search is superseding.

How Search Works

Ever since I was a child I have been a strong believer in the principle that to understand how anything works you need to take it apart and look at it in detail. This principle that worked with toys also works pretty well with search.

Search on Google's page is created by the complex synthesis of three basic components at the back end:

- A spider or web crawler
- A database (or index)
- A large network of computers

This is counterbalanced by the symmetry of three seemingly basic elements; the synthesis of which appear at the front end, right in front of us, as a matter of fact, every time we carry out a search on Google's search box:

- A number of search engine results pages (referred to as SERPs)
- A hierarchical ranking of the results from top to bottom in the 10 available positions on each search results page (referred to as organic results)
- A ranking algorithm that uses over 200 ranking signals to mathematically place each result that appears on Google search results pages in response to a search query in a position that best reflects Google's confidence in the answer that result can provide.

Spiders go across the Web collecting all the information they find on web pages at incredible speeds and then bring it back to be indexed in Google's database. Google's network of computers then serves up the information that matches a search query typed in Google's search box. There is a vital interdependency in these three elements. Without a high-quality spider Google would be unable to index the massive amount of information available on the visible web. Without its database that organizes all the data collected, there would be no way to store it, and without its network of computers Google would have no way of serving the search results it does now.

In reality these three elements are extremely complicated. Google's spider goes across the entire Web at speeds measured in nanoseconds, collecting terabytes of data. Its index can classify and store that information reliably, and its computers can maintain a 24/7, unfaltering presence despite the fact that, like all hardware, tens of thousands of them fail each day.

There is also equally vital interdependency on the three elements that make up the front end of search. Without the search engine results pages (SERPs) Google would have no practical way of providing a visualization of its index of information. Without the hierarchical stacking of pages and the hierarchical ranking of each result in them, there would be no easy way to present the most likely answer to a search query, followed by the next most likely answer, and so on. Finally without a search ranking algorithm Google would have no way of creating a hierarchy of results in its index that could present them on the search results pages with any degree of confidence.

Google does nothing like any other company. The computers, the spider, the index, the search ranking algorithm, and the data centers, all have an architecture that is ground breaking and unique. Different search queries are served to different countries in different languages, and, just to make the mix interesting, I can query the US index of Google for information that is located in the United States, typing in English even when I am in, let's say, Shanghai and get almost exactly the results I would if I were based in the United States.

Yet, despite all this considerable complexity the entire front end operation consists of those three elements that are, essentially, dumb. The search results pages present the information, the hierarchical ranking provides a signal of confidence in the results. The ranking algorithm determines where each result should be in the search results pages. The computer network serves it. Each of these elements powered by the ceaseless, sleepless back end set up that works with the tireless, focused tunnel vision of a robot, does what it is designed to do without thinking, and it does it well, up to a point.

The end result of all this complexity is the simplicity of the familiar look of Google search where 10 blue links, each with a brief snippet description, appear in the SERPs, ranked in descending order of quality.

The point where the system no longer works the way it is supposed to is when human interaction or rather the human motivation to game it begins to affect the ranking of the results on the SERPs so that websites begin to appear as the answer to a search query at a much higher rank than they should.

It's a no-brainer to understand that if search *is* marketing and if search is the only viable means through which we navigate the Web, a company that manages to rank high on search will benefit hugely as a result. The financial rewards involved in any such result were such that gaming Google's algorithm became the Holy Grail of practically the entire search engine optimization industry.

Ever since there was any kind of search to talk about there have been search engine optimization (SEO) experts who use the same mathematical logic that drives search to benefit their clients. Human nature being what it is, it's only natural to try to find weaknesses to exploit, and search technology and the way data is assessed in search, has had its share of them.

The cat and mouse game that has gone on between Google and search engine optimizers has resulted from the apparent inability of the search algorithm that determines the ranking of results (i.e. websites) in search to become, somehow, smarter and present results ranked in a smarter way that is less prone to gaming by those who understand how search works.

It's true that for every iteration of search programming Google introduced that was intended to increase the quality and trustworthiness of the search results pages, search engine optimizers found ways to exploit it in a manner that, in time, achieved the exact opposite result.

Each time Google introduced a refinement, a filter, or a penalty, SEOs would experiment, testing it for flaws and vulnerabilities, deducing its parts and then, inevitably, gaming it to achieve search ranking results that were perhaps a little better than what was deserved.

Theoretically this way of carrying on could have gone on forever. Google might have been able to tinker with the ranking algorithm that provided the ranking in its organic search results pages but without changing its nature to SEOs it would simply be a bigger, dumber beast, ruled by the same mechanics it had in the past, in some new combination perhaps, there to be studied and analyzed and, ultimately, gamed.

The introduction of semantic search has put a stop to all this. The factors taken into account by Google's search ranking algorithm that now determine how a website ranks in search have expanded considerably to include information that is a lot harder to game. This returns the function of search back to what it was intended to be: a helpful means of navigating the mass of information that is placed on the Web and of course it leads us, quite naturally, to the point where we can take a look under the hood and see what it is that makes semantic search hum.

How Semantic Search Works

Just like regular search, semantic search can be deconstructed into its component parts to see exactly how it works, where it is different, from the search we were accustomed to in the past and, most importantly, see how that difference comes about.

Before we get to the nitty-gritty it will serve us well to look at Figure 1.1, which shows the elements that help create semantic search in the first place.

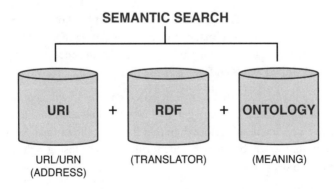

Figure 1.1   *The three basic elements of semantic search are a Universal Resource Identifier (URI), a Resource Description Framework (RDF), and an ontology library.*

To create a semantic search that understands words the way you and I do, three elements need to come together.

The first is a Universal Resource Identifier. This can be a URL of the type we are all familiar with on the Web, or it can be a Universal Resource Name (URN) which is a fancy way of saying that it is a name like that of a person, for instance. The URI is needed because this is where the initial set of data comes from, and, yes, a spider is still involved in the process. This initial set of data is not sufficient, however. It helps to think of it as massive amounts of raw data that at this stage is still pretty useless and needs to be further classified and refined.

Just like sugar cane goes through a refining process that turns it from something that looks like bamboo stalks to the fine white sugar grains that have the power to sweeten our drinks and desserts, so does the URI need to be refined further before it can be consumed. This refinement is achieved with the help of a Resource Description Framework (RDF). It helps to think of the RDF as a set of rules that allows the transportation (or translation) of data from one database, where the URIs are stored, to another without loss of meaning or a mix-up of value.

To illustrate this a little let's look at the simple example of my home address in the UK. The place where I live can be detailed by my name, my house number, the street address, the city, the county, the post code, and then the country. In a UK-based database a post code consists of letters and numbers. Now suppose my data is ported over to a US-based database so I can get a subscription of a publication printed in the United States. Straightaway, in the old way of doing things this would throw up a few glitches. First of all in the United States counties are replaced by states, second, post codes are usually called ZIP codes, and third, they have different formats that are usually all numbers.

If there was no way to tell the US-based database what kind of information it has received, it would be unable to make any kind of meaningful use of it, and I would be unable to subscribe to any US-based magazine, for instance, unless I decided to migrate to the United States and buy a house there.

Luckily for me the RDF translates my UK-based data into fields that make sense for the US-based database, so I can get my US magazines delivered to me at my home address in Manchester. More than that the RDF allows the US-based database to maintain my UK-based post code format without losing sight of the fact that it is a ZIP code.

So what the RDF does, in this context, is provide meaning to raw data that has been indexed by a web crawler, or spider, in ways that allow that data to make sense almost anywhere. I say almost anywhere because while data that is intended for machines to read can be pretty literal, words used by people are not. The same word can have different meanings and even different uses. The problem of this ambiguity is solved by ontologies that are nothing more than collections of meanings.

An ontology, for instance, could define that an address is defined by a city and the city is defined by a county and the county is defined by the country it is in. You and I understand this intuitively the moment someone asks us for our address, but machines can't, and without an ontology to guide them, they never would.

Ontologies are easy to structure into classes and subsets of those classes and then add an inference rule to them. One inference rule for instance could say that if an address is in a particular city and the city is in a particular county then that address is associated with that county, even if it is not specified. So by detailing my address and the fact that I live in Manchester, UK, a semantic search can easily deduce that I live in the county of Cheshire even if I do not specifically say I do, just like a real person would.

The computer does not really understand that I am a British resident, that my home is in the UK, and that Britain is divided into counties that have post codes instead of ZIP codes. But by combining the three elements of semantic search it learns to translate data and associate it with specific meanings in a way that appears to be intelligent. In a sense if I have my name linked to that address the computer would then "know" that I am a British resident without there ever having been a mention of the fact on any online document or piece of data. Semantic search would have deduced it. Better still, by associating my address with a means to contact me it could also pull up my phone number and email and present it right there in search without you having to go through tens of pages looking to find the best means to reach me.

Ontologies that appear cumbersome for humans work wonderfully on the Web. As web crawlers go through a website they can pick up massive amounts of data without losing focus or getting tired the way a person would. What they could not do in the past is make sense of the data they collected the way a person could.

Now, however, with the introduction of programming that uses the URI and parses it through both an RDF and an ontology, data acquires a more precise value that enables Google's search to actually infer meaning from the associations of the data it indexes and appear intelligent in ways we can recognize.

In Figure 1.2 we can see the power of the association of data with meaning by searching for "works of da vinci." In the past this would have thrown up an entirely different set of results, probably imprecise enough for me to have to go back and refine the search with the query: "works of Leonardo da Vinci."

Figure 1.2   *The results page gives us instant answers in the Knowledge Carousel at the top, the Knowledge Graph on the right, and the familiar 10 links that now drill deeper on the subject in the middle.*

Looking at the image of the search results in Figure 1.2, we can see that the search algorithm here is smart enough to understand that "da vinci" is Leonardo da Vinci and that I am looking for his artwork. It has given me some additional biographical information on the right-hand side and has even made some suggestions regarding additional, related searches.

Although this is a feature that is not directly associated with the core of semantic search, it is a valuable addition to the search results page. It is a little more officially called serendipity discovery; an entire field of search technology deals with serendipitous information retrieval and the dynamics that govern it. For us it is sufficient to know that it has huge implications in terms of the marketing of your business and the way you will be able to find customers in the future—implications that we explore in this book and formalize into a set of practices that can help you take advantage of it.

No More Games

Search and the tendency to game it seem to go together like bacon and eggs or cookies and milk. Companies that have engaged in SEO practices not approved by Google range from BMW in Germany (they got de-indexed) to JC Penney and Overstock (they were both penalized). Each time the losses were catastrophic. The BMW brand disappeared from the Web in its home market; JC Penney and Overstock almost went into receivership due to the losses suffered in the three month period Google deprecated their ranking on the Web; although operating in a downturn market they were more than likely facing a variety of issues, the fact that they lost their first page positions in Google's search probably exacerbated whatever difficulties they were going through.

Despite the risks of getting penalized by Google, to my knowledge, there has never been a shortage of companies willing to engage in risky SEO practices. The rewards are obvious, and the perceived risk is something that may not happen. So, the threat of a Google penalty (or even de-indexing for the worst offenders) is an insufficient deterrent.

What we learn from behavior economics is that the moment a metric is created it generates an incentive for people to pursue it. A high ranking in Google's search is a definitive metric and one that frequently has been the bane of the SEO industry. I have been present in corporate meetings discussing the value of search where the only question being asked was where the corporate website ranked for specific key-words. In this case there is also a strong additional financial incentive to gaming search to achieve rankings not usually reflected by the quality of the website whose rank is being boosted.

Faced with all this kind of behavior Google had one of two choices: A. Continue on the current, iterative path of filters, penalties and more ranking signals and play cat and mouse with the SEO industry, or B. Find a way to make gaming next to impossible and ranking redundant.

Since it was a tactic that has been in place since the beginning, A was probably the less expensive and more obvious option. Google chose B. One reason it went with this choice lies in the fact that developments within search rivals were leaving the company little choice, but also significantly reducing attempts to game its algorithm and dilute the quality of its search results must have been a motivating factor.

Semantic search, just like the search programming in place before it, relies on mathematics and can be reverse engineered to a high degree so that its component parts are exposed. The big difference this time is that the scale of the metrics is such that to actively pursue to game them requires greater time, effort, and cost than what the attempt to rank in search using legitimate methods would require.

For the first time, perhaps, in the SEO industry the cost of looking for shortcuts to ranking in search is higher than the cost of not doing so. That, in itself, has become a game changing development forcing those who work in search engine optimization and those who hire them to remain more honest than perhaps they might have done willingly. And just to make sure this continues to be the case Google is also slowly killing search ranking in the traditionally understood way.

The idea that ranking on search for a particular keyword is no longer a metric that counts is anathema to both search engine optimizers and companies alike. For one it removes a commonly agreed upon metric that the former could use to prove their ability and the latter could use to hold the former to accountability.

There are other, deeper, implications to semantic search that impact directly on the way search marketing was performed in the past. We will explore them in detail in following chapters but an overview helps show just how radical the change will be for traditional online marketing and how far-reaching its impact.

Google search answers one billion questions a day. It is the primary means through which businesses get their websites in front of their potential customers. To do that businesses traditionally rely on the use of keywords that help them appear in search and ideally in the first place position of the first page of Google's search.

The perception in the search marketing industry has always been that a first page position is valuable to a business and the higher you are ranked on that page the more clicks you get. Trying to quantify that perception, Compete.com, a media marketing company, in 2012 spent time analyzing "tens of millions" of consumer-generated search engine results pages from the last quarter of 2011. In a study published on their website they showed that when it comes to clicks on the search engine results pages, 53 percent go to the top result. The second sees 15 percent of the action, the third 9 percent, the fourth 6 percent, dropping all the way down to 4 percent at the first five results on the page.

From a marketing perspective this helps wonderfully to focus the mind into action-ables. If you really want to succeed online you need to:

- Have a website that is indexed properly by Google.
- Create the best means possible through which your website is ranked.
- Get your website to appear on the first page of Google.
- Get your website to appear on the very first position of the first page of Google.

The obvious strategy that these actionables produce however is now challenged by the fact that Google's semantic search displays results in ways that now make the Compete.com study obsolete.

The Knowledge Graph Carousel changes the real estate structure of search and diverts the end-user's attention away from the traditional vertical of 10 links, the first five of which received 87% of the end user's attention to a place where the horizontal scrolling of the Carousel adds considerable competition for clicks before we even get past the first link displayed on the page.

Marketing is a cause-and-effect world. Every small change in its technicalities produces much larger changes that travel along the chain and then make it necessary to do things differently. This seemingly simple change in the way the results are visually presented on Google search is a great example of this. By changing the way your target audience behaves it now changes the list of actionables you need to have in mind as you prepare your digital marketing in the semantic search age:

- Your website still needs to be indexed properly by Google.
- Find ways to get your website's true value to searchers recognized.
- Increase the means through which your website can be discovered on Google's search.
- Find ways to capture the attention of those who use Google search.

Although the restated actionables appear to deliver only a slight repositioning of what should be done, just like the small change in the visual display of Google search, the impact goes much deeper.

To understand just how nuanced all this is becoming consider that all this happens before we even begin to take into account the fact that semantic search also has computational capabilities. Many answers will now be given right there, on the search page, without the need for the end-user to click anywhere which means that many websites that used to rely on traffic that arrived in search of a particular answer will now experience a drop-off.

Google, of course, has not really done away with ranking as a metric. What has really changed is that search has both changed and fragmented. Whereas once we had desktop search as the sole area to gauge success in, we now have different search verticals in desktop and mobile. Google Image search is becoming a significant driver of traffic, Google Now and Google Voice Search are, again, different engines powered by semantic search, and just to further confuse the picture there is Google's social search that kicks in the moment you are logged in to your Google account and carry out a search. And let's not forget YouTube (a Google product) that is the second largest search engine on the Web after Google.

To truly wrap your mind around the way search is going think intense personalization and convenience. Google Now, a relatively new service, uses location-awareness technology to track where you are through your smartphone's GPS signal. It then uses Google's understanding of your preferences and needs, based on your Google Account opt-in settings, and it preloads information you will find useful that's just there when you ask for it.

In the following chapters we examine in detail what all this means in practical terms for your marketing efforts and how it changes your search engine optimization strategy, the kind of content you decide to create, the strategic positioning of your business and the guidance you give the teams and agencies working with you.

For now we build upon what's covered in this chapter and end with a practical guide of steps you need to take in order to prepare better. This final checklist of steps will be present at the end of every chapter, like a pre-flight checklist, to help you focus on the actionables you should be working toward.

The Semantic Search Preparation Checklist

Taking advantage of semantic search, paradoxically enough, requires a return to basic values. The fact that I detail this here is indicative of how far we deviated from that course over the past decade in the race to catch up to technical search engine changes and stay ahead of their restrictions.

Real search is about providing valuable information when it's really needed to those who are actually looking for it. This does not mean that there is no room for "optimization" tactics any more; quite the opposite as a matter of fact. The complexity of web design, browser technologies, and search indexing produces a few challenges that require optimization to overcome. The fragmentation of search requires a real strategy in order to save time, money, and still achieve the desired result.

The Semantic Search Preparation Checklist involves the following steps:

- Identify the Unique Selling Point (USP) of your business. What is it that sets you apart from your competitors? How do you define it, exactly?
- List all the platforms you have a business presence on, including offline ones as well as digital ones
- Detail who is responsible for coordinating search in your company. Explain how do they do it, how do they communicate their activities with the rest of your team?
- Determine how marketing initiatives are communicated across your business. Do you have a strategy in place for that? Is there a way to prioritize what gets communicated, to whom and when?
- Describe your content creation strategy—who is responsible and where does it then appear. Who contributes to it? How do you vet those involved? How do you make sure your company values are correctly articulated and presented, through content?

- List all your social media network activities. How do they get initiated, who is responsible for coordination, how are outcomes assessed? How frequently do you carry out assessments? How do you monitor effectiveness and what response strategies do you have in place?

- Describe where you think your potential customers are and how they find you. What do you think are their values and aspirations? Where do you think the common ground lies between what your company does and what your customers want?

- Describe your narrative, your unique message. All company marketing is a narrative, but it is, usually, a fragmented one. How do you make sure that the message your marketing projects is cohesive?

- Detail how you achieve consistency in your marketing message across all your digital assets.

- List all the possible ways you can intercept your potential customers across the digital spectrum. Be as comprehensive as possible here and include traditional marketing methods such as an opt-in newsletter, and so on.

2

What Is the Knowledge Graph?

Semantic search is powered by the Knowledge Graph. The Knowledge Graph enables websites and people to be discovered in the new Google search, and it also becomes the vehicle through which you can intercept your potential customers' attention with a new way of marketing. In many ways the Knowledge Graph is the brain of semantic search.

In this chapter we see what the Knowledge Graph really is, how you can go about being included in it, and how this then will affect your presence in Google's semantic search.

A Knowledge Engine Rather Than a Search Engine

Anyone who has ever watched an episode of *Star Trek* knows that on the *USS Starship Enterprise* computing is both ubiquitous and intelligent. There's never a need to manually input any data in the *Star Trek* computer, and the only way to interface with it is with voice commands. The captain speaks to it the same way he'd speak to an individual.

If that was not wondrous enough the *Star Trek* computer understands speech without any problem (and presumably speaks many languages, not just English), and it collects its own data through its sensors making it therefore both instantly scalable and independent of its operators.

More than that, being unable to forget, the ship's computer must get smarter and smarter with every *Star Trek* mission, until, I suppose, at some point its intelligence would surpass the intelligence of its makers and we will get the so-called singularity, where machine intelligence is greater than human. Trekkie fans might point to Lt. Commander Data whose positronic brain is capable of over 60 trillion operations per second (compared to 13 trillion per second for humans) and who has a total storage capacity of over 93 million gigabytes (humans have a capacity of about 1,024 GB). But Data chooses to limit himself and never really embodies the singularity in any meaningful way.

All of this is important because, right now, the search that Google has implemented is heading in that exact, same direction.

Amit Singhal is a Google Fellow and head of Google's core search team. Technology, these days, makes the kind of leaps and bounds that allow life to imitate art to imitate life. Singhal happens to be a big *Star Trek* fan, and like you and I, he noticed and was impressed by the ubiquitous presence and power of the Federation starship's onboard computer.

Unlike us, Singhal happened to be at the right place and had the means at his disposal in terms of training and resources to experiment with building one. Google's semantic search is the first step toward a search engine that is like *Star Trek's* onboard computer and the brains of that semantic search is what Google calls the Knowledge Graph. The word "Graph" here has been taken from mathematics but in this context it was coined by Facebook's founder and CEO, Mark Zuckerberg, who used it to express the social network of relationships within Facebook's digital boundaries. He called it the Social Graph.

The term has been used on the Web, since, to mean a group of linked data nodes. In this case Google's Knowledge Graph is amassing not just knowledge represented by facts (let's call them data nodes in the lingo) but also data about how these data nodes are connected to each other and what the connections actually mean.

Thanks to the Knowledge Graph Google takes our queries, typed in its search box, understands the words, and delivers results that approximate the kind of answers a human might give.

Allow me briefly to go a little math geek here: The Knowledge Graph does away with the inherent ambiguity of conventional search at Google's search box. It does not struggle with the word "Rio," for instance, which could be a film, a city, a hotel in Vegas, or an actual cinema in Essex, a county in Britain. Faced with such ambiguity Google's search presents results in a structured way that makes instant sense in terms of the possible choices and then helps us find the most likely answer. To do so, paradoxically, it relies on the mathematical expression of imprecision through something that's called fuzzy logic.

A holdover from the 1960s, fuzzy logic also does something that is mind boggling. It takes the language of mathematics, which by definition is very precise, and turns it into a probabilistic response that mirrors uncertainty. Fuzzy logic is particularly well-suited to semantic search and Google's Knowledge Graph because it ascribes a mathematical value to logic variables that have a range (usually between 0 and 1) as opposed to the hard "Yes/No" state of binary math.

This makes it particularly good at handling something math does not normally handle very well, like the concept of partial truth where a variable may not just be "True" or "False" but actually range from a state where it is completely true to one where it is completely false, depending on the variable and the context in which it is assessed.

When it comes to the Knowledge Graph, when we type a search query Google's index looks at all the indexed content associated with it and, because of the much wider net cast by semantic search, comes up with a huge number of possible choices. To narrow this down to the ones most likely to fit the search query it looks at the partial truth value of each and begins to narrow the choices down.

All of this is amazing because the moment we type "Rio" in search, the probabilistic response that is triggered by the uncertainty of our search query leads the search programming to associate the word "Rio" with all the likely answers. This is then reduced to some very precise results by being run through a set of filters drawn around the end user that help make sense of the intent behind the query and crystallize the results.

The effect of such filtering is that the search programming looks at what we have typed in search, looks at our personal search history, and tries to guess our intent behind what we are looking for. If it sounds a little involved, that's because it is, but it all happens at nearly the speed of light and the results appear to be almost instantaneous.

There are two separate searches typed into Google using the exact same search query: "rio." You can see the choices that Google has made for me in the first one (top) when I was not logged into my Google account (see Figure 2.1). The second search has been done when I was logged in. I am a bit of a travel nut and I also follow the Travel Channel page on Google+. Rio de Janeiro has been a destination I long wanted to try and recently the Travel Channel had a few photographs of the city which I spent some time looking at. Google noted that and the first high-confidence result it presented to the same search query, when I am logged into my Google account, was the city of Rio in Brazil.

Figure 2.1   *Google search results.*

The only way Google could "know" what I wanted to find when I typed in "Rio" in its search box was by taking into account my personal preferences and past history of search patterns. A Duran-Duran fan might have seen Rio, the second album of the British band, while a soccer fan might have seen Rio Ferdinand, the Manchester United center-back.

Fuzzy logic makes all this possible by connecting, right there on the search box, our probable intent behind the search query (pulled in by everything we allow Google to know about us) and the most probable set of answers, all matched through variable values of partial truth. What's more, with Google, there is the potential to add additional layers of filtering on this, all drawn from the end-user's perspective so that the results become even more accurate and personalized.

Geeky enthusiasm over; let's go and see how all this mathematical miracle gets turned into something we can use in the real world to get work done.

How the Knowledge Graph Works

A picture is still worth a thousand words, so let's take a shortcut to understand the actual mechanics of the Knowledge Graph that the math powers with Figure 2.2. This is what happens behind the scenes when I type the search query "da vinci."

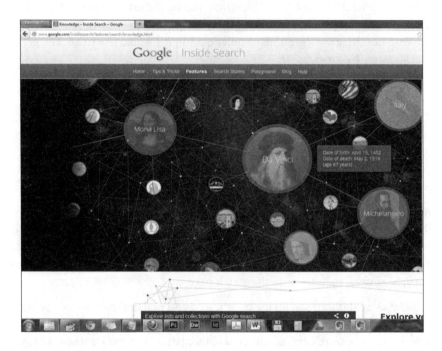

Figure 2.2 *The Knowledge Graph here has used cross-referenced information collated from all over the Web to create lists of objects associated with "da vinci."*

In Figure 2.2, for example, the words "da vinci" are not just associated with information such as the birthplace and date of birth of the great inventor but also with his contemporary artists and sculptors, his work, and even what's being said about it from an artistically critical point of view.

You understand, I hope, that once that kind of detailed cross-referencing of information happens about a subject all that is required next is the ability to be able to draw inferences (or make deductions) from it using mathematical rules, and all sorts of questions can be answered, such as

"When was Leonardo born?"

"What are Leonardo's paintings?"

"What are Leonardo's notebooks?"

Each time the answers are given there and then, right on the page, either as the Knowledge Carousel, at the top, or on the right-hand side where we see the true workings of the Knowledge Graph.

The current weakness of Google's semantic search, the extreme youth of its *Star Trek* computer, if you like, is given away by the gaps in its knowledge and abilities. For instance there are a great many other questions I would like to ask and get a quick answer to, for example:

"How old was Leonardo when he died?"

This search query still results in 10 little blue links where I have to go to by clicking each one, read the web page I find there and find out the answer to my question. A smaller search engine that also uses semantic programming, Wolfram Alpha (www.wolframalfa.com), gives me that answer in a second or two, right on the page: 67 years and 8 days.

By its very definition semantic search is all about computational answers rather than just discovering 10 top sites where you would have to go look for the answers to the questions yourself and as it grows and its store of knowledge becomes better defined and more reliable, we will start to see more instances where it provides an outright answer, right there on the search page.

Brilliant as all this is, it's of no use to us if it has no practical day-to-day application. Thankfully this is not the case. In our ever faster, time-poor world, there is real value in a search engine that could automatically recognize wherever you are in the world and answer the search query "What's my nearest restaurant?" or "What's the best pizza joint in town?" without you ever having to specify place, country, or restaurant type.

The magic through which this happens owes a lot to Google's ability to pull all the different pieces of data together; my geolocation, the GPS signal on my phone, and the address of the pizza restaurants near me alongside some great reviews about some of them.

If you were running a pizzeria in downtown wherever and I happened to be there, your business would benefit from my custom without either of us going to any effort to attract the attention of the other. This is the true value of semantic search. The search engine of the past that gave us "best choices" we needed to wade through now becomes an answer engine, a recommendation engine, even a prediction engine, understanding my intent behind my jet-lagged, fuzzy questions, and giving me answers like my best friend would.

That kind of search engine would not only command the lion's share of the market, but it would do so largely invisibly and ubiquitously, like the *Star Trek* computer. No one would have to program the answers, there would be no effort in communicating with it, and it would be trusted with the same degree of authority that the *Starship Enterprise* captains put in their onboard computer.

The kind of search engine that would be able to so seamlessly connect consumers with services would unleash a fresh "best of" value in the world where only the best businesses would do business, only the best places would get visitors, only the best cities would get clever people deciding to live in them, only the best information would ever surface.

If that thought excites you, you are right to be excited. From a business point of view it could significantly decrease your advertising and marketing budget and allow you to put time and effort into your business doing what you want: Make it the very best there is.

Traditional top-down, one-way marketing is an anachronism—a holdover of the last century. Marketing grew as a response to the problem of how do we make purchasing decisions when businesses have been scaled up across many local population bases and countries and new kinds of communication lines have not been invented to replace what we had in the small towns and villages of the past that got left behind.

The idea that as a business you have to spend heavily and try really hard to sway someone's purchasing choice is an oddity that has as a logical outcome frequently replaced quality with packaging, reputation with brand equity, and value with size. In the village of the past, the village square, ringed with stalls guided our purchasing choices along the lines of trust, reputation, and knowledge. We bought from trusted sources. We found out about new tradesmen from trusted sources. We bought from new people when their reputation preceded them. We chose how to buy based on the knowledge of what we wanted and what they offered, and if we did not know we asked someone who did.

It was a model that worked extremely well in the confines of the village square. But as that small-scale, bucolic world was left behind in the exponential scaling of markets, populations, and production processes that was the Industrial Revolution, its inability to successfully scale created the problem that modern marketing was created to address.

The beauty of semantic search and the Knowledge Graph is that it uses technology to make the world small again. In a global village where our "here" can have us standing on opposite sides of the globe within 24 hours, our village square has been replaced by an ever changing location populated by choices that are assembled by the same criteria of trust, reputation, and value that we used in our bucolic past to make purchasing decisions; the same criteria that we used to decide who we would trust with sensitive information about our life, who we would choose as a business partner, and who we would ask to buy our business when we retired.

The preface to the first chapter of this book boldly stated that search *is* marketing. The challenge we face is in getting past the geekery and obtuse terminology of the SEO world and understanding what does what, when, where, and how in terms that make sense not just now but 500 years ago, when Leonardo da Vinci was alive, and 500 years from now, when "search" will be a blinking dot at the corner of your eye, silently supplying you with overlays of data as you go through your life, or a whispering voice inside your head implanted at birth.

Going back to basics does not mean stripping us of our achievements. It means stripping us of our pretenses, getting rid of the inevitable hubris that comes with rapid development and understanding the dynamics of what makes things tick.

In this "Back to Basics" world businesses which do well in search are the ones who:

- Understand that the primary aim in using search is to capture and hold the attention of their audience.
- Seek to connect with customers not chase changing search algorithms.
- Deliver consistent value in ways that succeed in generating social buzz.
- Synchronize their online and offline presence to deliver a single, well thought-through marketing image.
- Communicate their core set of values well enough to establish a real, online identity.
- Manage to safeguard and grow their reputation through online engagement and interaction.
- Understand that content creation is more than just a need to create any old content just to put keywords in it that will help with search ranking.

Making the Connections

I am not for a minute glossing over the considerable challenges that the "bucolic" past I used in my example presented in terms of inequality, opacity, unaccountability, and corruption. Connections in that past were not always made meritocratically, and certainly purchasing choices often came down to choosing among the lesser of two evils as competition and choice were concepts not held in very high esteem.

The point is that what came after it, which was an improvement as far as competition and choice were concerned, but it also created a facelessness that generated its own problems—problems that are being addressed only now.

To understand how these connections are made in a new semantic world, let's look, once more, at the mechanics behind the search box.

We saw in Chapter 1 that to be able to give meaningful answers to our queries, semantic search, which is powered by the Knowledge Graph, requires three basic ingredients:

- A Uniform Resource Indicator (URI)
- A Resource Description Framework (RDF)
- An ontology

Here we need to look beyond the mathematics and the terminology to see how the Knowledge Graph really works to collect all the information it needs to build its lists.

On the Web information is collected from

- Websites
- Social networks
- Professional networks
- Profiles
- Databases
- From Google Search itself

But having all this information is not enough. Google uses inference rules to understand how the information actually groups together and what it means. These rules are activated by the way we use data in

- Social networks
- Web platforms (like forums)
- Google Search (with our search queries)

And by the data we generate in

- Social networks with shared content
- Social networks with comments and interaction
- Commercial websites with the creation of reviews and opinion
- Website platforms with the creation of content

Plus the way we use the Web:

- Personal data that we allow to surface
- Tracked behavior in terms of websites we visit and what we do there
- Personal search patterns

And it even includes our offline behavior:

- Location-aware services based around the GPS signal of our mobile device
- Geolocation based on IP address
- Machine collated data (when devices connect and talk to devices)

So this baby *Star Trek* computer of a semantic search is not just smarter. What was there before it could only present us with information based on lists and approximations. This new search is also capable of learning from our own activity and refining its understanding of what we do, why we do it, what our intent is and yes, it can even understand words the way we do. Once it learns something, it can apply it everywhere, so for instance if a combination of indexed and acquired data teaches the Knowledge Graph that the words "code red" are associated with a heightened state of alert, it is knowledge that it can then apply universally, not just in the context where it learned it.

In "The Semantic Search Preparation Checklist" in Chapter 1 I asked you to look at basic things in your business, like its unique selling point, for instance. I have lost count of the number of times I have heard executives supply their company's advertising line or its mission statement as the unique selling point, thinking that this is what the company did. It never is.

Google may have as its mission statement to "Index the world's information," but that is not its unique selling point, any more than the Coca Cola company is there to sell Coke or Bayer sells aspirin. Google's real unique selling point is that it gives answers, Coke sells happiness, and Bayer sells relief from pain. The reason it's important to get to the core of what a company does is that its current delivery mode is the result of technological constraints. Google may have a desktop-based search box, Coke may have a signature lifestyle drink, and Bayer a little white pill, but that's only because that is as far as our technology takes us at present.

A thousand years in the future Google may stream answers directly into our cortical synapses, Coke may have morphed into something else entirely, and Bayer may be manufacturing synthetic neurotransmitters that help block the signals of pain to our brain. What will not have changed in that fantastic futuristic scenario is the intent behind each company and its consumers.

Google will still be supplying answers to a population thirsty for information and continually asking questions. Coke will still be a drink that's a lifestyle accessory for anyone who feels that's what they need to complete their internal picture of what their lifestyle should be, and Bayer will still be providing relief from pain to those afflicted by it.

Companies that cannot successfully answer what they do fail to then understand how they can continue to do it in the face of a changing world. Semantic search is all about creating connections in a world where point A is actively looking for point B and vice versa. The proviso here is that there is a clear understanding of the dynamics involved—the need or want that is being answered by a product or service.

The real challenge is to be found in the areas where point A can connect with point B. The opportunities where a company can find its customers and the ways in which a consumer can find a product are multiplying, fragmenting, becoming a bewildering array of niches that frequently confuse those who focus too closely on them in a way that gives real meaning to the popular phrase of not being "able to see the forest for the trees."

Interestingly, the actionables for a business that is serious about taking advantage of the power of semantic search and Google's Knowledge Graph are, on the surface at least, simple:

- Find ways to prove your authority through a digital presence.
- Create a clear identity through content and online engagement.
- Understand how your reputation is created online and how you will safeguard it.
- Interlink all your online activities and make sure they are transparent.

Your Business and the Knowledge Graph

To my mind the value of knowledge has always lain in what can be achieved once you gain it. While knowledge for knowledge's sake is a valuable goal, it is also a monumental waste of time. For example, electricity is only good when it is activated to power something. Just having it does nothing to unlock its own value. It does nothing to benefit us personally or our world. If knowing something is not used we may as well go back to not knowing about it.

Technology, today, has set us on a path that is unified by intent rather than presence. We say the world is wired, massively connected, and those whom businesses want to target are "always on," but that has only made each potential market for businesses paradoxically smaller, tougher to crack, and full of high entry thresholds placed there by personalized usage.

The ubiquitous nature of connections has not created a brand new massive marketplace. It has started an ongoing process of nichification that is accelerating. Consider, for instance, your average target customer. Chances are you probably can't. He (or she) used to be on the Web, and the Web was accessible via the desktop computer. Even when laptop computing took off and added greater mobility to computing, little changed. The Web was still the Web, desktop search was still desktop search, and the "customer" was there.

Targeting that customer was easy. You needed a website, some form of online advertising, email marketing (perhaps), and some means to bring the customer back to your website. You knew that when the customer looked for information he or she would go to search, and search was governed by keywords. Ranking was governed by incoming links (so you needed to build more) and trust was governed, partially, by website design and PageRank (so you needed good design and a high PageRank).

This "connecting of the dots" made for a certain clarity of working that's already being missed. When someone searched for "the best pizza in the world," your website would come up only if you already had done the Web-savvy thing and optimized it for the words "the best pizza in the world." Your website would come up if you had created an aggressive backlink building campaign where many other sites linked back to you with anchor text that stated "the best pizza in the world." Your website would come up if you had created a ton of nonsensical content on why your joint made "the best pizza in the world."

Perhaps there were reviews somewhere that said "Hey, you know what, this is not really the best pizza in the world," but they were buried deep enough for most online visitors not to see them. And if they made the mistake of linking back to you the keywords you wanted were still there and actually did more good than harm to your search ranking. Perhaps there were websites that actually said that your "best pizza in the world" was really, really, not. But they could not be found. Your website was better optimized, your SEO team rocked, and you could always bury the negative results with fabricated positive ones.

You were the king of the search engine world.

In the pre-semantic search world success in online marketing was determined by one's ability to virtually shout the loudest. It was the search engine equivalent of outbound marketing.

This is what's changed:

Your potential audience is now found in

- Traditional desktop-based search
- Mobile search
- Voice search

- Predictive search (with Google Now that preloads information on the user's mobile device based on location)
- Customized searches (created by commercial websites like Amazon)
- Apps (that lock information and customer attention within the app walls)
- Personalized search (that presents results based upon the user's search history and social connections)
- Localized search (that uses location-aware technology to present information based upon your mobile device's GPS signal)
- Specific service search (like YouTube or even Google+)

The results your potential customers see are now served when they carry out a search are based upon an understanding of what they are looking for that is so precise that it makes the SEO efforts of the past a lot less effective. The social connections of your target audience and their personal online activity also feed into this complex loop affecting what people see when they carry out a search.

The net result of this is that the search experience that in the past could be controlled by just throwing money at it has changed irrevocably.

I appreciate that right now search, presented like this, sounds like a lost cause. Quite rightly, reading all this and realizing the magnitude of the problem, you are asking yourself that given the fact that information on search is now cross-referenced from so many sources, can anything be done to bring search back under the control of the business owner with a business to run, products to sell, and mouths to feed?

The short answer is "yes." The saving grace in all this is that semantic search in assessing the quality of the results it serves uses three criteria that mathematically simulate the decision making process of the village square of our past:

- Trust
- Reputation
- Authority

Like anything that has to do with search, there are also specific ways to establish these, augment them, and ensure that your web presence is robust enough to ensure high visibility across any search interface. In this mix I will throw in two more rays of hope: serendipity and citation. Both of these are actually terms employed within the algorithmic calibration of semantic search, and they impact the ability of your business to be found on the Web.

They are important because there is a specific set of actionables that trigger them. They then become the new smart weapons in your search engine optimization arsenal.

Here's how they work. As semantic search gets more and more precise in the results it serves us, there is a theoretical danger that it locks us out of knowledge we need because it lies outside the narrow boundaries of our search query. Most of us understand that frequently our description of what we search for is imprecise at best. There may well be something that could enrich our search or answer it better or help us discover something tangential to the problem we are trying to solve with our search that lies just outside our reach or our capacity to describe it when we carry out the search.

If semantic search had no way of allowing for this we would have to do several searches, trying to guess what we are missing. It is hardly a good use of our time or of search and it certainly does not improve the overall search experience. Luckily we do not have to and we have serendipity to thank for that. Wikipedia defines serendipity as "a 'happy accident' or 'pleasant surprise'; specifically, the accident of finding something good or useful while not specifically searching for it." And that is exactly how it is understood by search engine engineers.

In practice this means that the programming behind semantic search uses a number of signals to find content that may not directly bear upon our search but is related to it. The information comes from social signals in networks that arise from content that is shared and interacted with, but they also come from other search queries.

If you are familiar with Amazon's product suggestions at the bottom of each product that show that "customers who bought x, also bought y" then you begin to understand how serendipity works. Amazon's additional product suggestions leverage the activity of thousands of other buyers to divine an intent of sorts. The theory behind it is that if a sufficiently large number of people who bought a mouse also went ahead and ordered with it, or as a next purchase, wrist support then the two are linked through a value proposition that may also apply to you. In most cases this opens up your thinking in terms of what else you may need to buy and saves you time at a later date.

Amazon is a very closed world when it comes to search. Although the Amazon universe is pretty large it's still very small when compared to the vastness of the Web. Yet even Amazon has to sift through a massive amount of data just to get some degree of meaningful reliability in its suggestion of related products.

Google does a similar thing but instead of an online buying environment and purchasing patterns it looks at the entire vista of the Web and uses Google search and end user inputted search queries.

Regarding the way search queries are used, researchers Vera Hollink, Theodora Tsikrika, and Arjende Vries of the Wiskundeen Informatics Centre, in Amsterdam, published a paper titled "The Semantics of Query Modification" that demonstrates how, by comparing relations between large numbers of user queries on the search engine box, it is possible to identify semantic modification patterns that reveal, for example, that users often search for two entities sharing a property (e.g., two players from the same team). It is then possible to use this data to generate suggestions for queries that are better in terms of quality than the statistical method of the past that would look at the number of logged queries and generate a statistical model.

Serendipity, which in search programming circles is actually called serendipitous information retrieval, allows for the creation of methods that we will examine that enable your brand to come to the attention of potential customers when their precise search query excludes it. It basically allows for the creation of methods that broaden the search results in a way that visually at least is similar to Amazon's. The programming is vastly different but that is not really relevant to us here. What we examine is ways this feature can be used to help your brand come to the attention of potential customers when their precise search query excludes your brand by name, or any of the keywords you might have used to help your content surface in search.

Figure 2.3   *In this search for "Kathryn bigelow," Google's Knowledge Graph brings up everything it has, associated with the Academy Award winning Director. At the right-hand side, right under her movies there are a number of actors associated with her work that others have searched for and which Google's serendipity programming now suggests.*

You notice that in searching for Kathryn Bigelow I never even typed any of the names of the actors suggested by Google in the figure and yet I may click and find out more information about them, their careers, and other films they were in, discovering in the process information that is relevant, enriching from a knowledge point of view, and totally unlooked for while I was carrying out my search.

The potential presented here is that businesses that take advantage of Google's serendipity programming can find themselves with a wider reach than what traditional SEO techniques would have provided them with.

Actionables here include:

- Creating extensive content that connects everything your business does in a meaningful way (for example, if you sell leather jackets you may want to have content that covers the ethical sourcing of leather, or have leather care information, leather repair, or Hollywood celebs who absolutely love leather jackets).

- Guiding the online conversation in social media networks in ways that extend the boundaries of what your company or brand does.

- Using your social network profiles to link to content that adds further value to what you do (for example, sharing information that broadens the boundaries of your own marketing, like a bicycle business that links to cycling paths everywhere and has extensive information on cycling holidays).

If serendipity is beginning to look like a good way to break into your potential customers' awareness when they are not actively looking for your business, citation is another.

Citation in search looks at the mention of your website, business, or brand across the Web in association with particular qualities. If, to hark back to my earlier example of having the "best pizza in town" the name of your pizzeria is independently mentioned across the Web with some frequency in association with the high quality of your pizza, then it will come up as a choice when someone looks for "best pizza restaurant" even if you have done nothing to actually promote it as such.

It is astounding that it can work this way but only in the context of machine logic and search. In the real world of people where the three qualities of trust, reputation, and authority are the criteria we reflexively use to assess whether we want to be associated with a person or a business, this peripheral way of finding our information through tangential points of contact in our personal networks, is the norm.

To recap, the Knowledge Graph is the search engine result equivalent of the sum of your reputation on the Web (the information associated with your business), the authority you have (how influential you are judged to be), and the trust others have in you (the quality ranking of your offerings). Provided you have the kind of business that is focused on delivering value to its customers, improving what it does, and evolving to meet real needs with real solutions, then there are concrete steps that can be taken to ensure that your perceived trust, reputation, and authority help you make more sales.

The Knowledge Graph Preparation Checklist

The Knowledge Graph rests upon information that is discovered and indexed independently by Google's search engine bot. That information needs to be created specifically for the purpose. The catch here is that unlike in the past where search engine optimized content was created in order to artificially rank a website and all it needed was the right kind of meta tags, the right kind of keywords, the right keyword placement, and keyword density and a few links pointing to the page, now the content that's created needs to have real value for the end user.

The focus on core company values that was the main purpose of the Semantic Search Preparation Checklist in Chapter 1 now becomes the springboard that allows you to adequately prepare for the Knowledge Graph.

The Knowledge Graph Preparation Checklist involves the following steps:

- Identify a list of real problems your business product or service is designed to solve. Detail all the ways you get across, on the Web, the solutions you can provide.
- List all the ways you could possibly collect and refine the problems that your customers face. Detail how you propose to address the issues that come to the surface from the information that you gather.
- Decide what is the best way or the best combination to present information to your customers (i.e., text, video, podcasts, infographics). Explain how you plan to make sure that all the information presented helps deliver your company's or brand's core values; how you propose to check that there is consistency in your approach, across all the different formats of communication you use and how you will fix any that do not quite follow your plan.
- Decide how you will generate content (who is responsible for it, how, who will approve it, how will it appear). Detail frequency and intent. Explain how you will set goals and how you will monitor them.
- Describe all the different ways you have in place that will help you promote the content you create. Detail how you measure success in each area.

- List all the possible ways you have of getting customer reviews. Explain how you encourage customer interaction and engagement.

- List all the ways you have of connecting directly with your customers and assess each in importance of impact on your business brand and reputation.

- Detail your social media crisis monitoring and response processes. List all the tools you use, frequency, the person(s) responsible, the frequency of reporting, and what triggers you have in place in case a social media crisis surfaces.

- Detail all the metrics you use across your digital assets to measure their success. Detail all the different definitions of success that you use. Explain what exactly they indicate, show, or measure and the impact that has on the core activities of your brand or business.

- List all your competitors and detail how you do things differently from them. Be as detailed as possible and list all areas of similarity here as well. Show where your activities diverge and where they converge and explain how that fits in with your unique brand or business identity.

What Is New in SEO?

Search engine optimization (SEO) is changing. Once a "dark art" you could outsource and forget or buy-in as needed every time you noticed your website traffic dropping or your competitors' websites doing better than yours, it has now become an integral part of your business practices and is closely integrated in your business structure. Or, at least, I hope it will be soon after reading this book.

In this chapter we see what is different in SEO, what is the "new SEO" everyone is talking about, and what you can do to take advantage of the developing trends. More importantly we see what you should do to integrate SEO in the DNA of your business.

What Is the "New SEO"?

If you've been reading *Forbes*, *The Guardian* (in the UK), or *The Wall Street Journal* lately, you will have noticed the screaming headline: "SEO Is Dead" frequently followed or preceded in the editorial content by "How Google Killed SEO."

Apart from the fact that neither of these headlines is true the degree of consternation they cause is indicative of two facts: First SEO now plays a central role in marketing, and second it is undergoing radical change. Both of these developments are good. The first because when SEO is done right it is indistinguishable from being a public service: It allows the right information to surface at the right time for those who want it (everyone's happy). And the second because for too long the SEO industry was mired in the dark ages, hiding behind obtuse terminology and ill-defined concepts and beset by practices reminiscent of snake oil peddlers selling a cure-all to being found online.

In the SEO world that's being left behind many activities revolved around two primary constants: keywords and links. Keywords were necessary to get a website to show on the search engine results pages (SERPs) in response to a search query. Links were needed to help that website rise in the search rankings.

This is a bit of an oversimplification of the Google ranking process. Google's algorithm takes into account more than 200 separate signals before it ranks a website. However it is fair to say that without keywords content would not even surface in search; therefore your website would be invisible, and without inbound links it would not rank well. These two factors then became the primary drivers of SEO in the past.

They also became the focus of many of the practices that led to SEO abuses. Links, in particular, became subject to a number of sophisticated schemes to artificially boost the ranking of websites. Google's Link Graph is a record of the link profile of every indexed website linking to others and being linked to in turn.

The power of links and linking to boost a website's ranking in search was such that unwittingly it gave rise to an entire link economy. Whole online industries were built around the exchange and selling and buying of links, with professionals as well as amateurs engaging in the practice.

Things are changing. The days when almost anyone could claim to be able to sell you links that would drive your online business up in search rankings are practically gone. The few emails that I still get, with such offers, come from Hotmail addresses and have names like "SEOKing" and "Optimizer75." Anyone taking these seriously and getting burned should not be in business anyway.

The paradox here is that the "new SEO" that is emerging is not new at all. As far back as there was an SEO industry to speak of Google advised optimizers to focus on quality, content, navigability, and an excellent end-user experience. This is really not rocket science, and the search engine optimizers that came from a business background to begin with consistently put out the message that SEO and the way you do business are closely interlinked. They would say that the message of who you are and what you are about should be part of your search marketing strategy and that focusing solely on getting traffic to a website when the usability of it was less than optimum, was a waste of time and money.

Some of these SEOs were listened to. Many were not. The perception that search engines had nothing to do with business and search engine optimization was simply a quick-fix service that needed to be brought in to "fix" things was too ingrained in too many businesses to change. Search engine optimizers were not thought of as anything other than tech stuff.

To be fair there was an element of truth in that as well. SEO started out as a purely technical activity carried out principally on-page (i.e., on the website itself), and to an extent that technical nature has persisted. Its evolution, however, has been steadily adding layers to its toolbox so that just being "technical" is no longer enough.

In all this Google has engaged in a considerable amount of education of its public on what is considered ethical SEO. The company has published its Webmaster Guidelines (http://goo.gl/kAd7G), which are constantly updated, and it is engaged in an ongoing effort to help online businesses understand better what they must do to make search work for them.

Despite this, every Google search algorithm update that is designed to address abuses finds a large number of websites that suddenly suffer as a result.

It is a fact that Google's successive algorithmic changes over the last seven years and its switch to semantic search have hit hard many online businesses that relied on either shady techniques that skirted or broke the Google approved guidelines or poor quality SEO work to rank. As a result the days of being able to "wing it" are long gone. Businesses that are serious about succeeding in the new Google-dominated online world have to take search seriously and create a process-driven business strategy around it.

If you want to know whether your business is one of those who either on the advice of your SEO agency or out of your own in-house SEO actions have been placed in a position of vulnerability to search updates, work through the following questions:

- Is the online marketing of your company or brand based entirely on keywords?
- Do you only use keywords to check your ranking in search?
- Do you use a link building strategy as the core of your company's or brand's SEO?

- Do you use keywords to assess the effectiveness of your ranking in search?

- Do your SEO-planning sessions revolve mostly around spreadsheets of keywords and where each one ranks in search?

- Do you regularly research where competitors get backlinks from and try to adjust your link building efforts to match them?

- Is a "first page position on Google's search" the main thrust of your online marketing?

- Is "anchor text" in created links something that is considered crucial to your SEO activities?

- Are your SEO activities kept apart from everything else your company does, such as branding and marketing, for instance?

- Is your SEO strategy revised a lot less frequently than any other of your brand or company initiatives?

If you answered "yes" to any of these 10 questions you may want to start rethinking things a little. The sea change that's underway questions whether there is even such a thing as an "SEO strategy" these days. Certainly there are SEO activities, but the "strategy" part should spring naturally from everything else your brand or company does.

It is in this total alignment of effort that the difference and the strength of the SEO of today is to be found.

The "new" SEO that works now focuses as much on the quality of the business offerings, the online visitor experience once they get to the company website, and the perceived reputation and authority of the business itself as much as it focuses on the traditionally technical aspects of search engine optimization.

As such it has now been divided into unofficial but increasingly differentiated types of SEO: technical and nontechnical. Technical SEO addresses specific onsite issues that prevent a website from being indexed by search engines. Indexing issues can be caused by the website structure, the coding of the underlying platform it runs on, excessive use of javascript, ajax programming that does not permit a search bot to follow navigational links, slow server responses, slow website loading times, and even top-heavy graphics that affect individual page loading speeds. Typically there can be as many website set-up indexing issues as there are websites.

Each one is unique in that respect and many of the indexing issues that crop up are the direct result of website use that has not been factored into the SEO equation or the website's set up.

The good news is that a technical audit usually brings up all these issues, none of which are very difficult to fix. Technical SEO services, like this, can be one-off services, or they can be brought in as required, though keeping a careful eye on traffic figures and running audits at regular intervals is just common sense, particularly as websites grow in content.

Nontechnical and on-going SEO work looks at the company's or brand's marketing strategy, the evolving nature of marketplace communication, content creation, social media outreach, and the way a company connects with its customers in the online environment.

If that sounds a little intrusive to a business it is because that's exactly what it is. In the new SEO world of today a business can no longer afford the luxury of considering what it does as being separate from search. Search is how its online customers navigate the Web, discover products and services, and research the products and services they need on their way to making a purchasing decision.

Google, which thrives on data, released in July 2011 a free eBook authored by Jim Lecinski, Google's vice president of products and sales in the United States. Lecinski details how the traditional "first moment of truth" when a customer first encounters a product on the shelf and the battle to win this customer begins has shifted to an earlier stage now called "zero moment of truth" (hence the title of the eBook) that starts with search.

The startling statistic that Lecinski reveals is that 70% of purchasing decisions start with search, looking for product details and online reviews. The eBook is packed full of data pulled from Google's own research, and it creates a sharp moment of clarity for businesses everywhere. The digital landscape that had been seen by many as a bolt-on to the traditional business model is now key to driving business forward.

Search is center stage in all this. SEO has suddenly become the key to success.

The journey then from "there" to "here" has been one of maturation. Businesses have gone from seeing search engine optimization as something you could call in and action as an afterthought, to seeing it as a service that is inseparable from marketing and now required to be part of the company's DNA.

It has not been an easy journey, and most of the challenges lie ahead. But the very fact that now we are talking about SEO being inside a company is a major win in itself.

How SEO Is Changing Business Practices

Because search engine optimization itself is changing, when applied correctly now it impacts many ways a business operates, changing it in the process. A concise look at what used to happen in the presemantic search days and how things are shaping up now helps quantify some of the changes you should be thinking about in your company or brand.

Here's how SEO used to work in the past:

- You bought links because they increased the ranking of your website in Google's search.
- You told your SEO company you wanted a list of keywords for your industry to rank on search, preferably on Google's first page.
- You hired someone to write thousands of words with the keywords you were targeting, and you posted the content on your website so it would become more visible in search and aid in its ranking.
- You spammed social bookmarking sites with links to your keyword-rich content without any consideration for engagement or interaction.
- You thought that a good commercial website was one with a shopping cart.
- Your perception of a good customer experience was one that gave you a sale.

In the new SEO world the things that work and help a business take advantage of search and increase its ranking are

- Good quality content that delivers value to the end-user.
- Websites that offer an excellent online visitor experience in terms of ease of use, content, and navigability.
- Businesses that are being talked about on the Web, on blogs, and social networks.
- Businesses whose content is reshared on the Web across social networks.
- Businesses with a strong social component that actually engages their prospective customer in a way similar to a person.
- Businesses that stay current and generate consistently fresh content proving that they both have something to say and that they are part of the current online conversation.

Key to all this, driving all the activity, is content. Content marketing has become so vital to all aspects of search engine optimization in the semantic web that it underpins many of the activities that your business or brand needs to engage in. As a matter of fact in Chapter 6 we look in detail at the implications of this and the actionables associated with it.

To drive the point home let's consider a conventional brick-and-mortar business that sells an everyday necessity, such as baked bread. If you are a savvy marketer who along with a bakery has a website (because you know you ought to), you will suddenly realize that your traditional business that sells baked bread now also needs to become a multimedia business that pumps out online content to sell baked bread.

From a certain perspective it seems to be antithetical with what a baked bread business needs to do and where it ought to be focusing its time and energy. After all, baking bread is not rocket science. The production algorithm (if we can call it that) requires flour, yeast, and water (at its most basic) and the judicious application of heat. The struggle is usually in keeping production costs low through control of wastage to maximize returns at the point of sale.

It's hard to see where multimedia content is going to help in the sale of baked bread. So let's look at the baked bread example a little more closely.

If our baker is any good at all as a businessperson he already knows that baked bread, alongside any other good you care to mention, has been commoditized. No matter how good you are at what you do there is always someone else who is either better, or nearer, or cheaper, or smaller, or bigger, or gives out lollypops with each baked bread loaf purchase.

This is the same virtually across the entire marketplace, and the point is that no matter what kind of business you are in these days you will have competition and a lot of it. If you are unable to differentiate yourself sufficiently from your competition, your business will go under. If you are unable to create an emotional connection with your customers, your business will fail.

That emotional connection online can only happen with the production of content—great quality content that communicates something important. The question for a modern business is not whether any of the above SEO steps should be followed but how they can all be followed consistently (and bear in mind that each of them is itself made up of a number of steps).

Marketing has changed from the twentieth century Jerome McCarthy model that gave us the 4Ps to guide us: Product, Price, Place, and Promotion to the twenty-first century digital world one expounded by global advertising and marketing firm Ogilvy & Mather as the 4Es: Experience, Exchange, Everyplace, and Evangelism.

In the digital marketplace Product now stands for Experience. Price has become Exchange, where the value of creating, packaging, and selling something is exchanged for the value of what it means to the customer to receive it, which also then determines the price. The notion of Place has been replaced by Everyplace because the potential market, as we have seen, is now fragmented. Promotion has been replaced by Evangelism. This reflects the changing relationship between businesses and their customers that enables both parties to profit from the relationship beyond the transactional value of the purchase price and the product bought.

In the baked bread example, if the entire experience of buying a loaf of baked bread from your particular bakery does not successfully engage my mind and reflect my lifestyle, I am unlikely to even consider it. If the exchange of value in buying the loaf of bread does not include how special you make me feel, how well you have communicated with me the artistry that goes into making the best baked bread in the world, and how my money helps keep an ancient tradition alive, then what I will most likely focus on is how much more expensive it is when compared to the sliced bread I buy from the grocery store.

If you cannot capture my attention as I go from my LinkedIn profile to Facebook then to Twitter then to some website and then to Google+, you are unlikely to benefit very long from my willingness to buy the more expensive baked bread you sell. I will forget to come to you, my attention will be diverted, the reason I buy baked bread will wane, and I will either buy from a competitor who simply happens to be nearer, or I will revert to the supermarket sliced loaf again.

What you will have succeeded in doing as a marketer then is either creating a customer by fostering the need in me to buy baked bread and then failing to capitalize on it as I went ahead and bought bread from any bakery or, worse, making me decide that baked bread is one of those luxuries I could forego because it is so much more expensive than supermarket bread.

Finally, if your baked bread does not fill me with a sense of wonder in the way it has been produced, how it has been presented, and the way it tastes, then I am unlikely to even remember to talk about it to my friends, colleagues, and acquaintances. You will have invested all that effort in your relationship with me for the return of a sale of a single loaf of bread. Something that constitutes a totally losing proposition.

So selling something "simple" like freshly baked bread has now been transformed from an activity that entailed the production of a product and a place to sell it at a reasonable price to an activity that needs to engage the heart and mind of its target customer in such a way that the effort and attention that goes into creating a single sale begins to scale on its own, which is what provides decent returns.

Clearly this is a new way of doing business. It requires a change from selling a product to a customer to selling an experience to a customer with whom you now have a shared relationship. This is called the relationship economy, and guiding this transition to the relationship economy is the ultimate relationship machine: semantic search. The way it does this is what we look at next.

Your Business in a Semantic Search World

I hope you can see how important relationships with its customer base have become to a business. It is not wrong to think that the traditional buying of a product has now been replaced with an unwritten contract of shared values between a business and its customers. The relational exchange that takes place the moment money is exchanged for goods or services also involves an understanding that the business and its customers both stand for something more, something unique, something special even, and it is that that makes the entire relationship work for both.

To stick with the bakery of my example, here's how your successful baked bread business would look in a semantic world: On your fast-loading, mobile-device friendly website you would have fresh, daily content that would keep me coming back to learn about what's new in the baked bread world. There would be baked bread industry news and a blog where your passion for your business would be palpable. There might be special recipes for making my own bread whenever I want to, and there might even be speciality breads that I specifically have to remember to come in for.

On YouTube there would be videos telling me just how your bread is made from flour that's imported from a particular region of France, famous for its waters that help feed some of the ripest wheat on the planet. There would be a video of you getting up at 4:00 a.m. to make it to your bakery in time to put the first batch of bread in the oven. I would see you get that bread out of the oven and test it for perfection. All of this would add to the value of your work in my mind. I would not be buying just a loaf of bread from you. I would be buying a work of art. And because of that I would be willing to share that video and even your website content with my online circle of friends with whom I share my passions, including my love for baked bread.

On Facebook I would come across one of my Facebook friends talking about your baked bread because you recently ran a promotion there, and I would chime in, explaining that I am a big fan and have never considered going back to buying sliced bread since I switched to your product. Someone would tweet that on Twitter, and I would then re-tweet it because you have managed to make me an evangelist of your product through the passion and effort you put into baked bread.

On Google+ I would see a discussion going on that you started about the ethical sourcing of grain and the paying of a fair price to farmers. I would not join in, because it's out of my expertise, but I would feel proud to actually help create a fairer world with my money, and I would share your post with my friends explaining that we need more businesses like yours.

It's possible that all this attention would also get you some coverage from bloggers who cover the baked bread industry, and they would mention your business in their articles, perhaps even link to your website. Fairer pricing and the value we place on the creation of goods is a hot topic, and the blogosphere is always actively looking for "heroes."

Meanwhile all this activity is noticed by Google's semantic search bot. It sees that when it comes to baked bread you pump out more content than anybody else, and it is original. What's more it is reshared and commented on by many of those who come across it. Your content is associated with a fair price for wheat farmers and even the notion of a fairer world. Your website comes up in connection with both topics in mentions and online discussions. It also appears on Google search whenever equitable farming practices are mentioned. Both these subjects are now associated in Google's serendipitous information retrieval with your website so that whenever someone looks for baked bread and your company name they also find the gem that is fair sourcing of grain. Their world expands; they become better informed. They realize that the money they spend as consumers buying a daily necessity has a far greater impact than just paying a good price. Some of them will share this with their friends, expanding your reach and fame.

One or two of those who come across articles about you happen to be in the media. They remember where they saw fair pricing for grain and which bakery was associated with it. You may get a call or two from a local TV station; a staff reporter may want to interview you for a short newspaper piece.

Google sees that your company name is consistently associated with the notion "change the world for the better." It begins to serve your website to those who are researching the subject looking to find out more, some of whom are intrigued. They talk online extensively about how a small bakery has become a symbol for changing the world for the better. Some become your customers; others not local to you extol your product to those who are to become your customers. You begin to get offers for partnerships, and an entrepreneur or two approach you with the idea of a franchise run under the same principles as your local business.

In the meantime traffic on your website goes through the roof. You begin to experiment with selling bread online with orders placed days in advance and bread delivered locally within a certain, same-day radius. You launch an Android app to keep those on the move satisfied with content about bread and a fairer world. It is successful. You follow it up with an iPad app, and the Apple bloggers pick up the notion that "baked bread has come to the iPad" and write about it. After the first three months you extend the functionality of your app to include special offers, and, as a trial, you launch the ability to send someone a fresh loaf of bread anywhere in the United States. You cut a deal with a number of independent bakeries to fulfil orders where you can't, and you reciprocate.

You have to think about hiring more staff and extending your baking hours. You may well need bigger premises and more outlets. Your baked bread business has successfully leveraged the relationship economy through the connectivity of semantic search to

- Find new customers.
- Increase its reach.
- Grow its impact.
- Grow its market.
- Increase its visibility.
- Change the perception of the value of its product.
- Evolve the scope of its business relationship.

In the meantime your competitor, a more traditional baked bread business situated in the next neighborhood, is complaining. Business is slow. With so many choices in sliced supermarket bread no one wants to fork over money in these tough times to buy freshly baked bread. He is thinking of selling and closing down.

Sound far-fetched? Zappos shoes started out selling shoes online, a task many considered impossible. The dollarshaveclub became a constant on search for terms such as "razor blades online" and "razor blades via mail," and its YouTube video was watched millions of times. Both of these disrupted their industry, doing what was thought to be impossible because they approached the Web with what I call true semantic search values in mind.

To win in a semantic search world you need more people than you have on your payroll. You need your customers. You need fans. You need evangelists. A marketing plan and a budget, the staples of twentieth century promotion, no longer cut it. A top-down, controlled advertising approach won't work either; you will not get the online interaction you need to amplify your presence.

Kevin Kelly, founder and former editor of *Wired*, made waves around the Web when in 2008 he wrote a blog post called "1,000 True Fans." The proposition of it was that success on the Web does not necessarily entail having the "whole of America" following your efforts as long as you have 1,000 true fans.

Kelly's definition of a "true fan" is one who is passionate about what you do and is willing to give you the worth of a day's work (i.e., $100) in the year. Kelly was talking about the eCommerce side of things, which back then was the most contested and contentious issue in terms of development and success, but his concept is totally applicable in the social media age of the semantic web.

Change the word "fan" to "customer," add in social media and its ability to create immediacy, accessibility, and personalization, and the formula Kelly was talking about works in terms of amplifying your marketing message, your brand signal, and your sales pitch. Significantly, it is all done through content. The catch is that your content must now explain your brand values, establish the common ground between yourself and your potential customers, and be convincing enough to turn those who do business with you into Kelly's version of "true fans"—brand evangelists who will extol your products and services of their own accord.

In a digital world where search has meaning, content needs to as well, and that requires your business to also be able to deliver real meaning in what it does that goes well past the product and its sales pitch. Put simply just saying "buy my stuff" is not going to work regardless of how loudly or often you say it.

How Semantic Search Is Creating New Economies

Having used the example of the fresh bread bakery to illustrate the insidious power of semantic search to pick up and amplify your online presence in ways that are frankly quite unexpected, it is fair to quantify, here, the different types of economies that are emerging because of semantic search. While an economy is usually defined as a production/consumption model within a country that's restricted to goods and services, the behavior of digital transactions that extend beyond that fit the description well enough for us to use.

The economies emerging in the digital world are ones of longer value chains. They have names like relationship economy, collaborative economy, co-creational economy, or participatory economy, and they all mean the same thing: The divide between you and your customers has disappeared.

Now everyone is on the same side. You should want your customers to have a fantastic experience dealing with you, one that reflects the kind of experience my imaginary freshly baked bread company example offers.

It is the same with semantic search. Search started out in a push-pull kind of relationship where anyone who had an online presence struggled to get noticed. They used to do whatever it took to get to the first page of Google, cut every corner they could to get ahead of their competitors on search. It is questionable whether that served their customer needs first and theirs second. But if the question was ever asked it was never considered too deeply. In the helter-skelter world of the early days of search the struggle was to be seen and make the visibility work. That was also sufficient to generate sales, or at least some sales.

Clearly that is no longer sufficient.

As semantic search unleashes fresh meaning on the Web it demands of business the same three criteria we discussed in Chapter 2: trust, reputation, authority. These three are gained in exactly the same order, and in my example of the imaginary bakery, they emerged in exactly that order through the activities its owner embarked upon.

As Figure 3.1 illustrates, the three cogs of trust, reputation, and authority also make up your brand machine.

The Brand Machine

Figure 3.1   *Trust, reputation, and authority are central components in the establishment of brand equity.*

Writing in the *Journal of Theoretical and Applied Electronic Commerce Research* on the subject, reputation researchers Rehab Alnemr, Stefan Koenig, Torsten Eymann, and Christoph Meinel explained how the Internet is a distributed, decentralized environment where considerable risks are inherent in every transaction.

The absence of a central authority creates a currency out of perceived trust, which then acquires monetary value that translates into increased eCommerce and Internet services activity. This is a formalized way, perhaps, of saying that trust leads to reputation that leads to authority, and all three create your brand equity that makes you a trusted source of news and services, or a trusted place to buy something from.

Semantic search requires all three to work properly, and Google is putting in place precise mechanisms to establish them. In Chapter 4 we see just what these mechanisms are and how you can get a head start in creating them in your organization so that you benefit directly from the assessment semantic search is beginning to impose.

The New SEO Preparation Checklist

Brand equity is gold. It leads to a better amplified online presence, greater offline/online benefits, and real bottom line gains. Semantic search has mechanisms that measure trust, reputation, and authority through content creation and social interaction. Brands that are trusted enjoy a greater market share and better relationships with their customers and suppliers. They have an easier ride when markets undergo tough times and are quicker to benefit when there is a boom. Above all, they enjoy that most ephemeral quality of all, one that is incredibly hard to get and all too easy to lose: customer loyalty.

Each of our checklists so far has been designed to help you define the tools, concepts, and practices that you have to put into effect to take advantage of the benefits offered by Google's semantic search.

The New SEO Preparation Checklist involves the following steps:

- Identify the kind of content that is prevalent in your business vertical. Match it across different social networks and online content sharing channels, such as specific industry blogs or channels that deliver a specific type of content, for example, YouTube for video or SoundCloud for podcasts.

- Explain how you "listen" to your potential customers. What social media monitoring tools do you employ to do so, and what criteria do you use to filter the content you capture and then assess it?

- Explain how you plan to discover where your customers are in the social Web. What techniques will you use, which social platforms will you look at, and what metrics are you going to employ to gauge interest, engagement, and interaction?

- Explain what you understand by the concept of the "online conversation." How do you propose to initiate it and then how will you continue it?

- Explain how a realignment of values can help you remove any perceived barriers from what you do and what your customers want. Then detail how that realignment will be communicated to your potential customers.

- Explain how brand evangelists could help your business, and then detail three different ways you could attract, find, or convert potential customers to become brand evangelists.

- Explain the decision-making and approval content in your organization for content creation. Each time content is created you need to have some criteria in place that guarantees quality and professionalism. List what they are. Explain how they reflect the core values of your brand.

- Explain how you plan to monitor your company's or brand's performance in search beyond ranking for keywords. List the tools you will use, frequency of checking, and what decisions you made when you chose the criteria that will be used to judge success.

- Explain what brand equity means for your organization. Then detail how you assess the worth of brand equity, what choices you make, what criteria you have in place, and how they impact what you do.

- List everything you stand to gain if your brand equity increases in the future. Explain in detail the impact that greater brand equity will have upon your customer base, your marketing, your content production teams, and the bottom line.

4

Trust and Author Rank

The Web is changing. The transition is loosely described as going from a web of websites to a web of people. Essentially this means that authority on the Web and the power to gain visibility in search are shifting from something that happened exclusively through actions that had to take place on a web page to activities that now must be instigated through people, and by people, and they become the prime movers. This is a subtle change with far-reaching effects that we need to understand.

In this chapter we see just what impact this transition has on your SEO. We examine what visible metrics were in place in the past to help create trust online and what has replaced them now in the emerging semantic web. We also discuss what you can do to create a trusted online presence.

Trust in a Semantic Web

Trust is one of those qualities that you cannot easily define but is worth its weight in gold. Before the global credit crunch people used to trust banks because they thought they provided a valuable service and were too big to fail. The spectacular collapse of Lehman Brothers and the avalanche of revelations about corruption, mistakes, improprieties, and profiteering that affected most money institutions across the globe, killed off both those notions.

The importance we place on trust and the semantic web has become crucial for two reasons. The first, and perhaps the most obvious one, is that the traditional means we had at our disposal that were used to create a sense of trust no longer work. Fancy logos, sleek websites, and heavy advertising seem now to be the tools of potential conmen (like Bernie Madoff) rather than the badges of trustworthiness. The second is that in a world where social media creates radical transparency trust becomes an incremental quality that is built in a series of steps that take place at the point where a company or a brand meets its online target audience.

When size is no longer enough, apparent wealth does not count, honors and titles are suspect, sleek advertising and top-down control have the exact opposite effect than desired, and any kind of apparent authority produces suspicion, trust building becomes a much harder exercise.

To understand the challenge created by the notion of trust on the Web let's first examine why you need it and why it's likely that you do not have it, or at least you may not have as much as you need. One way of looking at the Web is as a decentralized, empowering machine that creates abundance out of scarcity. Scarcity usually implies direct value in something and the person or organization who provides it, and it is associated with a high initial cost.

When the only way to buy a pair of GORE-TEX boots was to drive down to a department store at the mall, the trust factor associated with the store that sold them was high because the cost of setting up shop was high—high enough to make it unlikely that the store would take my money and offer me poor quality boots. The assumption here is whatever the store would gain by selling bad boots was so little compared to the damage that would happen to its reputation if the customer's trust was lost that it was unlikely to be worth their while to try and offer poor quality goods.

My investment here was in a pair of boots. Even a thousand customers investing in a similar transaction to mine was pretty small change when compared to the operational costs of a department store. This means that to survive a department store had to become a destination of trust in the mind of each of its customers. It had to become the place I would unquestioningly drive down to and give my money in exchange for merchandise, and I had to keep on doing it all year round, year after year.

The only way the department store could survive and succeed was by getting my business again and again and again.

On the Web anyone can set up a website and can say anything about anything. What's more, they can also sell anything. While I will not go so far as to say that the cost of setting up a website is equal to a pair of GORE-TEX hiking boots, it certainly is not on the same level as setting up a brick-and-mortar department store. The Web is a more dynamic and open environment where the behavior of the participants is uncertain.

When the behavior of the participants cannot always be guaranteed because of the environment they operate in (in this case the Web), the calculation of trust that any participant has toward any other is based on two distinct types of experiences:

- Direct experience (which means that having dealt directly with a company or brand we now have sufficient information to know whether we can trust them)
- No direct experience (which means that our sense of trust toward them will now have to be generated through our assessment of third-party opinions or suggestions)

On the Web the most popular third-party "suggestion engine" is search. It serves results in direct response to our search queries, and it makes suggestions in direct response to its own assessment of a company's or brand's website's credentials. Google, as a brand, invests an enormous amount of resources to establish its credentials. As a matter of fact the investment Google makes in being Google dwarfs that of the department store in the mall of my example. This creates the interesting chain of association that if the end-user, carrying out a search, trusts Google to deliver the most relevant results, then a business or brand first needs to convince Google of its authenticity and trustworthiness.

This would make the task of marketing online fairly singular: Prove to Google that you are worthy of recommendation in search. Then sit back and enjoy the commercial success you deserve. Funnily enough this is not that far removed from the kind of success that traditionally was there to be had by companies or brands that managed to get on the first spot of the first page of Google's search engine results pages.

The modern notion of trust that carries weight on the semantic web is one that harks back to an age when communities numbered in the hundreds of members at most. In that environment people either knew each other or knew someone who knew the person they needed to deal with. This association is important. If you wanted to do business or get some information about a particular subject, in that environment, you went straight to a person whom you knew could be trusted. If they could not help you, they were usually able to direct you to another person who could.

What if I were to tell you that this old-fashioned, simplistic way of connecting is now machine-driven, scalable, and capable of sorting the wheat from the chaff on the Web?

This is pretty much what has happened, and the primary requirement for this revolves around a singularly simple concept that seems to be at odds with the way the Web works: identity.

Creating an Identity in a Connected World

Before Google introduced Google+ and insisted on real names being used on the social network, identity on the Web was a chancy thing. The original Web was the product of connections being made among members of academic communities where the question of identity (and trust) was not much of an issue. As a result no one really thought about the need to create a formal way of verifying who they were. As the Web grew exponentially, anonymity and the flux of being anyone you wanted to be online became one of its signature marks.

This is not to say that efforts were not made. In *Weaving the Web: The Original Design and Ultimate Destiny of the World Wide Web*, Tim Berners-Lee wrote: "The Web is more a social creation than a technical one. I designed it for a social effect—to help people work together—and not as a technical toy. The ultimate goal of the Web is to support and improve our weblike existence in the world. We clump into families, associations, and companies. We develop trust across the miles and distrust around the corner."

This was a sentiment many felt to be true and they saw the problem of identity on the Web as something that needed to be addressed. One solution was floated in 2003 with the introduction of Xhtml Friends Network, an independent effort. Shortened to XFN for convenience, the idea was to allow hyperlinks with specific attributes like rel=friend or rel=brother to be used, therefore creating an awareness of the relationships behind the people who run the websites.

XFN was notable because it also introduced the attribution of the author meta tag allowing someone to be identified as the author of a particular web page (something that has been incorporated in HTML5).

None of these efforts were destined to take off or have much of an impact. For a start they required some technical skill with code (when the majority of people on the Web have none), and they were decentralized activities that required a conscious effort of goodwill to take place. Someone needed to actually go to the trouble to insert links with specific attributes or meta tags in this way, and the pay-off for them was questionable in the short term and uncertain in the long term.

The majority of people on the Web were therefore left to experience it as a web of connections that provided no means of ascribing any value to them that they could see.

When it came to commercial transactions you took your chances. You could choose, for instance, to do business with someone called "NewLuddite87," but there was always a chance that since you did not know that person's agenda, per-sonality, or even identity, if things went south he could easily cut ties and resur-face using another name without any loss of reputation. The risks seemed too one-sided.

The problem seemed intractable. It became solvable only when we were in a closed community setting, like eBay, where the introduction of a feedback system that could impact on reputation, which then had a direct impact on sales, created a level playing field. In eBay the seller and buyer hold mutual power over each other, and each represents an equal half of a successful transaction. For as long as both the seller and the buyer intend to be active in the eBay environment they both have a vested interest in helping each other report a positive experience. But eBay is not the Web. Not everyone wants to go through a commercial transaction process to learn whom to trust, and there are still plenty of other relational exchanges that happen online and involve the exchange of data and information instead of money where trust is just as important. These have no feedback systems to help gauge reputation and trust.

The growth of the Web, the prevalence of search, and the need to create a sense of trust in the search results have made the problem as pressing for search engines to solve as it was for ordinary end-users who routinely accessed information online.

Although it is not immediately obvious, this is something Google had been work-ing on for some time, and the company's efforts came to fruition with Google+.

Google+ solved this problem by doing what few social networks have ever suc-ceeded in doing: It made it cool to use your real name, photograph, and details on the Web. Google achieved this through the usual means it does anything: by lever-aging the carrot (and stick) that is called search. Although it did not really become apparent what it had done until almost a year after Google+ was in place, the intention behind it started out a lot earlier, as far back as August 2005, as a matter of fact, with US Patent Application 20070033168. In that filing search engineers David Minogue and Paul A. Tucker filed for what the abstract describes as

"The present invention provides methods and apparatus, including computer program products, implementing techniques for searching and ranking linked information sources. The techniques include receiving multiple content items from a corpus of content items; receiving digital signatures each made by one of multiple agents, each digital signature associating one of the agents with one or more of the content items; and assigning a score to a first agent of the multiple agents, wherein the score is based upon the content items associated with the first agent by the digital signatures."

Translated into plain English this is the intention, by Google, to take content that is placed on websites and rank it according to who placed it there (or created it) and who they are. Obviously, the first step in achieving this was to find a way to actually identify people on the Web. The problem is that online there are no restrictions such as those presented in the offline world. There are no physical addresses. There is no face-to-face contact. Nicknames and websites and even online businesses represent a fluid environment where one easily can morph into something else, virtually overnight.

Facebook, to name but one large social network, has long had a real names policy in place. And yet in its first quarterly report to regulators since the company went public in 2012, Facebook itself revealed that it had 83 million fake profiles on its network. A "real names policy in place" clearly is not the answer to solving the identity issue on the Web. Nor is having penalties a deterrent. Most network users either don't think they will get caught or, if they do, they simply come back with another fake name and fake profile.

Policing the mechanics of the network or, for that matter, the Web is not a solution either. IP addresses and locations can be changed or cloaked. New nicknames can be invented, and new websites and business names can be worked up. Even the existence of a central account (like a Google account) is not sufficient to verify a real identity. Microsoft tried that for years, hoping that its Microsoft Account service that also eventually incorporated Microsoft Wallet, Microsoft Passport, .NET Passport, Microsoft Passport Network, and most recently Windows Live ID, would provide an online authentication service that would allow the online population to sign in on many websites with just one login and also help solve the question of identity on the Web.

It failed.

Although many dead trees as well as pixels have been devoted to analyzing why Microsoft's efforts in that direction failed, the reason is a simple one: gain. Prior to Google no one had provided the online population with any real motivation to reveal who they are. If anything, the "freedom" of the Web to be whoever you wanted to be was seen as fundamental to its identity, and any attempts to change this were perceived as a direct attack on the freedom of the Web and condemned as such.

The answer to the online identity question is that it had to be an effort undertaken voluntarily with some real gain to be enjoyed for undertaking it.

Prior to Google no one had provided the online population with a real motivation to identify and verify their identities or the reason to go into some effort to either link up accounts and clarify them under a single identity or abandon the multiple account syndrome and put in all their efforts behind a single identity that became their online presence.

Google's patent 20070033168 did this in a way that in retrospect appears blindingly obvious.

Trust and Authority

It is perfectly logical to assume that the validity of content on the Web, its trust-worthiness and its authority, rests more with the creator of the content than the owner of the platform where the content appears. Think about it for a moment. An article written by a faceless service that outsourced it to the lowest cost provider in a third-world country, when placed on a high-ranking brand website could easily outrank in Google search a highly detailed, authoritative piece that simply appeared on someone's personal blog.

Of such injustices is sometimes change made. In our case, though, it was more a case of relevance for Google and a real need to get rid of spammy websites with deep pockets that could buy links and order cheaply written, keyword-rich content that would then help them rank in search.

Prior to semantic search, authority and trust on the Web were calculated, primar-ily, through PageRank. Named after Larry Page, PageRank is a link analysis algo-rithm that looks at a set of websites and ascribes a numerical value to each based upon its perceived importance in the set. The set, in this case, could easily be the entire Web (as when Google search is looking for a list of possible answers for you) as well as a smaller subset (like the ranking that appears on Google search once the list of possible answers to a search query has been drawn up). This is the Link Graph that became central to many of the services that sprung up around SEO activities.

The public version of PageRank (called PR for short) was intended to indicate Google's trust in the authority and reputation of a website. It was updated two or three times a year, and it was easy to find and frequently publicly displayed. The nonpublic version of PageRank was calculated on a daily basis and sometimes adjusted within a subset of websites prior to them being displayed on Google's search results page. This way links pointing from one set of websites to a particular website acted as votes of confidence from one website to another and determined the perceived value of each.

The diagram in Figure 4.1 provides a good representation of how PageRank works. The size of each circle, representing a website, indicates its importance in the eyes of search.

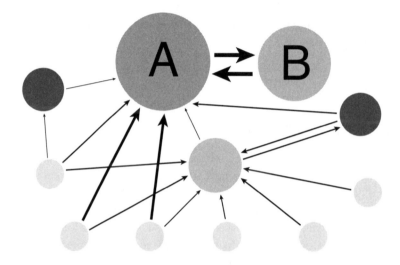

Figure 4.1 *Google uses algorithmic scales to work out the importance of a link and decide how to appraise the importance of a website. The arrows represent links, and the circles represent websites. Although website "B" has just one link coming to it, it is appraised as having greater value because it gets a link from a highly trusted, authoritative website to which it also links back.*

Just by looking at Figure 4.1 we can see the potential issues that such a model raises. In theory, of course, it should have worked flawlessly. In theory one website only links to another if it really believes in its authority and authenticity. In practice it gave rise to a link economy on the Web that revolved around the artificial boosting of a website's worth in the eyes of Google and the promotion of its ranking in search, beyond its real merit.

Behind each link, of course, Google introduced an ever more finely grained tuning that took into account:

- The topical relevance of the website providing the link
- The placement on the page of the link
- The anchor text used to link from

- The importance of the page that provided the link
- The age of the website
- The age of the page
- The age of the link

As a matter of fact this is the process in which the more than 200 separate ranking signals were used in an attempt to increase accuracy in the results, stop the gaming of the system, and establish a certain degree of veracity that could always be relied on.

Despite this constant refinement Google ended up fighting a losing battle. For each attempt it made to create trust and authenticity human ingenuity seemed to be able to produce a workaround. Left alone it's evident that it wouldn't really take that long to break the system, and the moment search broke, the Web would start to unravel at the seams. To break the deadlock, Google put in place through Google+ an online identity service.

The first real hint that this is exactly what Google+ is was given by former Google CEO Eric Schmidt at the Edinburgh International TV Festival in August 2011 when in reply to a question by NPR's Andy Carvin he stated that "Google+ was built primarily as an identity service, so fundamentally, it depends on people using their real names if [we're] going to build future products that leverage that information."

This echoes the comments made by Google's search chief Amit Singhal who in an interview with Danny Sullivan, editor of searchengineland.com, stated: "A good product can only be built where we understand who's who and who is related to whom. Relationships are also important alongside content. To build a good product, we have to do all types of processing. But fundamentally, it's not just about content. It's about identity, relationships and content."

This makes it clear that the transition from a web consisting of websites and their authority to a web consisting of people and a greater degree of trust began pretty much the moment Google+ was turned on and people started to join it.

Actionables at this point for a company or brand include

- Setting a monetary value to reputation. The definition of reputation is the willingness of total strangers to trust you when they have no direct experience of you. In a business environment that leads to an increase in transactional interaction.

- Sales that have a monetary value. It helps clarify your goals when you know, first what your reputation is worth to you in terms of sales. If you lost it today, would it impact your earnings and by how much? And second, if you improved your reputation so that your brand was widely known as a reputable one to do business with, how many more sales would you make? This value is obviously an estimate as you can only guess, but again, it is something that helps you with your goal setting.

- Understanding the need to build and maintain trust. This means that you have to break down into discrete steps how you will do this, i.e. content created and shared that has a certain style and authority. Your style of communicating. Your willingness to engage in specific discussions, online, and so on.

- Devising a way to assess the monetary impact of trust and reputation on your business. (The impact of eBay's visual feedback system is a great example of how reputation can impact trust and affect sales.) In order to progress you need to understand how each percentage point you lose or gain in reputation affects your business' ability to make money.

With all this in mind, the data being pulled together through Google+ also made Google's patent make real sense. Suddenly the words "linked information sources," "content items," "digital signature," and "agent" could be translated into plain English as websites, content, identity, and person, respectively. The foundation for the transition of trust and authority from websites to people was on, and it was largely voluntary and scalable. The real question of course is how?

Ranking and Reputation Scores

Having an algorithm judge your reputation is no easy thing. On the Web there are no gestures, voice cues, or body language. There is no easy way to judge the size and worth of your business or the tradition of the company that has hired you. Your intent, in other words, is a mystery. So you have to somehow work with what you have: people, content, and websites.

The supposition here, and it's a deep one, is that given sufficient time and enough social connections to follow, Google can learn to understand not just the meaning of individual words but also the real importance of content and those who interact with it.

Google's big pull here came with Google+ and more specifically a raft of gains that revolved from being in the social network and using a real name and picture there. As expected these had to do with search and the building up of trust in one's online presence, and central to this effort was the relatively unique idea of authorship.

There is a problem with the Web that is intrinsic to anonymity. If you have created a fantastic piece of content that you then place on your blog and use it to begin the promotion of yourself, it can be stolen.

Content "stolen" by mistake (because someone simply does not realize it's not the done thing), or by intent (in outright plagiarism), or unintentionally but by design (as in when someone uses an automated program called a scraper to pull content from the Web) was the Achilles' heel of the Web. It undermined the efforts of search engines looking for originality and quality, it disincentivized content creators who often saw content stolen from them used to outrank their own sites, and it made it difficult to establish any kind of deep trust in search or the content found on the Web.

Remember the XFN initiative we looked at earlier in this chapter? This is what they were trying to address. And they were not successful. The reason they were not successful is because they were not providing sufficient incentive for the verification action to happen in the first place. Just "for the good of the Web" is great as a notion but poor as a driver of action. You need something more.

But before we get to the nitty-gritty of what Google offered let's take one small step back and look at the bigger picture that contains the beast called Author Rank.

Author Rank is the natural outcome of Google's patent 20070033168. It assigns a specific value to a content creator and then uses that value to further rank, or not, the page that this person has created. There is a lot of speculation as to the exact extent Google goes into when brining all these factors together. Certainly the company indexes and stores the information, but the exact synthesis and the weight it ascribes to it is never made very clear. However it is fair to assume that the synthesis contains attributes such as

- Who created the content
- What else that person has created in the past
- The content creator's social media connections
- The content creator's online activity with further content
- The content creator's interaction with other people
- How the content this person created was received in a social media setting
- The content's quality, authority, and originality.
- The content's stylistics (language level, reading difficulty, paragraph length, use of headings and subheadings, overall length, embedded links, supportive links in footnotes, citations, images, and any multimedia embedded in it.

In addition to these there is the granularity provided by the Google+ Activity API (Application Programming Interface). The API is designed to allow developers to build applications and services that integrate seamlessly with Google+. It is of interest to us here because of the kind of data it is designed to capture. Captured data such as "Additional content added by the person who shared this activity, applicable only when resharing an activity," or "Comments in reply to this activity," point to engagement being the strongest metric that Google uses to calculate the weight of online profiles.

The Google+ API actually is detailed with no fewer than 81 different attributes that can be potentially captured for each interaction, and some of these have several subclasses of attributes of their own.

This indicates that in the semantic web, interactivity and engagement can become refined. By incrementally adding data attributes each of which represents a quality such as authority, originality, trustworthiness, we can use an algorithm to judge the quality of an online profile (i.e. a person) or a website in a very nuanced way. As a matter of fact if we think that this approach mimics, to some extent, the process we employ as individuals in the offline world to judge people and businesses, we would not be wide of the mark.

Google uses Google+ as a primary source of information to gather all this data, particularly where the person's name is concerned, but it also uses other points on the Web like Twitter, Facebook, and comments on forums and blogs to cross-reference everything in an effort to flesh out the "identity" behind the name.

All this data gathered is what Google calls "the social signal," and it includes activity on social networks. It measures influence, reach, and the quality of connections on them, and it is used to calculate a digital reputation score with the intent to gauge how much it can be trusted.

So now we've come to the meat of all this. The fact that trust and reputation in the online world can now finally be algorithmically assessed, independent of social network platform, is of vital interest to any business. Success at achieving a high enough level of trust means a direct increase in the likelihood of conversions from online visitors to paying customers at your website. Trust matters because it governs search rankings in SERPs. More than that, it matters because it governs how frequently and how prominently your website is served in Google's semantic search results as an "answer" to a need. It matters because now, it means money. It really comes down to this: businesses that are trusted get more visitors and make more sales.

None of this would really work if Google had not managed to solve the most important issue here: content ownership. In the new semantic web, results in

Google search frequently come attached with thumbnail pictures of their creators. A picture of the content creator, next to a listing of the page associated with him, visible on Google search to hundreds of thousands, even millions of people across the globe, makes for a powerful brand message. A strong marketing angle.

The pull is undeniable for anyone working online, and that's just how Google's verified Authorship, a feature that initially was available only through Google+, became the carrot that convinced online brand marketers, writers, and authors to play the online identity game. The picture in Figure 4.2 perfectly illustrates why.

Figure 4.2   *Content creators who have gone to the trouble of verifying the authorship of their content have a thumbnail of their picture displayed on Google search, alongside information regarding their popularity in Google+ and a link encouraging the viewer to find more content by the same author.*

In what has to be the cleverest move in mutual gain, Authorship allows content creators the opportunity to leverage the global power of Google search to market themselves to their audience. In return they help Google weed out the low-quality spam sites that polluted the Google search results and diluted the end-user's trust in the brand.

The steps that lead to your personal picture being displayed on Google's search are simple. Here's what you need to do:

- Have a Google+ profile (not a page).
- Link that Google+ profile to your content (the pages you write, blog posts you create, or website you own).
- Place a Google Profile Badge (http://goo.gl/d9lAr) on your website or blog page (that contains the rel=author tag that identifies you in Google's eyes as the creator of that content).
- Go to Google's Rich Snippet Tool (http://goo.gl/AhPN), input the URL of your site or the page you have, and check to see whether Google recognizes the connection. If it does, it will tell you, and a thumbnail of your face will appear in Google's search results within a few weeks.

As Authorship becomes more important and Google wants to encourage more people to implement it, it has begun to offer different ways it can be set up. On Google+ there is an Official Authorship Page that contains all the necessary, up-to-date details and is well worth a visit: https://plus.google.com/authorship.

Notable in this is the fact that Authorship verification works only for people, so you need to use a Google+ profile, not a Google+ page to set it up, and the thumbnail image you use must be of a person. Google has face recognition in place that is sensitive enough to work even with caricatures. Logos and brand images do not work and will not show on search.

What this allows the clever company or brand to do, of course, is to leverage the people who work in its business to increase its importance on the Web. There is, of course, an additional element at work here that is almost a side effect. The use of real people to front a company has begun to humanize corporations and brands. Because people like interacting with people, as opposed to faceless corporations, it is increasing social media engagement between businesses and their target audience who now can identify a little better with them, and it is accelerating the impact of the social web on businesses and search.

The benefits of Authorship do not stop there. As if the promise of exposure on Google search is not enough, Google has created additional benefits for author creators who go to the trouble necessary to verify and claim their content by suggesting to end-users more results by the same author if they have looked at one of the pages created by that author and have then spent some time reading it (see Figure 4.3).

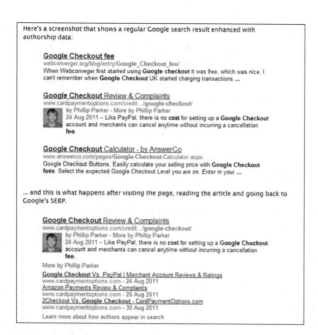

Figure 4.3 *In the image at the top we see the results returned by Google search, and below that we see the results returned by Google search after some time has been spent reading the article and then clicking the back button to return to the search page.*

The idea behind this is that, first, provided sufficient time has been spent by the end-user on a page, the person is engaged and therefore finds the content to be of value, and second, for authors who create consistently great content, this is a way to allow more of it to be discovered.

This is a radical departure from anything we have had in the past. To understand just how radical it really is we need to look under the hood of Google's search engine. The moment we type a search query in Google search that query is ranked according to two sets of criteria. One is called query-dependent criteria, and the other is called query-independent criteria (usually called signals).

Traditionally, the former includes the search terms used, their association with a particular web page, where they are in the document, how fresh that content is, and its keyword density in relation to the search query. The latter includes an assessment of the importance of the website through PageRank, its age, reach, and the quality of its connections on the Web. Semantic search, with its introduction of the range of assessed activities that are loosely grouped under the "Author Rank" label, changes both how search query-dependent and search query-independent signals work by filtering everything through the content creator.

Now, instead of keyword density (an on-page search engine optimization technique) and PageRank (an off-page search engine optimization technique) determining the ranking of websites in search, we have the reputation, perceived trust, and authority on a particular subject of the content creator influencing both search query-dependent signals (how trusted the content is and how relevant to the search query) and search query-independent signals (the perceived trust, authority, and validity of the website containing the content).

The rationale here is that if an algorithmically calculated reputation score is hard to attain and relatively easy to lose, then it begins to acquire value worth safeguarding. This happens through the judicious creation and sharing of content on the Web. In other words, people suddenly have the ability to influence ranking by the quality of their digital presence and association with particular content. If search is marketing as I stated in Chapter 1 of this book, then content marketing is how you get found in search.

A much deeper implication to this change goes beyond Google search and seeps into the way organizations structure themselves and determine their offline operations: Author Rank takes time, effort, and energy to build up. By placing real power in ranking on the online authority of individuals on the Web, Google challenges the notion of the traditional employer/employee relationship. The traditional power dynamic of a company that took the work of a group of individuals at one end and gave it value through a sausage-factory production process that brought a collective outcome also assumed that they were all expendable and interchangeable components of a larger whole.

A company's online presence is no longer the direct result of the faceless collective efforts of a number of departments like, for instance, marketing, products, PR, and SEO. In the semantic search Web, the company presence is guided and aided by the accumulated authority and trust that resides in the algorithmic calculation of the profile of the individuals who are engaged by it.

When these are members of its workforce it raises questions such as what happens when one resigns, on what terms and under what conditions? Can an individual with a particularly well developed online trust and reputation score withdraw her support for the content she has created by removing the link pointing to it from her Google+ profile, thus affecting the standing of the company's website?

The answer to that question is not immediately clear. It becomes even more challenging when we consider that beyond its efforts to get individuals to put their real identities online and claim ownership of the content they have created, Google is refining and improving its own means of identifying content creators and ascribing Authorship to them, making them appear in search in association with content even when they themselves have not expressly gone through the steps required to link their Google+ profile to it.

Currently this process is imprecise, providing some instances of amusement, such as when a 2010 story about abortion on *The New York Times* website, written by Emily Bazelon, was wrongly attributed on Google search to deceased writer and author of *Breakfast at Tiffany's* Truman Capote, or some instances of frustration when Anthony Pensabene, a blogger and content marketing consultant, had a piece written by him in May 2012 for his own eponymous blog wrongly attributed to digital marketing specialist Chris Countey on Google search.

In each case the errors occurred because Google, lacking clear signals by the authors who had created the content, was working to fill in the blanks. When ascribing authorship attribution on Google search without the benefit of the Google+ profile link, Google picks up all the possible signals it can find. Most blog posts and articles have a byline, for instance, and Google knows that this is the name of the person. The challenge comes when it has to match the name to an image and present it in search without any help from a Google+ profile link.

Semantic search is a lot more complex than it sounds. It is, however, capable of learning, and, unlike humans, it does not forget, so mistakes are not repeated, and the more relationships it maps, the better it becomes at inferring the importance between them. These are, indeed, human qualities. Semantic search is computational in nature; it retrieves answers based on inferences rather than statistical analysis. Because computations take up more resources than traditional analysis semantic search has a clever caching system that allows it to store answers it has already worked out, almost like a human memory, and retrieve them faster when necessary. More than that, fresh answers that require answers that have already been worked out and have been semantically cached, now become possible, allowing a scaling of complexity in computations that looks very much like human learning.

Cases such as the ones above where semantic search gets it wrong highlight the importance of not leaving things to chance and assuming that somehow Google will get it right, regardless.

The route that has led search from a cat-and-mouse game of applying techniques that game Google only to have them deprecated and then have to discover and apply new ones, to this point has been powered by the need to rank high in search. The temptation to say that semantic search is impossible to game is high, but inaccurate. Like anything that has to do with machine learning, semantic search can also be gamed.

What has changed, however, is that now the energy, time, and cost it would take to successfully game semantic search is high enough to make it impractical. Offered with no discernible shortcut, it makes sense to do things "properly" anyway and try to rank high in Google's search based on merit rather than through technical shortcuts. One of the benefits of the semantic web seems to be that the transparency of connections between authors, content creators, content curators, and websites is making us all a little bit more honest.

The Author Rank Preparation Checklist

The ranking of websites based on their association with content creators and the way they, in turn, interact with web pages is radically different from anything we have had until now. Successful preparation for the semantic web requires a number of steps related directly to "Author Rank" (a.k.a. the measure of reputation and trust Google puts in a personal profile).

Leveraging Google search to promote your brand as a content creator is not just logical, it is also smart. Using your company personnel to amplify your digital presence makes total business sense and creates a valuable, additional layer to any paid efforts you already have in place.

The Author Rank Preparation Checklist involves the following steps:

- Identify company staff with a key online presence.
- Decide how you can leverage the online presence of your company personnel as a whole to help promote your website and digital marketing efforts.
- Decide how you can coordinate everyone involved in your digital marketing effort to "speak" with one voice.
- Detail how you will educate everyone within your business on the value of Authorship and linking from their Google+ profile to the company website.
- Detail how an amplification of your company's digital signal through everyone working in the business will be managed correctly.
- Decide whether there are areas of content creation in your business that are currently being overlooked and that could be better used if more members of staff blogged or became involved in the effort.
- Decide how you will encourage your staff to share content they are passionate about and find ways to include your company content in some of that sharing.
- Detail what metrics you will use to help those involved in the company's digital marketing amplification effort gauge the effectiveness of their contribution.
- Discuss how you can more closely link your company's reputation to those who work in it.
- List all the different places your company content appears in, or your company has a digital presence in, and describe how you propose the content amplification effort will be used.

5

What Is TrustRank?

Google search is getting smarter, and as it gets smarter it gets more judgmental. The greatest defense against poor search results on the Google search results page is the capability of Google's semantic search to ascribe a trust value on the results it serves. To do that it requires as much help as you can possibly give it in making the right connections.

In this chapter we examine the concept of TrustRank, how it affects your SEO efforts and what you can do to increase the likelihood of your organization's website coming up in search.

The Concept of Trust on the Web

In his popular book *The Tipping Point*, author Malcolm Gladwell looks at the way information flows in social networks based on the associated trust the members of the network have for their peers. Before we go any further here's a thought that I want you to keep in mind: Real trust is the belief in a positive outcome in a transaction that takes place in an asymmetric relationship.

If I place, for instance, the positive outcome of an event, such as acquiring a critical piece of information, in the hands of a total stranger who I have never met before, I need to have an incredible amount of trust, bordering on faith.

I am not even sure that degree of trust can work in real life between five friends let alone the Web in all its breadth and depth. So trust in a connected web, to work, has to operate in a way that completes a symmetry of sorts in transactional relationships even if the transaction in question is one of exchange of data or the simple consumption of information. Right now it's important to note that any kind of trust model on the Web without an implicit symmetry in the relationship is doomed to failure.

Symmetry implies that somehow there is a roughly equivalent amount of mutual gain to be had from the successful completion of the transaction.

This is a crucial notion because it helps us understand how semantic search assigns TrustRank to websites and people and how you can then maneuver your company or brand in a way that it gains trust in the semantic web.

The classic model of symmetrical trust on the Web is eBay where buyers leave feedback that is reflected in the reputation score of the seller. That reputation score acts as eBay's TrustRank, and even a relatively low number of negative feedbacks has the ability to significantly affect sales for a seller.

As a result sellers have a vested interest in remaining engaged with their buyers right up to the point that the transaction completes and the feedback score is given. In eBay, sellers and buyers have their TrustRank expressed as the percentage of positive feedback they have over a certain number of transactions. This allows for a nuanced approach.

Someone who, for instance, has only ever sold 27 items may not enjoy a high level of trust, despite having 100% feedback, while a power seller with more than 1,000 completed transactions will enjoy a much higher level of trust despite his positive feedback score being 99.9%. The importance here is that the feedback score on its own does not hold the swaying power we might expect. It only works when it is associated with all the other factors such as the number of transactions the seller has completed. This implies that in deciding whether to trust the seller we take into account his experience, the volume of his business, and the statistical certainty that as the volume goes up there are likely to be some unsatisfied customers or transactions that ended in a poor end-user experience.

Trust then within the eBay ecosystem is a sophisticated metric, which can be refined further based on the complexity of the item being sold (postage stamps might be easier to sell as a standardized item than, say, eighteenth century hand-painted collectors' figurines).

The numbers I have given here are arbitrary but closely reflect real-life examples I have encountered. Within the limited world of this example where a consumer is faced by two sellers selling the exact identical product, his choice will be governed by his ability to work out who he trusts more based on a complex, internalized assessment of the feedback score each seller has received, the number of transactions he has carried out, the price of the item, and the consumer's own understanding of the four separate elements that make up the feedback.

As Figure 5.1 shows, the choice between even two relatively simple items with low transactional risk becomes complicated.

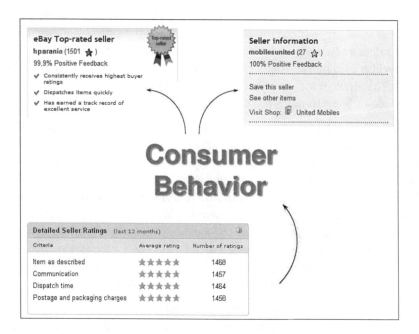

Figure 5.1 *The consumer has to make a choice based on his perception of which of two sellers is most trustworthy. What becomes apparent here is that there is no such thing as absolute trust and therefore there cannot be such a thing as an absolute TrustRank. Trust, each time, is relative to other factors prevalent at the moment of evaluation.*

In this case a recent negative feedback may have a disproportionate impact on sales despite being statistically negligible, due to its freshness. The reason for this is that it affects our assessment of trustworthiness and has an impact on purchasing behavior. The recency of the negative feedback increases, in our minds, the statistical possibility of something going wrong with our own transaction because it may indicate a change in the way the seller operates that has only now come into effect. The power of that one negative feedback, stacked against many other positive ones, shows how the time it happened makes it relevant to the consumer's intention to make a purchase in a time frame adjacent to the one the negative feedback was left in.

In 2004 Stanford researchers Zoltan Gyongyi and Hector Garcia-Molina partnered up with Yahoo's Jan Pedersen to publish a paper called *Combating Web Spam with TrustRank* where they used PageRank, the traditional way of ranking websites in search, filtered through a TrustRank algorithm of their own devising, to help them filter web spam results on the search results page.

Carrying out a limited trial they were moderately successful. Their experiment, which did improve the search results somewhat, also helped highlight the persistence of spam (or poor quality) results in search and the difficulty of assigning trust values on web content without the assistance of humans. In their trial the researchers used human-tested pages to seed the results and provide a baseline for trust. The problem with the approach is scalability across a much bigger data set of websites, such as that represented by the open web.

Incidentally human raters are also used by Google to establish a baseline in the results delivered by changes to its algorithm. Raters are paid by Google to do exactly what their name implies, rate web pages. Instead of being used to directly influence the ranking of a web page by saying "this is good," or "this is bad," they are part of the Search Quality Evaluation Team. They are used as a test of the search algorithm's accuracy in rating websites. Working from a very detailed brief (120 pages long at the last count) they establish whether a website is a good or a bad result in response to a particular search query. Their responses are then used by Google's search engineers to change the search algorithm, run comparison tests and bring out fresh search algorithm updates, like the Panda update.

While search may be hugely complicated as a subject, the results it delivers aren't subject to the same level of complexity. If you are thinking about search for the first time and are wondering just how your website can rank high so that it helps your marketing and branding ask a simple question: "Would a human rater rank this page if it came up as a response to a search query relevant to my business?" Make sure you give yourself an honest answer.

The one other remnant of the experiment carried out by Zoltan Gyongyi and Hector Garcia-Molina was the notion that TrustRank, as an algorithm, was something that Google also adopted and started to use in its rankings. This misunderstanding arose out of the fact that just a year later, in 2005, Google trademarked the term, and Googlers, when discussing how their search engine ranked websites, frequently used terms such as reputation, authority, and trust.

The facts are that Google let the trademark on "TrustRank" lapse in 2009, and the terms reputation, authority, and trust that Google uses internally are employed in a somewhat loose definition to signify the different factors that Google uses in its semantic search ranking of websites.

Again this is an important distinction. TrustRank as an algorithm suggests that this is something that has a specific entity in search, which can then be gamed. By keeping it as a guideline to what needs to be achieved in the search results in terms of quality Google also made it more robust as a guiding concept in the development of search.

If you're not thinking it already your search marketing plans then should be:

- The establishing of trust on the Web
- The establishment and safeguarding of reputation on the Web
- The need to closely associate your company or brand with trust and a great reputation

If you are wondering how this can be achieved in a way that is directly scalable across your business, hold on, we are almost there.

A vital clue as to how you can go about doing all this is found in another Google patent. In October 2009 Google was awarded patent No 7,603,350 authored by Ramanathan Guha where the words "Trust Rank" were mentioned. It's worth noting that this is the same Ramanathan Guha who in 2004 while working for IBM coauthored with Ravi Kumar a paper titled *Propagation of Trust and Distrust*.

The basis of his paper back then, which now echoed his current one, is that "a network of people connected by ratings or trust scores" is the fundamental block for building trust. The patent awarded to Google states that:

> A search engine system provides search results that are ranked according to a measure of the trust associated with entities that have provided labels for the documents in the search results. A search engine receives a query and selects documents relevant to the query.

> The search engine also determines labels associated with selected documents, and the trust ranks of the entities that provided the labels. The trust ranks are used to determine trust factors for the respective documents. The trust factors are used to adjust information retrieval scores of the documents. The search results are then ranked based on the adjusted information retrieval scores.

In other words human interaction with web pages is going to be used as one element of their assessment, and, at the same time, the reputation of those who interact with these websites may be used as one of the signals that determine their ranking in search. The fundamental difference between Google's approach is that not only is there a role for trust in its ranking model, but there is also a role for distrust.

The actionables here revolve around the magic words interaction and reputation.

People interact with websites in a combination of ways, which in descending order of importance are

- Commenting in a blog post on the website
- Responding to comments on a blog post on the website
- Commenting about a website in social networks
- Responding to comments about a website in social networks
- Resharing the content of websites and adding a comment to the reshare
- Resharing the content of websites without adding any comment
- Following websites that have a presence on a social network
- "Liking" or "+1-ing" the content of websites
- Interacting with the social network posts of websites

In their totality these are the activities that produce the "social signal" that Google uses in its semantic search indexing to help rank websites in search. They are also a blueprint of sorts when it comes to the marketing activities that produce results in the semantic web.

Building a Web of Trust

We've seen that trust cannot really be successfully built in a system that does not support a symmetry that can confer value for all parties engaged in a transactional exchange (like in eBay with its feedback to the seller and buyer approach). The problem with the Web is that it is a largely open system with a large subset of unique interactions. In that respect the idea that symmetry can be created based on the mutual benefit of monetary transactions is insufficient to ensure a defining motive for all the different subsets that exist within it.

A fitness forum where members go to share training tips and information, for instance, has no monetary value for any of them. A community of people of different backgrounds, levels of experience, and motives for being online drawn together by a perceived shared interest offers no monetary transactions of any kind. A large social network, like Facebook, that draws in hundreds of millions of people with the promise of keeping in touch with close friends and relatives and perhaps meeting new people offers no perceived mutual gain, particularly the moment people extend their circle of contacts to create a pool that is no longer bound by their everyday contacts of people they know. All of these are examples of asymmetric relationships that extend beyond the narrow sense of buying and selling.

There is a small paradox here that drives the point home even more. Buying and selling, activities that are of some transactional value in terms of money, may indeed become evident at some point, somewhere within some of these systems or even in a digital space tangential to them (like, say, eBay). I, for instance, could come across a contact in a fitness forum who is selling a bicycle. As we engage in what is a commercial activity in a system that is not really designed for it, we begin to be bound by the symmetry of both of us wanting a positive outcome, yet the environment we are in is a sort of free-for-all place that is not really conducive to that sort of transaction going smoothly. The moment that happens the existing asymmetry of relationships within the system becomes even more unequal with some of the members now being bound either by an existing symmetry outside the system (if I meet a forum member in eBay, let's say, and decide to buy something from her) or by the new one that is introduced by the person's commercial activity within the system itself.

This makes the point that without a means of establishing a symmetry of expectations and mutual benefits in transactional relationships that extends beyond the dynamics of the eBay system, the Web soon becomes unruly and ungovernable. Yet symmetry does not always rely on the exchange of money and the mutual profit reward. It can be created in systems that do not have a clear monetary value as long as there can be found a way to successfully address the question of symmetry of mutual gain within the relationships that occur. Failure to do so unbalances the system as the temptation to game it (for a variety of reasons) or simply cut off ties, disappear, and re-emerge fresh under a new identity every time things become difficult, is too great to resist.

In the pre-semantic search world, web design companies would die overnight, after taking cash advances and leaving customer projects hanging, and reappear weeks later under a different name and URL with none being the wiser. Personally I've come, over the years, across three SEO companies doing the same thing. Where monetary transactions are not involved in social environments, such as forums, or networks such as Facebook, trolls can delete their identity and come back using another fictitious one.

It should be clear that without having some implied or explicitly stated mutual benefits in play, symmetry in a transactional relationship on the Web is hard to establish, and without it, trust is hard to find.

Consider an example where a book lover, called Alex, comes across a used books seller, called Alice, on Facebook. Alex, a respected professional at his work, is very new to the network and has only two friends so far on his profile. Alice is an established Facebook pro that not only uses Facebook to keep in touch with friends and family but also to find new customers.

Alex contacts Alice directly and expresses an interest to buy a book she has for sale. Alice carries out her due diligence and, given Alex's very new status on Facebook, has some very serious concerns. While she is established and known to the network, he is new. There is very little she can use to verify that he is who he says he is and that makes her unwilling to take a risk. Her solution, of course, might be to bring Alex into eBay where she also has a well established presence there, but if he is also new to eBay then, again, the relationship is asymmetrical. Alex could easily take the book and disappear without any harm coming to a reputation that for him does not exist yet.

A professional in Alice's shoes would be very reluctant to embark on any transaction with someone like Alex without some cast iron guarantee of the outcome (like using an Escrow account for the book transaction) or creating a symmetry by having Alex take most of the risk by paying in advance in a way that does not allow for chargebacks. Given the scenario, Alex might also suspect Alice's behavior. From his point of view he is earnest, wants to pay and is willing to go through with the transaction yet the difficulties thrown up by Alice make him a little suspicious.

The solution to both of course resides in something that is as simple to state as it is difficult to achieve: what both Alex and Alice need is some way to be able to carry trust and reputation they have gained in one domain on the Web, to others.

The ingredients then, for establishing the kind of symmetry that promotes online behavior that generates trust and adds value to the equation are at the minimum:

- A means of establishing one's identity
- A commonly accepted mechanism of transferring value from one person to the other during the transaction process
- A means of establishing mutual gain (symmetry) in the transactional relationship
- Some way of capitalizing on the value that accrues when the conventions or rules of the system are respected (like in eBay's accumulating reputation score)

Let's take this again into the eBay environment so that it becomes easier to visualize. eBay offers the umbrella term of "eBayer" as a way of establishing a framework of commonly accepted values for every member in its platform. In real-world, face-to-face transactions, a physical presence and a legal system perform the same task.

eBay is a commercial environment, and value within it is primarily conferred through the exchange of money with each transaction.

Within the eBay environment symmetry is established in a mutual feedback mechanism that is used to work out a reputation score for both sellers and buyers.

Both sellers and buyers who obey the eBay rules get a higher reputation score than those who break them, which is indicated through a variety of mechanisms: the positive transactions that accrue through feedback, power-seller status, special badges for successful sellers, and different levels of feedback with different color stars.

Unless something catastrophic happens to a person within the eBay environment and his reputation score as an eBayer ceases to matter to him personally, the system does a pretty good job of creating an environment where those who are in it are tied together by largely symmetric relationships that provide them with a mutual interest in making it work.

Stepping outside the confines of the eBay environment, into the wild west of the Web it now becomes evident, I hope, that in order to create a more equitable online world where the online experience is mutually respectful, largely positive, and scalable, the four ingredients already outlined previously, are essential.

In the semantic web, navigated by Google's semantic search the four requirements can now be pithily translated into

- Authorship
- Content
- Influence
- TrustRank

Right now, I hope, you are either jumping up and down with excitement in the privacy of your home or struggling to stop yourself from doing so in a public place. The "Big Deal" about social media, and it is a big deal, is that it allows us to create globally an environment that has significantly lowered the cost of connection and interaction with each other.

It keeps on lowering it in a process that constantly strips away any perceived barriers. With an entry threshold that's being lowered all the time, there is a fresh influx of converts. Pretty soon anybody that's anybody, which pretty much makes it largely everybody, will be online, active in a social network.

The influx of people on the Web is paralleled by the influx of content being created. From tweets, to comments, Instagram photographs, Vine videos, and Facebook status updates, everyone's a publisher, producing content that has specific intent, even if that intent is largely subconscious. Life logging, the trend to increasingly chronicle and upload everyday facets of our lives that become publicly viewable, is generating massive amounts of content and the information that comes with it.

The point is that whether acting consciously or subconsciously, everyone's behavior will be affected by the four characteristics of Authorship, Content, Influence and TrustRank. Right now, this seems a stretch, I admit. But only because we are still used to the notion of the Web as a place where we go to free ourselves from the burden of our offline identity. In the offline world we already accept these four characteristics that govern behavior to such a degree that they are used to establish a definition of order and civilization anywhere we go, from Kathmandu to the projected colony on the Moon.

As the Web matures, as social media continues to add transparency in online connections and relationships, and as semantic search creates meaning out of all that information, online will become indistinguishable from offline. Already we see a seamless integration happening through mobile with Google's Mobile search, itself closely informed by Google's Knowledge Graph. The connectivity of the cloud and the prevalence of tablets and smartphones have eroded the traditional online/offline divide. Within a short time we will most probably stop thinking of it as "online." We will simply be connected, all the time, everywhere, and the online world will be notable only by its absence when that connection breaks.

In his research paper, *Propagation of Trust and Distrust*, Ramanathan Guha noted in his summary of results that "Typical webs of trust tend to be relatively 'sparse': virtually every user has expressed trust values for only a handful of other users." In closed environments there is a real need for wholesale participation in the system because that provides the connective matrix that helps generate trust.

In the semantic web the connective matrix that makes the system work is provided by search itself. As search creates visibility, TrustRank extends beyond the narrow confines of a feedback score that is good only in a particular setting and acquires a much more nuanced approach—one, which I suspect, Guha (now working at Google) probably appreciates.

As ranking in search increasingly confers an instant advantage of trust (and the potential benefits for increased conversions that this implies), it is logical to assume that developing an eminently trustworthy online presence that can be assessed as such, will translate into an advantage in search ranking and deliver very real commercial value.

Building Up Your TrustRank in the Semantic Web

The question of how trust is built up on the semantic web is underpinned by the unasked question: "What can I do to build it up?" In the past this approach led to a problematic relationship between search engine optimizers chasing Google's search algorithm changes and Google who was concerned with the quality of the end-user experience.

Funnily enough this is not the case anymore. In what is indicative of just how radically things have changed we are now at the exact opposite end of the scale. For the system to work correctly we need to actually work with the system as closely as possible.

This change of attitude, which leads to a real change of approach, is the result of a realignment of benefits. Just like eBayers gain more by working within the eBay reputation guidelines, so does working with semantic search requirements deliver more gain than trying to find workarounds to subvert them.

So, it is worth analyzing at some depth just how the online connections we make become visible and create the ability of a company, person, or brand to become trusted enough for its online presence to positively impact Google's search rankings and become more prominent.

To make what is an involved, detailed process easier to assimilate we will work with lists of four. The first set of four actionables you need to concentrate on in your trust-building efforts are

- Have a fully formed presence in digital platforms.
- Enrich your digital presence with all your details.
- Network your presence within each digital platform.
- Fine-tune your connections to reinforce your identity.

In a little more detail:

Digital platforms can range from Facebook to Twitter and Quora. Not every digital platform is equal, and not every digital platform is capable of being of use. Yet they all require time and energy to work properly, and you need to be judicious in your choices. So, the first step is to actually draw up a list of the platforms that are most likely suitable for your business vertical. A marketing company that hopes to reach the business world, for instance, is unlikely to find Pinterest or Instagram to be of the same value to its online brand as LinkedIn, so that's where a marketing firm should focus its efforts. Conversely, a company that targets the consumer will find that a strong presence on Facebook, Foursquare, and Pinterest pays more in creating brand awareness than a presence on LinkedIn where it is most likely to have a limited audience.

Once you have a presence on a digital platform make sure it is fully fleshed out. Companies need to mention in their profile not just the company but also the company website and, wherever possible, key personnel whose profiles or biographies are also on the Web. Individuals need to mention and link up to brands or companies with which they are associated and include links to all the online places where the content they have created can be seen.

Having a presence on a digital platform that does not work to engage those who are already present on it is a waste of time. Once you have a presence and have fleshed it out, develop a plan on how it will engage those who are on the platform already. Basically the question your activity needs to answer here is: Why Do You Matter? Everything you do must be able to answer that question in a concise, logical way.

Finally, since you have a presence on a digital platform and want to now make it work for you, you need to fine-tune it through the connections you make. A company with a presence on Facebook, for example, will link to some of its employees. Employees there will link to the company. The company will link to the activity of its suppliers or major customers who also have a presence there.

The point is that in the connected economy, meaning and its value, semantic or otherwise, is unleashed only through the power of connection. Without interconnecting our digital presence we miss out on the opportunity to rank for specific search queries, but even more important than that we miss out on the opportunity of being serendipitously discovered, in search, by association.

This is one of the biggest benefits of the semantic search world. In the past if someone looked for, let's say, Coca-Cola, and I happened to be involved with Coca-Cola in helping it develop its social media presence, the only way my name would have come up on search was if I had specifically included keywords and backlinks with anchor text that reinforced that connection. Even then it would have been, statistically speaking, tenuous enough to maybe not even register unless I was prepared to spend considerable time and effort optimizing a page on my website to come up specifically for such a search query.

With semantic search I don't have to. Provided the network of connections is there and they are sufficiently explained the chances of my name coming up in association with Coca Cola's social media marketing increase the more I flesh out the profiles and connections I have with the company. For instance, I would

- Link my Google+ to the Coca Cola company and put in my work association with them.
- Connect with Coca Cola on LinkedIn and fill out employment history there.
- Follow the Coca Cola page on Facebook and interact with it there.
- Comment on Coca Cola marketing efforts on my own blog and make sure I linked to the company's profile or marketing videos as necessary.

- Draw up a list of opportunities where the Coca Cola name and my association with them could come up: blog posts, comments, interviews.

By making the connection as transparent as possible, incrementally, I would ensure that Google becomes aware of my relationship with the company without my having to go to great lengths to specifically optimize my website for that.

The next four elements we need in the building of TrustRank are:

- The establishment of authorship
- The creation of content
- The establishment of influence
- The establishment of trust (as in online credibility and authority)

Looked at each in turn these also provide a granular picture of activities designed to assign attributes of value and meaning to what we do online.

Authorship, established primarily through the connection of the Google+ profile, enables us to claim content we have created. It is our digital signature on the Web, leaving a growing, accumulating, digital footprint that becomes our past and our present. It informs not just the digital platforms we are active on and what we do there but also the connections we create as part of our identity.

Authorship is only officially attributed to writing on the Web, but content creators can be identified with their content in the semantic search index by making sure that their online profiles are clearly labeled and linked to that content. This can include YouTube videos, Picasa or Instagram photographs, Tumblr shares, and Twitter posts.

Content is key to everything. It has become the currency of the connected economy. The kind of content that you create now needs to be guided by a content creation strategy that operates within a specific framework of aims, targets, and intent. As an example, comments I leave on an article are signed with my name and link to my online personality, I share a specific type of content on Twitter and Facebook, and I choose to interact with a specific type of content, again, on Google+. All of this forms an online behavioral pattern that in its totality accurately reflects who I am in terms of interests, likes, and dislikes. A company or brand that follows this kind of strategy begins to establish a clearly defined online identity that sets it apart from its competitors.

Influence is the closure of the symmetry gap that drives online transactional relationships. Anyone who is online wants to feel that the empowerment of the digital world allows her presence to matter. Social media connections, the ability to broadcast messages to the world through Twitter, the capability to hold Hangouts

On Air through Google+ like a TV station, these are all tools that allow people to explain, subconsciously, why they do matter. Whether it's comments shared in an online stream or an interaction in the Twitter feed, the creation, sharing, or resharing of content all happens within the framework of influence—those we influence, those who are influenced by us, and those we help be influenced. In the semantic web this creates a powerful mutual gain that acts as a normalizer of sorts, just like eBay's feedback system.

To be a little more specific influencers and those they influence either through their reach (follower numbers) or depth (follower interaction) both gain from the exchange. The influencer gains a certain amount of status in the online environment where he has influence, which is then converted to something else (interviews, importance, book sales, speech bookings), and those being influenced acquire a trusted shortcut to discovering things of interest and following trends before they peak. The balance is a tenuous one and indicates just how powerful symmetrical relationships are in keeping everyone in check. An overstepping of the boundaries by the influencer may strip him of followers and loss of influence and status, and an overstepping of the boundaries by a follower may exclude him from access to the influencer, which he needs.

Credibility is what Swedish writer and sociologist Alexander Bard singles out as being one half of the attention economy. The attention economy is an approach to the management of information that treats human attention as a scarce commodity and applies economic theory to solve various information management problems. Given the fact that we only have so much time available, as consumers, to actually notice something and then act upon it, it seems reasonable that our attention then becomes the scarce commodity that needs to be addressed first.

The other half of the attention economy is awareness. Awareness is created through semantic search where you are found either because you rank for specific search queries and appear in search or are part of Google's serendipitous discovery content. Either way, once found, if you cannot appear credible either as a person or a company, then you have wasted your time and effort. It is worth noting here that traditional marketing techniques were also predicated on the establishment of credibility (through sleek advertising) and awareness, and although semantic search adds a much more nuanced layer to the mix, it does not invalidate the marketing methods of the past. It merely deprecates them.

Reputation on the Semantic Web

Google's head of Web Spam, Matt Cutts, has, in his regular webmaster videos on YouTube, said on a number of occasions that there is no such thing as TrustRank in the sense that there is a single algorithm, like that envisioned by the Yahoo research team, that calculates trust and uses it as a ranking factor.

Instead, in a verisimilitude of real life, the reputation of people and websites on the semantic web is calculated through a variety of factors that include the value and originality of content and its social signal plus the digital footprint that accompanies credibility.

This is also roughly the formula that Alexander Bard stipulates when he says that

> Reputation = Attention × Credibility

Where in his equation Attention stands for visibility in search and Credibility is TrustRank.

The building blocks of reputation in this context are drawn directly from Google's graphs which are, again, four:

- Social Graph
- Knowledge Graph
- Link Graph
- Engagement Graph

The dictionary definition of "graph" is a diagram showing the relationship between typically two variable quantities, each measured along one of a pair of axes at right angles to each other. It is a pretty good one when it comes to understanding what is meant by each of the four graphs just listed.

Typically each one has to do with a person, website, company, or brand (which I shall collectively call "entity" for the rest of this chapter) and, in turn, a cache of data pertaining to a specific activity.

The Social Graph details all the social interactions between an entity and other entities that are found across the Web (direct links from one to the other, personal connections, shared group activities, mentions, and more direct interactions in terms of shared content).

The Knowledge Graph contains as much knowledge as is available, linked to an entity. The early classic example of typing "works of da vinci" in Google search and getting the Knowledge Carousel at the top listing all his works as well as his biography and the serendipitous discovery links generated by people's related search queries beautifully illustrates the point (see Figure 5.2).

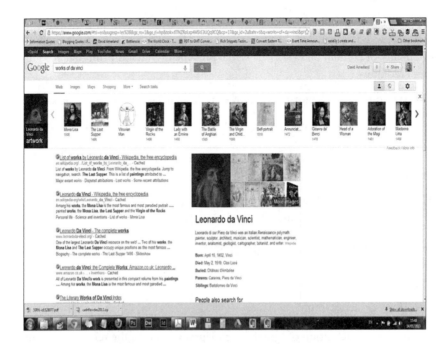

Figure 5.2   *The search query "works of da vinci" activates Google's Knowledge Graph around the subject of Leonardo da Vinci and gives me the correct choices right there on the search results page through the Knowledge Carousel.*

The Link Graph is all the information accrued through PageRank. It contains who links to what and how as a determinant of the importance of the relationship between two entities and the value one places on the other.

The Engagement Graph charts the level of engagement between entities. This includes comments, "conversations," "+1s," and Likes. The difference between engagement and social connections lies in the degree of interaction. For instance, I may link to a past employer from my Google+ profile and that would make me part of her Social Graph. But if I never mention her again anywhere in my online activity, and if my general direction on the Web is in an area far removed from what my former employer does, I am not part of the Engagement Graph associated with her.

The four graphs, in their totality, also sum up the body of work that must be performed for a company, brand, or individual who wants to be in control of their online reputation.

The TrustRank Preparation Checklist

In retrospect the old ways of search engine optimization, which focused primarily on the Link Graph, must seem both a little primitive now and a little nostalgic because they were much simpler.

Taking responsibility for your online reputation requires nothing less than a total effort from the person, brand, or organization that involves everyone remotely associated with the production of content, online posting, and brand amplification.

The TrustRank Preparation Checklist involves the following steps:

- Identify the digital platforms that are most likely to help promote your expertise, brand, or business vertical.
- Identify the influencers on each digital platform you are on and connect with them.
- Detail how you will involve or link to company staff and business contacts online.
- Detail your content creation strategy for each digital platform you have chosen; explain how it is platform-specific and how it serves your brand.
- Explain how you will ensure continuity of tone and message across the different digital platforms you are on.
- Explain your brand amplification efforts using your online connections in each digital platform you use.
- Detail the data that you think each of Google's graphs contains about yourself, brand, or company.
- Detail how you propose to track progress across Google's graphs in terms of brand equity.
- Explain how Authorship can be used to help your company's digital presence.
- Detail your engagement strategy across each of the digital platforms you are active on.

How Content Became Marketing

In the age of semantic search content has become the transactional currency used to unleash real value on the Web. When everything revolves around its existence traditional businesses are forced to become publishers and broadcasters, individuals need to become writers and photographers, and brands have to become more personable and direct. Everyone needs to remain current in their quality, fresh in their output, and constantly be producing content to define who they are and what they do.

In this chapter we see just how content production, once an SEO necessity that ticked a requirements box, suddenly became the axis around which now revolve all your marketing efforts.

The Currency of the Semantic Web

In order to successfully work in any medium you need to understand its tropes. What is it that powers it? What are the rules of conduct within it? How does one navigate through its different levels? What are the constituent elements that go into creating trust and authority within its confines? These are questions the answers to which we know intuitively in the offline world. When we understand the answers we also understand the dynamic that drives our environment. We use that knowledge to moderate and fashion our own behavior accordingly so that we achieve our personal and professional goals.

The dynamics of our behavior create our reputation, which we have seen already is an element of trust, because it measures our trustworthiness. Depending on our success, trustworthiness and reputation then scale into influence. All of these, in their different make up, comprise the construct that we call identity.

The Web mirrors the offline world, and offline we are adept at calculating a person's monetary worth, reputation, and identity based on visual clues. On the Web visual clues suddenly disappeared. There is no accent, dress code, physical address in a fashionable neighborhood, or a car in the drive to help us.

When everything on the Web is "free," or at least it does not have a direct monetary value, a new currency system is needed to step into the vacuum. That currency is content.

However, the value placed on information, advice, contact, ideas, opinions, and interaction depends directly on the context they are given in. Context then provides the key necessary to turn all the information contained in content, into a solution that has real value for the receiver. To give an example, the perfect BBQ steak recipe that someone posts on a forum has zero value if that forum is about knitting or coding. Those who are there, even if they are partial to perfectly BBQ-ed steaks, are highly unlikely to be in the right frame of mind to engage in exchanging recipes. The context of their online interaction is at odds with that post, and the post's value drops alarmingly, even though the recipe may, indeed, be the best in the world.

Seen in this regard then information, advice, contact, ideas, and opinions—what we call content, in other words—became no different than a form of currency. Just like dollars and pounds and yen can be used to buy something that will solve some problem we face, so is content, in that context, used similarly. And just as an accumulation of monetary transactions can result in a stream of cash that makes us rich, so does an accumulation of content related interactions, in the right context, result in a stream of appreciation that makes us reputable. Reputation, then, as the end result of the new currency being peddled, becomes the measure of this new form of digital wealth. And just like riches in real life, reputation in the digital domain is hard to build up and easy to lose.

Right up to the point where semantic search came along, this digital wealth was concentrated in the hands of relatively few people in very specific domains. It was possible, for example, for someone with great technical expertise to rise to great prominence in a forum whose subject matter was coding. Due to his generous nature and helpful posts he could gain a reputation that would allow him to become an influencer within that domain. His opinion would count, his suggestions could set trends. His word carried real weight. Yet, outside that domain he would remain a total unknown. More to the point the closed nature of each domain created a siloed digital ecosystem where the natural competitiveness that exists in humans would only permit a relatively few to rise to the very top. When you are competing for the attention of a finite group of people it is only natural to see most other contenders as competitors and want to eliminate them, or at least make it harder for them to rise and compete with you.

So the Web, which was supposed to be a unifying, level playing field for its participants, became a fragmented, hierarchical one. The reason we had such a fragmented result in what is, for all intents and purposes, an open web, can be found in the way data is stored, categorized, and then shared.

While the bits and pieces of content, information, and advice we could share as individuals are, indeed, portable and can be used anywhere across the Web, our digital history of interaction, the relationships we form, the connections we make, and the kind of content we become associated with, is not so easy to transport. This kind of data was platform-dependent so that, for instance, our reputation, credibility, and influence earned in one particular forum remained locked behind the forum walls. It could neither follow us to another digital platform nor could it be read and used outside the narrow digital environment where it was contained. Simply put, the moment we stepped outside the digital space where we were well known, we became just another anonymous surfer among the massive tide of people online.

Marketing, in that sense, then became a time-consuming effort that actually worked to keep those of us active in particular platforms locked within their walls. The time and effort invested in producing sufficient content to get anywhere within each digital platform was such that it became both tiring and prohibitively time-consuming to start all over again somewhere else.

Those digital marketers who felt particularly brave would spread their presence across several digital platforms and would create specific strategies, manned by teams, to help them achieve a multilateral presence. The majority, however, were left with little choice but to focus their efforts on specific digital platforms and the demographics they attracted. Creating a virtue out of necessity they also elevated niche marketing into an art form, identifying areas where they had few natural competitors to work in, or developing a marketing message that appealed to a very specific part of the digital platform they were active in. Both of these were tactics that allowed them to build their identity and reputation quickly and hold onto them.

This is no longer quite the case. The power of the semantic web lies in the fact that data attributes that could not be exported between digital platforms in the past, have now become portable. More than that, relationships have become both transparent and linkable. A powerful presence in terms of reputation and credibility developed in one digital platform like, let's say LinkedIn, can now be transferred across the Web, following the digital marketer just like reputation and credibility do in real life.

That's not all. The ability to transfer attributes attached to your digital identity across the Web can create a brand new means of branding and an entirely fresh digital currency of value predicated on the quality of the content that is created, produced, found, curated, and shared. The content we produce or use now has the ability to help us achieve greater brand awareness, deeper marketing, and more sales. What's more than that, because it helps create our digital identity and drives our reputation, it also becomes key to appearing in search and achieving greater online visibility.

Content Marketing and Semantic Indexing

Before we even begin to examine in detail how content helps in marketing and search ranking it is important to understand what content does. To do that we need to examine how marketing worked before content became an issue and, even, how it worked before the Web came along.

Everything that has always been done in marketing, from TV ads to radio, newspapers, billboards, and packaging, is driven by the need to help establish a sense of identity of a company (or person) that is then anchored by the twin vectors of

- Authority
- Trust

Traditionally, using mass media as the main communication channel meant that the flow of information that used to establish identity and its attendant sense of authority and trust were strictly one way. Television ads could not be interacted with, billboards could not be reshared, radio could not be commented on, and packaging could not be used to start a meaningful conversation with anyone without the risk of appearing deranged.

In his popular book *Thinking, Fast and Slow* Nobel Prize Award winner Daniel Kahneman explains how the hard-wiring of the brain that ascribes identity to everything we observe creates an interesting effect that frequently leads to a cognitive bias in the value judgments we make, particularly where issues that are not directly influenced by identity are involved, like judging whether an act is right or wrong. In such situations our perception of whether something is "right" or "wrong" for instance, will be biased by our assumption of who was involved, rather than the facts of the situation. As such it tends to be fast, instinctive, and biased as opposed to logical, thoughtful, and fair.

This is an important point because its logical extension shows how our responses validate the effort and huge expense that companies went to in the pre-Web days to advertise their brands and influence the consumer as he formed his purchasing decision. A sense of perceived identity carries with it an implicit, and mostly subconscious, judgment value that generates a halo effect. If I know you, for example, and have had some experience of what you do, and I trust you, I am a lot more likely to want to do business with you and buy your products even if my direct experience of you has nothing to do with what you do professionally. This is exactly how the halo effect works, and for it to happen you need to convince me to trust you, in some context in the first place.

The halo effect that perceived identity has on personal choices results in the creation of an unavoidable bias when it comes to critical judgment, and this creates an interesting paradox. Specifically, if little is known about you, the judgments people make tend to be unfavorable even when the evidence used to make them is in your favor. RAND Corporation analyst and British author Simon Sinek uses an interesting example that perfectly illustrates this point. Suppose you meet with a fellow businessman to close a complex deal, and you produce a bulky detailed set of Terms and Conditions. You ask him to agree to them and sign them, and after going through them all he does just that. But on finally standing up to leave he refuses to shake your hand. Would you trust him? Would you then have faith that the deal just agreed to will go smoothly?

Despite the fact that a detailed and binding set of Ts & Cs have been agreed to and signed the refusal to shake hands at the end destroys the sense that we know who the other person is. Without being able to divine his motives for the refusal of a simple handshake, our minds attack the sense of identity that we have constructed of him. The result is that now we have no trust in him, our relationship with him, and our sense of his reputation.

This is because the cognitive bias generated by the apparent comfort of knowing who somebody is, what he stands for, and what he does generates a positivity that creates a circle of trust. Anyone within that circle enjoys instant credibility regardless. People who find themselves outside it because they are new to our list of contacts are instantly distrusted. It appears then that identity, authority, and trust are closely linked to the amount of information readily available about a company or person.

The ways we get that information offline rely on popular media, hearsay, and friends and colleagues, and online on search, social media, and the content and opinions being shared by friends and colleagues. We have seen already instances of how collectively all that information is filtered to create the three attributes we call identity, authority, and trust, which then combine to form a fourth: reputation.

The popular phrase "better the devil you know" beautifully exemplifies the subconscious drive used in our judgment process and, as it happens, now brings us around to understanding the true value of search. Search, or rather the list of search results we see when we carry out a search query on Google, perfectly exemplifies the mental processes that psychologists frequently refer to as System 1 (an autonomic function of the brain that intuitively extrapolates from scant data to reach quick conclusions) and System 2 (a slower, more task-driven analytical, cognitive mechanism that arrives at decisions only after deliberate mental calculations).

Google has a way of calculating the perceived trust ordinary users place on the results displayed on the Google search results page through a variety of metrics. One of them is the Click Through Rate (CTR). CTR scores, these days, are one of the means used to assess the quality of a particular page presented as an answer to a search query by recording whether a particular result got clicked on, and how many times, and then anonymously tracking the behavior of those who clicked on it. If, for instance, a website that consistently comes up on the first page of Google for a specific search query attracts clicks but the visitors leave that page within 30 seconds, chances are that their experience has been unsatisfactory, the website does not adequately address what they are looking for, and, in all likelihood, does not deserve the high search ranking it has.

CTR scores are one of the metrics Google uses to automatically test whether its algorithm has correctly assessed a website in terms of authority and trust, and it is one of the signals that help the search giant decide whether a website belongs in a top tier subset of sites that provide a high quality end-user experience. If the accumulated data indicates that it doesn't, the website is then placed in a subset of low confidence websites that might still provide an answer when no other alternatives are available; but will make the visitor work harder to find what she is looking for.

You probably have already, correctly, deduced that identity-related cognitive bias in human judgment is the result of the influence of System 1 (intuitive) in our thinking over System 2 (analytical). When it comes to the presentation of results in semantic search, then the way a sense of trust is created in the mind of the viewer has a lot to do with the way identity is created through the descriptive snippets and titles that appear on the Google results page. These snippets and descriptions have a direct impact on CTR scores and traffic to a website. And all of this is intimately interlinked with content.

Figure 6.1 shows the impact a picture and description can have in terms of generating a higher degree of authenticity and trust.

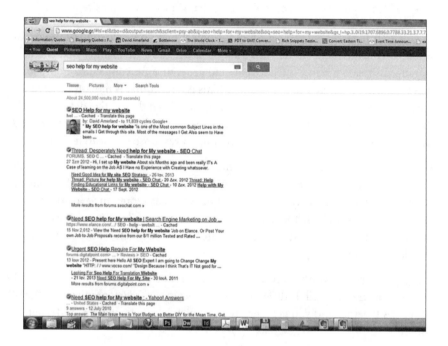

Figure 6.1 *The results for the search query "SEO help for my website" return an image of me and a post I wrote some time ago. Compared to the less visual, more generic nature of the rest of the results this generates more click-throughs for my website.*

Content, on the Web, then, is the data we use to achieve a number of things that feed into the attributes that matter:

- Establish a presence (Identity).
- Generate interaction (Trust).
- Define what we do (Identity).
- Establish our credentials (Authority).
- Propagate our message (Trust, again).
- Increase our digital footprint (Authority).

Content can come in many different formats:

- Text (blog posts, website content, articles, comments, tweets, Facebook status updates)

- Pictures (shared on Instagram, Flickr, Facebook, Google+, Twitter, YouTube)
- Audio (podcasts on websites, SoundCloud, YouTube)
- Diagrams (shared on Tumblr, Facebook, Google+, Twitter)
- Video (uploaded to Facebook, YouTube, Vimeo, own website)

In whatever format or combination of formats it may come in, content is data, and when we consider data on the Web then the attributes and qualities that enable us to gauge its relative value, categorize it, and generate a functional taxonomy for it are frequently referred to as metadata. This is a term that is often translated as meaning "data about data," and it's nothing more than descriptive data that makes the indexing of information in search easier. It also makes it easier to understand exactly what has been indexed and serve it up in response to a search query.

Posed a little more formally then, in semantic search, the ambiguity that is usually found in words can only be reduced by giving the search engine what humans use for disambiguation, namely knowledge of the world as represented in an ontology. In other words, by helping a search engine connect all the metaphorical dots between content and how it is used we enable it to understand it the same way we do: via its context.

Bring this into your work space and it becomes reducible to a simple formula: The content you create, in all its different pieces, becomes a fragmented puzzle. Put all the pieces together and you get a pretty good picture of who you are and what you do.

As a guide consider that every piece of content you produce, to work as part of your content marketing strategy, has to answer at least one of the following questions:

- Does it promote your brand?
- Does it promote your company values?
- Does it help you stand out from your competitors?
- Does it create a better understanding of your business?
- Does it help customers better understand the value of your products?
- Does it help potential customers understand why they should buy from you?

Many of the pieces of content you produce will overlap, and some will probably answer a lot more than just one or two of these questions. The upshot of all this is that the new semantic web with its insistence on fresh content and social media network engagement is forcing you, just like the imaginary bakery of our very early example in Chapter 3, to become a publisher. You're right. Despite the fact that you did not go into business to learn how to publish content on the Web, the fact is that now this is how you can achieve the best kind of marketing. The trick to becoming a publisher is learning how to think like one.

How to Think Like a Publisher

There is only one reason why you need to understand how semantic search works and that is because once you understand it you will be able to translate it into a particular set of steps, pertinent to your company or brand, that will help you to either increase sales or amplify your brand impact.

In most corporate talks I give at this exact point I usually see the battle lines being drawn between those responsible for the production of content and those charged with search engine optimization activity. The main reason for this is found in the way the two activities have been approached in the past. In the pre-semantic web age content was produced largely by marketing and PR, and search engine optimization was an outsourced activity farmed out to an agency.

The agency worked from a carefully worded brief that was, at best, reviewed every quarter, and marketing worked with the kind of lead times and pressures that every marketing department works under. And never would the twain meet.

This is not how the game is played now. Although technical SEO that has to do with the way websites are coded, pages designed and laid out, and information is stored, is still important, a large part of search engine optimization in the semantic search age is done through content marketing. To think of content creation and SEO as two separate activities at this stage is to miss the opportunity to gain all the natural advantages that a closer alignment will bring.

To help us establish some guidelines let's take a look at traditional or print publishers. Print publishers are in a business guided by a primary philosophy: to bring out books. The success of publishers depends on their ability to fulfill this basic requirement. On the first day of the first month of the year, a publisher may bring out a book that wins a Nobel Prize for Literature, but the painful fact about publishing is that if the publisher cannot also bring out a great many more books that month and every month after that the publisher will vanish.

Print publishers understand that the business of publishing books depends upon their ability to be everywhere, publish content across the board of interests that would appeal to their target audience, and build brand equity through a constant stream of products (i.e., books) that also serve as content. It's a difficult situation because publishers cannot wait for good books to just come to them. They need to be proactive and create the kind of presence that ensures they have a supply of writers at hand. If their content stream dries up, so does their business.

Because publishers sell only one type of product—that is, books—they also provide a great example of integrated synergy. Their production line (writers and editors) work to create the best possible product; their marketing department seeks to understand what it is, what makes it different, why it is unusual; and their entire selling pitch is aligned behind each book they sell. That's every book. There are, of course, differences between a book that has the potential to sell millions of copies that will be heavily promoted and one that may return a modest profit, but those are differences of scale rather than approach.

To succeed in the semantic web you have to think like a traditional publisher and then bring that mindset to your online publishing efforts. If your marketing department, PR people, copywriters, packagers, and sales teams are not perfectly aligned in the content they produce, you will get a diffusion of your sales message. Every one of these departments produces some kind of content, whether it's text, or sales pitches, or graphics, or brochures, or even product demonstrations—even newsletters and emails to potential customers.

In the past this diffusion did not matter so much because content addressed an audience that was contained in a silo of sorts. In the age of search, however, the silos themselves are porous. Those who consume your video message or your graphics may well next come across your blog post, news about your company, a new product press release, or a Twitter message about some event. They may receive a newsletter they subscribed to at one of your websites, or they may be at the receiving end of an email as part of a regular communication with your company.

The uniting thread here is that everything that is digital is visible to search, and it is through search that you stand a good chance to do two things at once: First streamline your every effort to work in sync so that everything you do amplifies everything else you do, or have done. And second, use search to increase the serendipity factor of your findability.

This second part is truly important. As search has become the way we navigate the Web, semantic search is the only way that the Web acquires some kind of structure. And with structure we get meaning. And meaning is derived through content.

The power of content and its impact in the digital domain are illustrated in Figure 6.2. This graphic was put together as a training aid by British business coach Bob Barker and Google+ evangelist Thomas Power of Frontier Coaching.

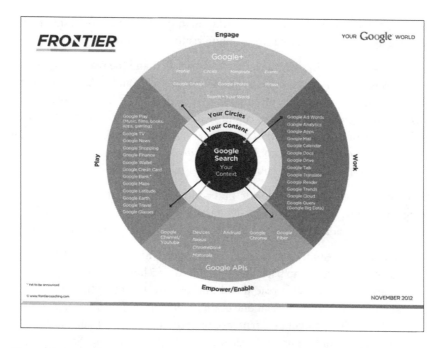

Figure 6.2   *Content becomes the layer that enables interaction to take place. By the same token it allows your digital presence to seep into all the other layers of the digital realm where it increases the likelihood of discovery and can amplify the impact it has.*

Considering that content is used to create, drive, reinforce, and maintain the reputation of a company, brand, or individual on the Web, we can see just how it has become the primary force behind the generation of engagement with its target audience.

Its new role then casts content as the layer that unlocks all the attributes we need to establish a sense of identity and authenticity. It renders it the means through which the connection is made between people and websites, consumers and brands, researchers and information. To truly work, this requires content to have real value in terms of what the end-user requires.

In many ways the distinction of the semantic web, typified by semantic search, and what was before is in that in the pre-semantic search days we could get away with producing content that was created exclusively for search engines. As such it was

- Bulky
- Repetitive
- Keyword-rich
- Difficult to read

The emphasis back then was on bulk rather than quality, repetition rather than value, search engine bait rather than online visitor interaction.

Semantic search requires a focus on the end-user first and the search engine second. This is partly how you build up trust in your brand, and as Daniel Kahneman frequently notes in his book, information that comes to you from a source you trust and like generates a sense of cognitive ease, and this affects your perception of the quality of existing as well as new content. In other words, if I know you and like you I am prepared to cut you some slack if you slip up somewhere, but if I don't know you, or don't like you, you'd better make sure you never slip up.

In an online discussion about how to best address this issue of content and trust, Sergey Adrianov, the CEO of a web design and web services company based in Mississauga, Canada, highlighted the trap even seasoned professionals can fall into:

> We started cleaning our blog a few days ago...Unfortunately we fell in an even bigger trap back then—we hired a $5 blogger to write our blogs. Worse, we never read them! But recently, I went on to read some of those. Almost each one of those blog posts speaks about... nothing! There might be a sentence or two getting close enough to the subject. And we proudly called it our blog, our thinking! Shame. Shame. Shame. Luckily, our portfolio is something that spoke for us better than the blog itself.

Beyond the power of this candid admission lies the fact that until recently most professionals were guilty of the same thing. When you had to produce content just to tick a search engine optimization requirement, you did just what was needed to achieve the desired end result.

The importance content plays on the semantic web right now is evidenced by an explosion of book titles that tell you how to generate it, categorize it, make it sound more authentic, and use it. The Web itself is awash with content marketing seminars, how-to lists on content strategy, and content placement and content management platforms that allow you to make better use of the content you have.

Getting Technical with Content

The first question I am asked when I discuss the importance of content that has real value in the semantic web is whether keywords are now suddenly redundant. In the corporate world search engine optimization used to revolve around keywords to such a degree that the notion of "money words" grew and was perpetuated from one marketing meeting to the next.

"Money words" is the term applied to the 12 to 15 keywords that purported to drive 85% to 90% of the traffic to a website. While this may hold true for some business verticals that have a narrow focus in terms of the products or services they offer, it is highly unlikely that the approach would serve well, let's say, the needs of a multinational.

The persistence of the idea highlights the danger of demanding quick-fix metrics to gauge success in search. Using a handful of keywords, understandably, is much more manageable to deal with at the corporate marketing level than to assess and then track 200 or more keywords whose positions in the search engine results pages fluctuate daily, but it also produces a false sense of security regarding the control one has over search marketing.

Luckily semantic search does away with some of this nonsense. Certainly keywords still play a role and this is in no way a call to overlook them, but the emphasis in semantic search is in divining the intent behind the search query, so the search query itself now becomes important.

Creating an entire page of content that convincingly answers the question of "How do you maintain quality in the menu of a restaurant chain?" for instance can produce great results in search for the query: "What's the best restaurant in town?" despite the fact that the words "best," "restaurant," and "town" are never mentioned in the web page itself—particularly if the restaurant chain in question has managed to generate a number of independent reviews on its restaurants.

This means that keywords, when used in the creation of content, should be used in an entirely natural way rather than being artificially crammed into the writing, and the overall emphasis has to be on the value of the content being produced.

The new search engine optimization list then goes from ticking keywords that are used in content specifically written to use them, to writing content that answers at least one of the following questions:

- Does it answer a specific question the reader may have?
- Does it create a challenge for the reader?
- Will it leave them feeling enriched?
- Is this content that helps establish your company's authority?
- Is it going to help generate greater equity for your brand?

These are the questions that have now replaced the traditional: How many keywords did we use? What keyword density did we achieve? Are the keywords in the title of the page? Are they in the opening paragraph? Have we used them in the anchor text of links?

There are a few more technicalities as far as content is concerned that we will cover in more detail in the next chapter. For now it is sufficient to consider that content that fails to satisfy the human visitor to your website will not help your company or brand rank high in search irrespective of how technical you get with its structure.

In the semantic web, meaning, in the fullest sense of the word, has to be your starting point.

The Content Creation Preparation Checklist

Content is key in the semantic web. Beyond ranking in search it has become the means through which companies and brands create brand equity, identity, authenticity, and a sense of trust with their target audience.

Because content can be reshared it can go viral becoming a tremendous amplifier of a company's marketing message.

In the semantic web content takes many more forms than just text, and its creation is the job of more than just one department.

The Content Creation Preparation Checklist involves the following steps:

- Identify all the different types of content your company or brand produces.
- Decide what message or marketing values you need to communicate with your target audience and explain how these will be implemented in the types of content your company or brand produces.
- Explain how you build, project, and safeguard your company's or brand's reputation through content.
- Explain how you communicate common values across all those responsible for content creation in your company.
- Explain your content creation strategy in terms of the type of content your company produces, its frequency, and the way it is used.
- Identify your main content channel and explain its impact on your brand equity through engagement and reach.
- Explain how you plan to integrate the different types of content produced by your company in the platforms where you maintain a digital presence.
- Detail the metrics you will use to gauge the impact of the content produced.
- Explain how you will identify the main traffic drivers in terms of content produced to your website.
- Detail how you identify suitable subjects to create content around.

7

Social Media Marketing and Semantic Search

Semantic search draws much of its power from the nuance of the connections it makes between different data points through interactions in the social web which it calls the "social signal." The social web is made up of a number of popular social media platforms that play a key role in how search results rank in semantic search queries.

In this chapter we see exactly what the "social signal" is, how it is used, and how it relates to the content that you produce as part of your search ranking efforts. Most importantly we learn exactly what you need to do to generate it and use it to your advantage.

The Social Signal and Its Power

For most of the twentieth century power and status were signaled and defined by the scarcest commodity of the time: data. Data is knowledge, knowledge leads to power, power allows dominance to emerge. Knowing the right piece of information at the right time is as crucial to, for instance, an investor considering where to place his money as to a company CEO considering his next strategic move in the marketplace. Having the ability to mine data, analyze it, and work from the inferences that could be drawn from it used to be the exclusive province of governments and secretive institutions, military analysis organizations, and global think tanks.

We don't live like this anymore. The twenty-first century is marked with data abundance. Each of us now has the tools necessary to create and publish an incredible amount of data, the online tools and mobile apps that have made it easy to publish personal pictures, videos, and blogposts have turned each of us into a data node. We publish where we are, through location-aware devices and sites like Foursquare, we Tweet pictures of our lunch, sharing them with the world. We videotape instances we like, from sunsets to rock concerts, and upload them on YouTube. Our individual data streams are aggregated in the social media platforms where we publish our content.

Twitter, Facebook, Google+, LinkedIn, and MySpace are each busy creating a world awash with social signals that in themselves generate a challenge. A surfeit of data is as bad as none at all. It generates a background of noise that makes it harder to find the signal of meaningful data you are looking for.

How to get meaning from all this noise is an issue that's being faced both at the personal level of the individual active on the Web today and the deeper, contextual level of relationship linking that marks semantic search. In both cases there is a clear need to isolate the signal from the noise with a clarity that allows meaningful, actionable conclusions to be drawn from it.

In a paper titled "Cognitive Modeling of Human Social Signals" presented in 2010 at the second international workshop on social signal processing held in Florence, Italy, Roma Tre University researchers I. Poggi and F. D'Errico made the case that "social signal" is a communicative or informative signal that, either directly or indirectly, conveys information about social actions, social interactions, social emotions, social attitudes, and social relationships.

Whether you are an individual or a search engine the challenge is the same and so is the solution. To increase the signal to noise ratio in the social signal you need to establish a framework that views the actions of mind (people) and social action (data) in terms of goals and beliefs.

Facebook does it through Graph Search where a very determined attempt is being made to map relational data and understand the meaning of the connections that have been mapped so that meaningful inferences can be made, algorithmically.

In semantic search the goal is to map the interaction of relationships between people and websites across the Web. The belief is that signals have an inherent meaning, and if a sufficient breadth and depth of captured data is mapped we will end up with a scalable, ever evolving picture of connections across the Web that will allow a search engine to understand the true meaning of a word through its associated connections.

The money question for us here is simple: How? The mechanism that allows this to happen is remarkably straightforward in concept. To have a signal we require an emitter and a receiver. The emitter in this case is a data node (and online we are all data nodes now). It can be a person, a group of people as in a community, or a virtual character, as in a company or brand. A signal then is defined as an action (an ad, a message, a comment, content posted) that allows an emitter to transmit information that allows the receiver (usually us, as individuals) to formulate a belief.

To illustrate this better consider that you are at a party and everyone is talking. Each of those conversations may have meaning for the individual participants engaged in them at close range to each other, but for you, standing across a busy room, their totality generates a lot of unstructured, garbled noise. To reach a particular person with your voice across the room you have two options. Option A says you could try yelling as loudly as you can in an attempt to use your voice to overpower the noise. That will, however, create more noise and may not necessarily work. Option B says you find a way to get the attention of the person you want to talk to. Throw her a can attached to one you hold via a string, or do the modern day equivalent and text her. The moment you have the person's attention, whatever you choose to share with her will help her understand something.

What is interesting in this model is that at some level all signals appear to do this. It is not necessary to suppose that there is a conscious intent behind the mechanism of connection. For instance a person looking in a particular direction for a minute sends a signal to whomever notices this action that says something of interest may be happening in that direction. To distinguish between signals that have real intent we divide them into informative and communicative.

A signal is classified as informative when there is no real intention behind it and the meaning we derive from that signal is purely interpretational, and a signal is classified as communicative when there is a clear intent behind it to communicate something of value. If you text someone for instance (or use two tin cans and a piece of string to communicate), there is a clear intent to communicate something to them.

Social signals across the Web, just like the "noise" at a party, tend to be user-generated and predominantly communicative in value. Simply put, every time we communicate with someone across a social network platform, share content, place a comment on content someone else has shared, generate a Facebook Like or a Google+ +1, or a re-tweet on Twitter, we have a specific goal in mind and intend for our action to create a specific belief in their minds.

A 2011 research paper submitted to the *Semantic Web Journal* by School of Computing, University of Leeds researchers Dimoklis Despotakis, Dhavalkumar Thakker, Lydia Lau, and Vania Dimitrova titled "Capturing the Semantics of Individual Viewpoints on Social Signals in Interpersonal Communication" points out that "There is a plethora of user-generated content on the Social Web containing user opinions and experiences expressed in terms of comments, stories, tweets and tags on a variety of events, activities, objects and services." This user-generated content can be used to draw a refined understanding of what these interactions really mean and what value they have.

Semantic search then uses the social signal to better understand the intent behind the actions. It maps this to specific content so that, let's say content I share with a friend on Google+ that contains "Techniques for tying a cravat," becomes mapped to cravat and a specific dress code and, once indexed, can appear on a related search without someone having to specifically ask for the exact keywords of "techniques," "tying," and "cravat."

As Poggi and D'Errico note in their paper: "What characterizes 'social signals' as 'social' is not that they convey information from one entity to another, but that their 'object'—the type of information they convey—is 'social.'"

This directly impacts two things we have been looking at for some time in this book: First, the type of content that is created in the age of the semantic web and, second, its quality. The relationship between content and quality, when aligned to context, becomes a road map for creating a comprehensive search ranking strategy.

Google's reading of the "social signal" helps generate

- A clearer understanding of the meaning behind content.
- Better indexing of the content.
- An assessment of authority of the content based on social interaction.
- An assessment of trust of the content based on social interaction.
- An assessment of the contextual value of the content indexed.

When Google used PageRank (PR) to establish authority and trust in a website and rank it in search the company inadvertently invited every search engine optimizer to try to game the system for the benefit of their clients. PageRank was based on incoming links, and it created an entire "link subculture" as well as a link economy where the buying and selling of links proliferated and the search became susceptible to being gamed.

Rather than adding to the "signal" PageRank gaming added to the "noise" creating the exact opposite effect of what Google intended. Understandably Google is reluctant to repeat the experience with the social signal. A clear, linear indication of ranking in search based on social sharing in social platforms would invite the generation of such massive shifts of data that it would blur a picture that's far from clear.

So Google is going the other way. By establishing the importance of authorship, which revolves around real people and their online activity and allows them to claim content they create on the Web, it creates a handy means to filter spam content and establish some veracity. Google's assessment of individual online profiles through the set of criteria that loosely form the notion of Author Rank helps it determine a sense of authority and trust in the profiles' digital presence and activities. Using these two sets of tools, Google is now busy creating a web of trust. Website content that cannot be readily and willingly created, shared, commented on, and reshared by real people, is, in Google's eyes, of scant real value and eventually will have no place on the search results pages.

Social Media Marketing and Search

There are inherent benefits to having your website in good standing in Google's eyes. Here is a short list of them:

- Your content gets indexed fast.
- Your content ranks high.
- The website is considered to be authoritative.
- Its content is increasingly, socially shared.

In an attempt to guarantee information from trusted sources Google treats websites that it trusts a little differently from run-of-the-mill ones.

A perfect example of a website that pushes all the right buttons and is hugely respected by Google is Stack Overflow (see Figure 7.1). By its own description Stack Overflow is "A language-independent collaboratively edited question and answer site for programmers." Unless you're a programmer you probably have never heard of the site, yet such is its size, popularity, authority, and the level of trust Google holds it at that, as Stack Overflow's co-founder, Jeff Atwood, reports, it gets indexed 10 times every second.

That means that Google's bots crawl the site at the unheard of rate of 10 times a second! Precious few websites warrant this kind of close attention. This begs the question as to what exactly is it that Stack Overflow does so well that Google loves.

An analysis of the site's web profile reveals some interesting facts:

- Its content is heavily reshared by the site's visitors.
- It has a strong following in social networks where it is mentioned frequently.
- It is heavily linked to by programmers and websites that deal with programming.
- It has a high level of traffic.
- It has a lot of content-producing activity.
- It has a lot of interaction within that content, on the site itself.

These are elements that govern the activity of the site's visitor profile.

Figure 7.1 *A Twitter search on the #stackoverflow hashtag brings up thousands of hits where the site is mentioned by name and linked back to its content. Even more interesting is the fact that many of those who are mentioning it have above average Klout scores (the influence measuring service on the Web) that indicates that they have some authority in their field and thereby add further weight to the importance of the sharing activity.*

When it comes to search engine optimization the reverse engineering of success-ful sites helps us understand how to structure winning online profiles that Google loves to rank. Stack Overflow is exceptional enough to be able to stand in as the standard for indexing excellence, authority, and ranking, and in this respect there is much that can be learned from it. We've already seen that the site's visitors mostly fit within a visitor profile that describes their activity and that indicates a high level of engagement with the site.

In the semantic web people interact with websites through their content and the way they consume it. Every website that is successful can trace that success to a unique online visitor profile (based upon the visitor activity) and a unique content profile.

Here are the elements that make up Stack Overflow's content profile:

- The site has a lot of unique content.
- The content is very much solution-oriented. It is there to answer specific questions, and this means it will rank high for search queries rather than just keywords.
- The content is sticky, managing to keep visitors on the site for pro-tracted lengths of time.
- The content invites interaction by way of further clarification or addi-tion, increasing the initial value to the online visitor.

In Chapter 6, "How Content Became Marketing," we saw the importance content plays in the semantic web. Content becomes the principal means through which a website acquires traffic, authority, and trust, and it also becomes the means through which the website's influence is spread in the social web.

The social web is made up of social networks. Some of these are professional, like LinkedIn; others are purely social, like Facebook; and some are a mix, like Google+ and Twitter. Content that goes through the social web is important because Google can see the website it came from. It can see who is resharing it and what kind of reception that content gets on the Web once it is reshared.

I've mentioned that the real characteristic of the semantic web and, with it, seman-tic search is that it is transitioning from a web of websites to a web of people. This can be a little hard to comprehend at times, particularly as the Web is still made up of websites and links, and it is websites we go to, rather than people, to buy stuff and consume news and information. The emergence of social networks from 2004 onwards and the ever-increasing role they play in the spread of information is key to actually understanding the nature of the transition.

In the pre-social web days websites promoted themselves. To rank high on Google search, for instance, you needed to have content that had a specific keyword frequency with keywords strategically placed in the opening paragraph of the content, the main title, the page URL, and a subheading or two. You also needed keywords in the anchor text of links linking back to that page. All of this was website-centric. A website that had a good enough SEO adviser to help them tick all the boxes was going to rank high in search, regardless.

That was the Web of websites. They held all the power. Google ranked them according to their activities. Not ours. What is happening now is the reverse. You could have a website that uses only traditional SEO techniques and is search engine optimized to the gills, and it still may not rank high in search. As a matter of fact unless its content is of sterling quality I can pretty much guarantee that it won't rank high in search.

The reason it won't rank high is because in the age of the semantic web Google forms an opinion about the quality of a website based on factors that, in their predominance, take place outside the website itself. They involve links (again) but also the way those links are created in social media networks, how they are shared, by whom, what that person is known for generally, how widely they share those links, and what happens to them once they are shared.

This approach places the balance of power squarely in the hands of those who are online. A heavy Twitter-user, for instance, who has a large following on Twitter has the ability to promote an item of content and drive to a website tens of thousands of visitors faster and better than organic search would have done. Google sees this, and depending on the subsequent behavior of the visitors who click on the Twitter link to go to the site decides whether the site is worthy of a high rank in search.

The visitor behavior that Google takes into account includes

- The type of personal digital profile the visitor has. (Is the visitor known for that type of content or is that irrelevant with what she does online generally?)
- How the visitor interacts with the content. Does the visitor reshare it? Does she stay on the site a long time? Does she access more than a page on that site? Does she leave within 30 seconds? Does she mention the site independently afterward?
- How the visitor interacts with the website as a brand. Does she mention it? Does she share any of its content after her first visit to it? Does she return to the site frequently?

These are important considerations that Google uses to discover just how relevant the website is in terms of a particular search query. The principle behind the approach is that by recognizing the quality of the pattern of sharing and interaction around a particular link Google can then ascertain with a high degree of confidence the quality of that link in relation to a specific search query.

The expectation here is that if Google has gotten it right then the person who reaches a website following a link Google has ranked high in search will find exactly what he is looking for, right there and then and not have to go back and check out any other links or do another search.

Incidentally both of these behaviors are now considered to be frustrating to the end-user. The faster pace of life that technology has made possible has resulted in more pressure being felt by online users to find the right kind of information quickly and less time to do an ever increasing number of tasks in. A study released by Google showed that the predominant majority of search users today expect to find the answer to their search query right on the search page (leading to what Google calls "good abandonment" of the search) or within the first 10 links.

This places some pressure on companies and brands that are seeking to rank high in Google search to

- Create content that answers specific search queries, as opposed to simply accumulating keywords.
- Have in place a social media sharing strategy that is intended to produce engagement and interaction with their target audience.
- Find ways to identify and attract the social media influencers in their particular business vertical.

The bottom line here is that semantic search signals the end to the part of SEO that relied on autopilot activities such as keyword-rich content, headings that matched keywords, and indiscriminate link building. In the age of the semantic web, SEO is closely integrated with the marketing of a business or brand and closely aligned with the goals they are trying to achieve.

In the transition from a web of websites to a web of people we also transition search marketing from SEO-by-the-numbers to SEO that delivers real value to the end user. One relatively small but significant change in this is that if you now work with a search engine optimization agency you will need to find one that actually understands your business. In the past all that was required was for an agency to simply know about search engine optimization. This is no longer enough now, and a good SEO agency becomes a virtual business partner that will amplify your brand-building efforts and online marketing and help you discover areas for further improvement.

How to Make Your Content Go Viral

Given what we know about the way Google ranks websites it seems obvious now that content that goes viral has some significant impact on a website's ranking in search. Viral content is content that is widely reshared and commented on. It has the ability to influence search rankings because it delivers the following:

- Traffic to the website as the content link is followed.

- A sense of authority in the website as the content that has gone viral is reshared and commented on.

- A sense that the website is trusted because at least some of the site visitors who reshare the content are trusted by Google.

- An increase in the number of links leading to the website. This is mainly because at least some of those who reshare a viral article will also blog about it and link back to the site it came from.

- An increase in visibility in search of the website. Its increasing mention in blogs and social media channels triggers Google's co-citation rule that looks to rank websites for specific content even when there are no direct links associated with them.

Although it is difficult to predict just what kind of content will go viral, the same cannot be said for the path a viral article follows. Essentially every piece of content that goes viral follows a similar path that takes it from its point of creation to the moment of broad discovery by one or two social media influencers who provide their "blessing" by sharing it with their followers.

What happens next is that because those followers consider the source of the reshare to be trustworthy and, perhaps, trend-setting, they both access the article (or piece of content) and reshare it in turn.

This generates the first wave of buzz that ensures high visibility. This then leads to independent discovery by many others who are not influencers. Unless you have your own strong following that is large enough in terms of numbers to enable you to "push" content to a large number of people, you need an influencer's help to promote it. This is not to say that it's automatic and just about anything goes as long as an influencer is willing to push it. Quality here is paramount. Influencers achieve their position in social networks by being picky about the content they share and being selective on the subjects they specialize in.

Google+ has an analytics feature called Ripples that enables the visualization of the spread pattern of an article. Figure 7.2 shows how an article that made it to the social network's "What's Hot" list started out by being reshared by a couple of its largest influencers first.

Ripples can be accessed when logged onto Google+ by clicking on the drop down arrow situated at the top right hand side corner of a Google+ post and choosing "Ripples" from the menu that appears there. The feature is only available when the post has been reshared, not before. On the plus sides this is a publicly visible feature so you can view the ripples on any post not just your own.

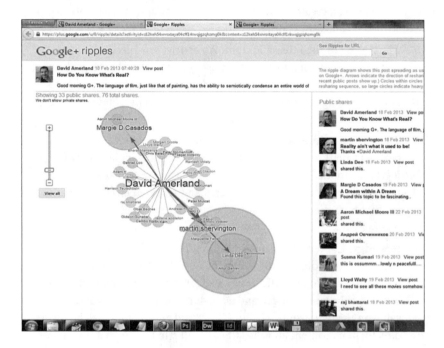

Figure 7.2 *The Google+ visualization of the spread pattern of an article that went viral shows that it was picked up by some of its larger influencers first. Their importance is signified by the larger circle. Within them we can see some of their followers resharing the article. Subsequently, as it rose in visibility, it was reshared by many other members of the Google+ community.*

One of the questions most frequently asked at this point is if there is a formula that can be applied to content (articles, blog posts or video) that can make it go viral. The easy answer here is no. But that is not entirely true. While there is no formula that can be applied to content that will guarantee it going viral there is a formula that reveals itself in retrospect in content that has gone viral, which, if applied, can help almost any kind of content go viral.

Every piece of content that gets discovered and succeeds in drawing attention from a large audience has all of these ingredients:

- **The subject matter is popular.** If it's trending then you have a little bit of a head start already. If it's not, then you will need to work a lot harder and with a much lower common denominator to have as wide an appeal as possible.

- **The treatment of the article hits all the right notes.** It is important that what you create or what you write about contains elements that spark a response in your target audience.

- **The timing of the release is right.** An article, or a piece of content, that gets released at a time when most of its target audience is likely to be offline (or busy doing something else) is likely to get buried in the stream of things that happen across the Web every second regardless of how well written or well produced it may be.

- **There is some interaction with the audience.** Content that goes viral benefits from interaction that amplifies its original impact, for example it gets mentioned and reshared by people who are far from where it first appeared and it gets rediscovered and reshared afresh, long after the first buzz dies down. Those who rediscover it give it a fresh lease on life by introducing it to new audiences.

- **It is edgy.** Content that catches the attention of the Web audience succeeds in standing a little above the rest of the content around it. It pushes the envelope a little. It has a slight controversy about it without being openly controversial, and as such it usually succeeds at delivering value on the twin fronts of information and entertainment. The former directly in its content and the latter, usually, in the interaction and "play" that's made of its sharing. (A classic example of this is the official picture released by the White House of President Obama shooting skeet.)

It is difficult to try and craft every piece of content you create with the intent for it to go viral, but if you keep these rules in mind and have on your radar the influencers in your business sector, then you are stacking the odds in your favor.

Websites that frequently have posts that go viral create a digital footprint that search engines love.

Figure 7.3 is the visualization of the digital footprint of a page on my own website. Over a period of 12 months I was lucky enough to have several articles go viral on the Web. The average traffic these pages received was 100,000 visitors over a three or four day period.

You can see the links that have been generated as a result of such activity.

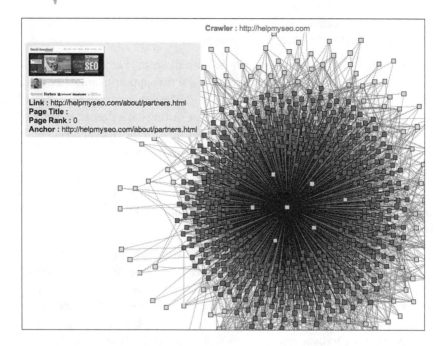

Figure 7.3   *With my own website at the center you can see in this visualization the links coming in from all around the Web and the interconnections between them. The lighter colored ones are linking to websites that make a mention of my content, referencing it, while the darker colored ones provide direct links to my website. Creating such a digital footprint on the Web is necessary if you want your company or brand to achieve good ranking on the search results pages.*

In terms of marketing your website the semantic web requires you to use social media networks to propagate your content. In turn those social media networks create a social signal that is generated from the pattern of sharing, resharing, and commenting on the links of your content that enable Google to understand the importance of that content. This naturally brings us to the final part of this chapter that creates the boundaries within which your content, indeed, any content that you create, will work.

Context and Relevance in the Semantic Web

It is no accident that the very word "semantic" is based on an ancient Greek root that means, meaning. Actually the real meaning of the word is importance as pertaining to meaning, and on the Web this is derived in the exact same way that importance is derived in the offline world: through the relationships connecting different people with the addition of the connections made (thought the sharing of content and linking) from one website to others.

Connections only acquire meaning when they are of value. Value only comes into play when it can be seen through the twin filters of context and relevance.

The best piece of writing in the world, the most technically accomplished video, or the most beautiful illustration are of zero value if they appear in an online setting that only accepts entries written in binary code. The semantic web reminds us that every picture, every video, every single piece of writing has a deeper, underlying meaning encoded in it that is designed to resonate with the right audience at the right time. That's exactly what context and relevance mean.

A piece of writing on real estate and SEO is of little value to a multinational corporation that faces decidedly different concerns when it comes to the visibility of its online presence. Similarly content that contains information useful to bankers may be of zero value to online grocery store owners.

The way semantic search unlocks the value of each item of information is by understanding its relationship to a search query and presenting it within the relevant context. This also shows the value of specific search engine optimization strategies that only make sense in a semantic web. The ability of semantic search to work out the meaning of information through this relationship analysis method also means that a website can now rank high in search because it has a broad enough reach in its content to become associated with specific types of search queries.

There are a few different ways that this can benefit you in search rankings and increase the chances of your website coming up in search in response to a relevant query:

- Personalized search (Google's Search Plus Your World, frequently abbreviated to S+YW)
- Suggested or associated results (Google's serendipity discovery mechanism)
- Search Query related search results (Google's understanding of your website's value in answering a specific search query)
- Google related searches (search suggestions based on what other searchers who had a similar search query to yours, looked for next).
- Google autocomplete suggestions (a little similar to Google's related searches this also takes into account your personal search history, plus the relevance of your location if your IP information is passed to search).

Each of these should be central to your thinking when it comes to using search to market your business. It is well worth looking at them in a little more detail.

Personalized Search (or S+YW) is what appears in Google search in response to a search query that is drawn from the end-user's personal social media connections. This is a little like seeing what your friends like in Facebook done better with Google's indexing of shared content and its understanding of the relationships and connections between people.

To achieve this Google uses predominantly Google+, but it also looks at Twitter and the wider Web seeking to index the information it needs to better understand the relationships between the people's profiles it has in its index. Obviously Google+ gives the company a much easier ride here in that respect. It also highlights the importance of having a Google+ profile in the first place and engaging in some Google+ interaction as part of your social media marketing efforts.

The end result of this is that if you've succeeded in getting your content to have a wide enough reach, if it has found an audience in social networks, or if you have been lucky enough to see it go viral, you also increase its chances to appear on someone's personalized search results when it otherwise wouldn't.

The personalization of search is an element of semantic search that is gathering momentum. Google has figures that the right kind of information appearing from the end-user's social network is perceived as being more trustworthy and produces more clicks as a result. Although currently it informs only a small percentage of search results, there may well be opportunities for it to grow in future as Google gathers data and its confidence in what it serves, as part of it, also grows.

It must be noted that this comes into play only when the end-user is logged in to her Google account. Some may indeed choose not to, but even then the strength of social media connections affects search results, particularly in voice search, and mobile devices where Google uses location-aware and even device-aware services to produce some of its search results. Even when you are not logged in to your Google account Google uses some stored cookies and your IP address to deliver a more tailored search experience for the sake of relevance and quality in the search results.

The non-logged in personalization trend is growing, particularly where location-aware or device-aware services are concerned and it must be noted that this will have to be taken into account when a search engine optimization campaign is planned.

Suggested or associated results in search are results that increasingly appear in semantic search and are drawn from Google's understanding of the individual's search history and interests, his association and interaction with people in social networks on specific topics, and the search patterns and behavior of other users who carried out similar search queries. It is then broadened even further by a factored serendipity algorithm that takes into account that when we look for things through search we may, sometimes, find something we like that we were not looking for.

There is only one way that you can try to get your website appearing in these results and that is to have its content appear in as many social media networks as possible and be talked about, discussed, and its content reshared.

Search Query Related Search Results in SEO tech jargon are frequently called co-citation results. This is when a result appears (or is suggested) in search that is only there because it has been mentioned enough times in the social web, even though no, or little, link sharing or linking to the website occurred. If, for instance, the once popular TV show *The X-Files* is mentioned enough times in the context of science fiction series, Google can understand that it is a science fiction series even if there is absolutely no content in *The X-Files* website itself that labels it as such.

A perfect example of how all this works is given in Figure 7.4, which takes a generic term like "sci-fi series" and uses Google's semantic search to power the Knowledge Carousel that appears at the top of search. What is worth noting here is that on the far left-hand side a black rectangle has appeared that says: "TV Shows – Frequently mentioned on the web" that shows just where the search results that appear in the Knowledge Carousel come from and how their ranking order is determined.

This is complex, but a quick moment spent here looking at the broad strokes of the engine beneath the hood will be useful. Google uses a technique called Entity Extraction to index web pages in its semantic index. An entity has a real world meaning. It can be a person, for instance, or a city or, in this case a sci-fi film. Google needs to understand this fully not just as a keyword, so it uses an Entity Extraction process to automatically extract document metadata from the unstructured text documents found on the Web. Entity Extraction uses programming (usually called Entity Extractors) to read an unstructured text document (i.e. one that has no semantic metadata but has relevant keywords) and enrich it by adding intelligent, relevant metadata to it. This, in addition to two more uniquely semantic indexing activities, Linking (mapping the relationship between entities) and Analysis (categorizing information about an entity from the content) allow Google to build its Entity Graph that powers semantic search results.

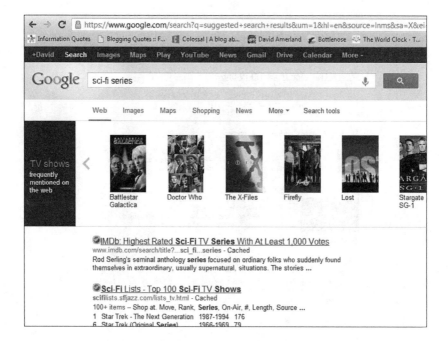

Figure 7.4   *The "frequently mentioned on the web" tab on the left-hand side of search highlights the fact that the results that are generated across the scrolling Knowledge Carousel are due to their social signal in the semantic web. Their popularity and engagement in social media networks also determines the order of their appearance there.*

When I carried out the search for sci-fi series I deliberately used a generic term to see what Google's semantic search would suggest, and I also stayed logged in to my Google account. What is interesting is that as Figure 7.5 shows, halfway through those search results is a personalized search result (marked so by the outline of a head and shoulders profile image) that points to a link that has obviously been shared in Google+. Right under the snippet that describes the link on the search results page, in a slightly grayed out font, is the source of who shared it. In this case it is Boston.com. The link appears in search only because I have chosen to follow the Boston.com Page in Google+ and the terms I have searched for appear on that page, making the return of this page a query-dependent signal.

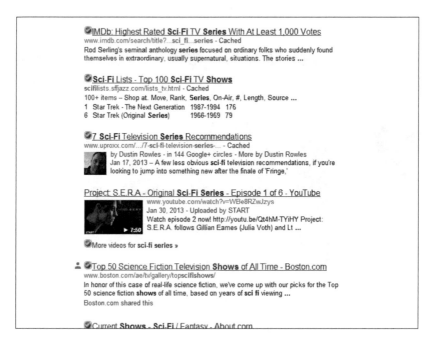

Figure 7.5 *The reason this search result appears here is because when I carried out this search I was logged in on my Google account, and I have also chosen to actively follow Boston.com on the Google+ social network.*

The idea behind the appearance of the link and the detailing of its source is to remind me that I am already following Boston.com in the Google+ social network. I presumably like or trust its content and this is its website.

Context and relevance in the semantic web have the ability to repurpose content and make it appear in relation to search queries that perhaps the content producer had no idea of. This turns the focus back on what you need to do to create content that works. You need to have a clear focus on

- Quality
- Authenticity
- Value

Never create content just to fill a website, tick a box of activities that you think you should engage in, or use as bait to draw traffic to your website. It is highly unlikely that it will have the desired effect, and, more to the point, it is likely to turn off human visitors and get your website cast with those low quality websites that Google tries to keep off the first page.

The Social Media Marketing Preparation Checklist

The whole reason you have this book is to help your website rank high and appear on the first page of Google. To achieve this you need to go back to basics a little bit and work out exactly why your business is in business, what makes it different, what makes it special, what fires up your passion, and what makes you get to work each day.

You then need to look at your answers, look at the kind of content you are producing, and decide whether the content adequately reflects all your answers. If not, you need to fix it.

The 10 points listed here are designed to help you do just that.

- Detail just how your content reflects your company or brand values. Think about tone and style in how you communicate in the online world.
- List all the different ways you get your message across to your target audience.
- Detail your plan for building a following in the social networks your company or brand is active in.
- Detail just how you will create an authentic voice in your online content and social media network sharing and interactions.
- Detail your strategy for identifying and soliciting social media influencers who can help you spread the reach and depth of your content.
- Detail the techniques you will employ that will help you amplify your social media impact.
- Explain how you will best prepare your corporate or brand website for semantic search.
- Detail what you need to do to increase the opportunities for your content to go viral on the Web.
- Explain in detail how you think your current SEO agency can best help you attain your search marketing goals.
- Explain how strong you believe the social signal of your website to be at the moment and list all the different ways it could be improved.

8

There Is No Longer a "First" Page of Google

Search engine optimization was never "simple," but it used to be a lot more straightforward. You knew when things were working because your website ended up being on the first page of Google for a whole lot of critical keywords. In retrospect those were the Halcyon days of SEO. Things now are much, much harder with the "first" page of Google's search being different for almost every end-user.

In this chapter we learn exactly why the concept of a "first" page in search has changed, what has replaced it, and what can be done to increase the opportunity for search to deliver targeted traffic to your website.

"Get Me on the First Page of Google"

The request to get a website ranking on the first page of Google is one that search engine optimizers and SEO agencies have been hearing for a long time. A first page listing on Google search is required for many different reasons, all of which make total sense at the organizational planning level but not at the front end of digital marketing.

Examining the reasons why the "First Page of Google" was such a ubiquitous phrase for online businesses gives us the opportunity to really understand what's changed in search and what we now need to do instead.

The list goes a little like this:

- **Clear metric.** A first page listing on Google search for a specific keyword was the kind of metric anyone could understand. Search engine optimization may have had a whiff of the magical about it, but none of it mattered when you had the clarity of going to Google search, inputting a search term containing a keyword there, and seeing if your site appeared and how high it ranked.

- **Comparison.** Everyone has competitors, and they are also aware of Google search and SEO. Seeing how your competitors ranked for the same keywords provided an easy set of targets that allowed a gauging of performance for the search engine optimization team (if the work was carried out in-house) or the SEO agency, if it was outsourced.

- **Implementation.** Implementing a ranking strategy based on keywords and website positions on Google search was the kind of thing team managers and CEOs could grasp without thinking too deeply about it. Plus it looked really good on color line charts.

- **Research.** Looking into what keywords are popular for a particular product or industry, in general, and compiling a list is one of those activities that made everyone feel that they were achieving something important.

- **Looking at competitor backlinks.** Playing sleuth on the Web and finding out what websites have linked to a competitor site and how, was one of those activities that were a little challenging to carry out and, when completed, provided the satisfaction of having learned a valuable trade secret.

The fact that none of these activities will be quite as useful as they were in the past, is testament to the impact the introduction of semantic search has had on SEO. But it is not only semantic search that has brought changes. The semantic web, these days, is fully mobile. Browsers access the Web from a number of devices (popularly called "screens" due to different screen sizes that define them) and the "three screen browser" who begins a search on his desktop, follows it away from his desk on his tablet or iPad, and then closes it on his smartphone have become the norm.

When the Web was website based and browsing meant a large screen and a laptop or PC, search engine optimization was an easier business to tackle for everybody (though it certainly only seems so in retrospect). A website based Web also meant that websites were where all the action was.

If you were doing search engine optimization you were essentially optimizing a website. Your content strategy was website based. You created a linking strategy designed to drive up the PageRank of a website. Your efforts were localized and cumulative. Both of these points are important because they highlight the depth of the change that's rocking the search engine optimization world and is creating the SEO challenges we are seeing. When you went offsite you did so to create links that pointed back to the website. As a matter of fact, with few enlightened exceptions, offsite work meant creating content and comments that pointed back to a website.

The practice led to some of the worst excesses in digital marketing and search engine optimization history the Web has seen. Without contravening Google's guidelines and engaging in banned optimization techniques (called Black Hat SEO), search engine optimizers would create legit profiles in numerous forums with the express intention to join the conversation and supply, through the forum signature or forum profile, a link back to the website. In relevant posts there would be the required precisely worded anchor text that would point a link back to a website using some of the most highly contested keywords that website was fighting to rank for.

Apart from generating tens of thousands of fake profiles (not all SEO agencies played completely fair) and inflating the traffic of forums, the practice also generated massive amounts of content in poorly written, keyword-rich articles that would appear in article repositories, the same article repositories that Google would later seriously penalize for harboring some of the worst quality content on the Web.

It all made sense at the time of course because it worked. Websites that cumulatively had specific keywords repeated in a specific keyword frequency per post ranked higher in search. If they had thousands of links coming in from all over the Web, their PageRank rose. They were deemed to be more trusted. They received more traffic, and they ranked higher in search. The longer those links pointed to them, the more power the website acquired so there was not much incentive to wait to get links naturally through quality content. There was no point.

What website owners demanded was a quick rise in search and a permanent place once a website got there.

How is this relevant to us now? Well, if you are looking to optimize your website today you can no longer rely on doing work just on your website alone. You can no longer use suspect linking strategies, poor quality content, anchor text in your links, or countless similar articles posted across the Web. Keywords and keyword frequency (often called keyword density) are no longer of much use. Certainly the latter has become largely meaningless as a search engine optimization technique, and it's more likely to work against you than for you.

Stripped of many of the tools and techniques that SEOs had at their disposal, the work at hand became even harder with the realization that not only could search engine optimization work no longer be localized, but it now also could not be cumulative. Google took the view that websites left alone without freshly created content were forgotten and abandoned, and it deprecated them as out of date and probably unlikely to produce any kind of satisfactory end-user experience.

Google's "freshness" algorithm, introduced in November 2011, took a long look at what search engine optimizers had called "the obsolescence of the Link Graph" that was made up of all those links website owners were counting on and said it was time to solve the issue of out-of-date content. And just as search engine optimization was no longer about working on a website, creating some links, and writing some content, the first page of Google, a ranking that had become the sole deciding test of success, began to fragment.

Those in the search engine optimization industry who still retained some semblance of sanity, soon began to feel like a threatened species.

The Fragmented World of Search

The title of this chapter raises an interesting question: How is it possible, you ask, for the first page of Google to just disappear? After all, from a visual point of view, the first page is still there. We can carry out a search query on Google, and the first page will appear and then all the other pages behind it, each numbered in sequence.

What has disappeared is the notion that there is just one first page of Google for a given search query—a place that has just enough room for 10 links and a few ads. A place that is the same for every person who carries out that exact same search query, irrespective of who they are and where they are, began to grow a little anemic the moment Google started to introduce localization and personalization in search.

Google first introduced localization in search in 2004 when it started to offer "relevant neighborhood business listings" and offered personalized search, as an experiment, a year later. The intention behind the former was to deliver the best possible search results to queries that had a local aspect, the latter to address the increasingly personal nature of search for the end user. In taking this path Google began to customize the search engine results pages, taking into account factors that would personalize search for the end-user, and began the fragmentation of the search presentation page for the marketer.

To be completely fair the Google search results pages were never identical in the results they returned for the same search query across the globe. The results were always drawn from Google's local index, and for that Google relied on its capability to recognize where you were through your IP address. So a query for supermarkets would return different results in Manchester, UK (where I live), than it would in Manchester, Indiana. But while the results would be different for those across the different indices that Google was building from its indexing of the Web, those living within the catchment area of a Google Index would expect to see largely the same results for an identical search query.

This is no longer the case; not by far.

The reason for this is surprisingly simple: stickiness, or rather the concept of trying to make a site as utilitarian as possible that's described by stickiness. In the Internet world stickiness is described as the average minutes per month visitors spend at a site or network. Occasionally it is page views (for a website) or visitor numbers (for a search engine like Google).

The point is stickiness only happens when the site itself becomes largely invisible. It fades into the background of the consciousness of the end-user and what emerges to the forefront is what the site does. Google wants to make search a seamless experience, and to do that it has created one of the largest vertical environments in the world.

Creating a vertical environment that is somehow "fenced" is every web company's dream. It allows it to capture the end-user usage data that can be used to create sense in the pattern of online behavior. It helps it create stickiness to its brand through a variety of seamlessly integrated services. It is a great strategy for ensuring brand loyalty and a great way to introduce a steady stream of data-based products and services.

Apple has done this with its virtually airtight hardware/software environment that locks its customers into its services and products. Facebook has done it by making its social network into what the inventor of the Web, Tim Berners-Lee, has called the web's largest "walled garden." Microsoft is attempting to do it with its Windows 8 environment. In short, this is a strategy that makes sense for a tech business.

When it comes to Google the accomplishment is phenomenal. Globally the search engine holds 80% of the search market share. Its own browser, Chrome, has overtaken its opposition to become the leading browser in the world in terms of usage. YouTube is the second largest search engine on the Web after Google, and Google+ is the second largest social network after Facebook. Its mobile operating system, Android, holds 70% of the global market share of smartphones.

Collectively all this adds up to a massive, digital, connected environment that allows Google to deliver a seamless search experience that is further contributed to by web applications such as Google Maps and Google Translate. Central to all this, holding it together, is search. Search is key to making the Web useful, creating order out of its chaotic data, and making it navigable.

Google search is no longer just the familiar Google search box that helped desktop users find what they wanted. In keeping with end-user preferences and usage, Google search has itself fragmented across interfaces. On mobile, for instance, end-users frequently use Google Voice Search. In tablets they use a combination of Google Voice Search and regular search. The search that powers YouTube and Google+ draws from a different index than the one that powers desktop search. Google Now, essentially a predictive search engine that preloads on your Android device what you may need to search for based on your location, draws heavily from localization and the end user's personal web search history.

If you are beginning to think that suddenly search has become a little ethereal—it appears to be everywhere but in different forms and formats—you are right. Imagine that for your company or brand name to get in front of the consumers you are targeting, it must somehow inject itself into all these different indexes that Google has built and then arrange it so that your website actually comes up in relation to a potential answer they may have. If the task appears, at first sight, to be monumentally difficult, that's because it is.

Search marketing and search engine optimization have become an increasingly time-consuming, expensive activity that, if performed traditionally in a top-down approach becomes so expensive, that no company has the budget to maintain it for very long.

The saving grace in all this is the fact that search, in all its possible formats, is powered by the same common denominator: data. The information you place on your website, the online behavior of those associated with your business, the connection between the different kinds of data you create, and the way that data is then used are what Google needs.

Content creation is the point where Google's need for data and your business's need to be found on the Web suddenly come together. The deciding factors are, as we have already seen, context and relevance, and the defining characteristic is quality. Google, of course, has been beating the drum about quality in content ever since there was a Google to speak of, so why is this now news? It's because of semantic search. The shift in the balance of power from websites where you controlled everything to people profiles across the Web means that you also cede a large amount of control over your marketing message.

Put a little more simply, the fragmentation of search and the reliance on content produces an interesting dynamic where success for content marketing (and visibility on the Web) hinges on the overlap between what you have to say as a business and what they are interested in as a target audience, as illustrated in Figure 8.1.

Content Marketing

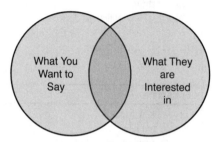

Figure 8.1   *The success of your business's online visibility hinges on the quality of its content marketing. The greater the overlap between what you have to say and what your target audience is most interested in, the more successful you will be in generating the kind of online buzz and engagement that produces a presence across many of the search verticals.*

Given how straightforward the path to search engine dominance was in the past, the natural question here is whether there is such a thing as a success equation that can be applied now.

As it happens there is one (see Figure 8.2).

Success in Search in the Semantic Web

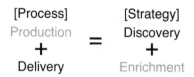

Figure 8.2   *Success in content marketing depends on you having a production and delivery system in place (a process) for your content and then being able to get it discovered and work to get it enriched (a strategy).*

The process part of your content marketing depends entirely on the raw materials you have to work with: your manpower, your web platform system, your team's experience and expertise, your management skills, and your ability to make it all work together.

Production	Delivery
• Articles • Videos • Podcasts • Infographics • Product releases • Press releases • Product features • Services • Presentations	• Website platform • RSS Feed • Mobile devices • Social networks • Second screen/companion devices
Discovery	**Enrichment**
• Social network • Social recommendation • Search • User profile • Serendipity (search)	• Engage and discuss • Search and filter • Annotate and segment

What becomes evident from this model of working is that in terms of implementation there is a symmetry in the number of activities associated with production and delivery on one side and discovery and enrichment on the other. In terms of functionality production and enrichment are part of the same activity as the skill set of the one is applicable to the other.

If you can make your process work seamlessly in sync with your strategy, you then are more likely to have the kind of business that enjoys a natural advantage in search. The approach also demonstrates that in the semantic web, where consumers jump from one screen to the next and one web vertical to another, your best bet at being discovered, creating engagement, and generating a buzz, lies in your ability to successfully interrupt their online journey.

Capturing Online User Attention and Search

If you are to successfully interrupt the online journey of the target audience you address and capture their attention you need to have some of the tools of the new semantic search in place.

These are divided into Features you can implement, Activities you should undertake, and Metrics you need to keep track of:

Features

- Snippets
- Content description
- Structured data
- High quality images
- Local listings

Activities

- Social sharing
- Engagement

Metrics

- Click Through Rates (CTR)
- Amplification
- Depth

Each of these is designed to help you get your website content, company message, and brand in front of your target audience as they surf the Web looking for information, sharing stories and content, and checking out potential online purchases.

Knowledge is always empowering, and understanding in detail each of these elements goes a long way toward helping you formulate the winning synthesis of process and strategy in your digital marketing.

Snippets   Snippets are the brief extracts of information that appear in Google search in relation to a search query (see Figure 8.3). Usually the combination of the displayed URL, the title with bold face keywords matches to the query, and the description under it are what motivates the end-user to click on a link. This makes snippets critical in terms of influencing clicking behavior.

With most of the attention usually going to the creation of the content itself proper descriptions and titles are frequently overlooked. Sometimes descriptions are not put at all in the meta tags of the article on the web platform where it is published. At other times they are hastily written, simply to tick the box of having done so rather than spending some time thinking about how they will appear to the end-user.

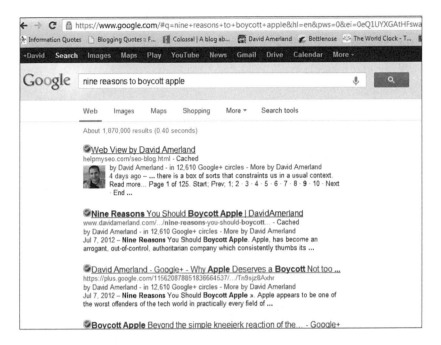

Figure 8.3 *I frequently use my own website to experiment. In this result you can see that in response to the search query "nine reasons to boycott apple," which is a very popular opinion piece I wrote, the snippet from my website (deliberately left blank for this experiment) provides a description that is a lot less likely to appeal to the end-user. The description of the same article on another site where I actually filled in the meta description creates a more compelling clicking experience.*

In March 2012 Google was awarded a patent that details how on the search results page it can rewrite the title and snippet if the description has not been filled in, or if Google feels the existing title is too generic and therefore not a good motivator for someone to click, or the existing meta description is not good enough, with insufficient keywords to cause someone to click on it.

Google uses code to rewrite the title and snippet, so knowing where it draws its information from is critical to always getting good titles and snippets in search.

The patent details that Google, in writing its snippet description, uses the following sources:

- The beginning of an article
- The end of an article
- The length of paragraphs
- Stylistics on paragraphs (like the use of bold, italics, or color)

- Other paragraphs based on their distance from the opening and closing paragraphs

The important things to remember here are that the titles and meta descriptions placed in created content are an important part of your marketing message. They influence clicking behavior and the traffic that gets to your website and should not be left to chance. Equally the opening and closing paragraphs need to be more than just literary works of art. Because they can be used as a source to rewrite the title of the page in response to a search query and its snippet description, there has to be a clear understanding of what they are intended to promote and what message they send.

Content Description   The description of a piece of content is called the meta description, and it is there to help search engines display in search a good summary of the page. It frequently gets added as an afterthought. So much effort goes into crafting quality content that when it comes to describing it concisely in 150 characters or less in the description and a maximum 70 characters in the title, the one responsible often fails.

Writing great titles and great snippets is an art, just like writing great content. Make sure that every piece of content generated has a concise marketing or branding message and that this is then reflected in the title and description tags.

Structured Data   One day soon the Web will revolve around structured data. Essentially structured data is a way of detailing information about a website in a more dynamic format. This allows a search engine to pull out not just the relevant details to display but also some of their functionality such as the price of tickets for a concert, the reviews for a restaurant, or the booking form for a hotel. Rich snippets, as structured data snippets are frequently called, such as those shown in Figure 8.4, add functionality to a listing right on the search results page and increase the likelihood of engagement with the end-user.

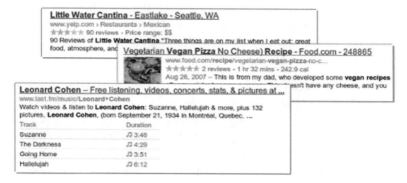

Figure 8.4   *These examples of rich snippets show reviews, ratings, and playing time for a song.*

There are three different ways to use structured data: Microdata (an HTML5 based way of doing it), Microformats (where coding conventions are used on pages to describe the information), and RDFa. The latter stands for Resource Description Framework, and it is a W3C recommendation. It adds a specific set of attributes to existing web pages that help describe the information they contain.

The use of structured data is still rare on the Web, though it will continue to grow. Currently Google does not appear to give preference to websites that have implemented it, in terms of ranking, probably because the prevalence of properly marked up websites is so low that to do so would create an unfair, two-tier search that would distort the quality of the search results. Obviously it indexes them and ranks them according to the same criteria as any other website and then uses their structured data format to display rich snippets from them, when appropriate.

Social Sharing   A website whose content does not appear on social networks is probably of low value, quite possibly of low quality, and may be, even, largely abandoned. Google's use of the social signal to find and index links and gauge the importance of the links it finds makes it necessary that you have in place a clear, measurable social media sharing strategy that defines what you share, when you share it, who you share it with, what impact it has, and how you can tell. Every business will be a little different here, and the social footprint of each will also be different. It is up to you to decide what yours should really be.

Engagement   The way your links and content are received in social networks is part of your website's "social footprint." It tells Google a little about the quality of your links and content and the subject matter, authority, and trust that your website enjoys. If there is no strategy on how to generate and sustain engagement, you are missing out on an important element of the new search engine optimization techniques you need to have in place.

High Quality Images   The Web is a hugely visual medium. Google has refined and enhanced its image search to produce deeper engagement and promote websites with better pictorial content and original illustrations. This shows that your content creation must now include a professional approach to sourcing and using pictorial content. Used properly this can become a welcome, additional, source of targeted traffic to your website.

Click Through Rate (CTR)   The Click Through Rate (CTR) score your articles and content get on the Web goes toward the overall assessment of the quality of your website. As such it is then hugely important, and it is something you can both monitor and control. The average position of your content in the search engine results pages (SERPs) is found in Google Analytics. Because your website is made up of individual pages of content and each of these now impacts the overall quality of your website, poorly performing pages tend to drag you down a little in your ranking.

What you do is

- Find the poorly performing pages on your website.
- Improve titles and descriptions to improve the way they appear on the search results pages.
- Implement authorship using the rel=author tag, if you haven't already.
- Make sure you don't have any weird characters in your title and content.
- Improve the content by updating it or rewriting it to make it more relevant.

It is worth noting here that it is a valid SEO technique to prune content that is not performing well and cannot be salvaged through rewriting.

Local Listings   Making use of Google's local listings through Google Places for Business adds one more data point to your digital presence and provides an additional means of engagement and interaction for your potential audience. More than that, however, local listings appear in local searches on mobile devices as well as desktop ones and can become a valuable means of guiding business right to your door. Although this is part of adding one more data point of what you do on the Web, for a bricks and mortar business with a local presence this has disproportionate importance to the rest of the features you can take advantage of. Google's free service (http://goo.gl/S7ww8) allows any local business to create a presence on the Web, adding information about itself that will appear in Google search, maps, and mobile devices. Google Places for Business has quite a few benefits. It enables a business to take advantage of Google Offers (an important element of any local business mobile marketing strategy), and it allows customers to place reviews on the business products or services, that appear on the listing page and on Google search. Local business listings are also visible within Google+. Beyond the obvious, direct appeal this has for potential customers, the integration of reviews allows Google to better understand what a business does and index it properly in its semantic search index. Local listings feature prominently in Google's local search and Google Voice search on mobile and should always be an integral part of a bricks and mortar business search marketing strategy.

Amplification   When you are active in social media platforms what you really are trying to do is amplify the social signal of your website through increased interaction, engagement, and sharing. This is where you need to have a strategy worked out how to achieve this. Amplification is a direct result of engagement in the online conversation in a way that it turns your interlocutors from potential customers to brand evangelists. This is no mean feat, and achieving it requires that you carefully and precisely determine what your brand values and message are and how you are going to communicate them.

Depth   This is the final tool you need to have in place for successful interrupt marketing. The best way to think of depth is in terms of commitment. You may have, as an example, a million followers on Twitter or be able to get thousands of +1s on Google+, but if you cannot get past the one- or two-word length in the comments your posts receive then you are highly unlikely to be able to exert much of an influence in the way they see you as a business or brand, or be capable of gently guiding their purchasing decisions. Generating deeper interactions is particularly useful because it allows you the opportunity to make better use of keywords and marketing in ways that would not really be possible conventionally.

All this sounds a lot like Marketing 101. Search is marketing. Every time someone carries out a search on Google and your website comes up in the listings you are marketing to those who see it. You are generating a greater awareness of your brand and creating opportunities for real engagement.

The New Rules of SEO

The thing to remember about SEO is that nothing dies off. As a practice it gets deprecated and further refined by an additional signal (or two). That means that the "traditional" SEO techniques listed at the beginning of this chapter are still valid. What no longer works is the blatant abuse to which they gave rise and the ability they offered to game search.

So, you ask, what are the new rules that must be kept in mind?

They are mostly conceptual, though each has specific, implementable tasks:

- **Think mobile.** Mobile search is at the heart of much of what is happening in search. Location-aware applications like Google Now pre-loads data you may need on the go. Google Maps and Google Local Search are also used by many people on the go. If your website does not work on mobile you are cutting yourself off from a large slice of your prospects.

  On the debate of whether you should have a separate, additional mobile website Google came down, after some vaccillation, on the side of responsive web design that is suitable for all screens and serves content to all devices from the same location on the Web. Creating a mobile strategy requires some involved thinking regarding identifying mobile audience needs and perhaps the creation of an app for serving specific content, or services to mobile users. The key elements to bear in mind in terms of optimization are site stability, loading speed, and the quality of the end-user experience across different "screens." Getting any of these wrong has the potential to derail any search engine optimization drive.

- **Think search query.** Consider how to create content that answers specific problems your target audience may have. By all means use keywords as you optimize your content, but keyword frequency that tried to "load" a page and take advantage of Google's statistical analysis in traditional search and rank high, is a thing of the past as an SEO technique, so write naturally. Because the behavior of the online visitors now counts as a metric (through the CTR scores and the way visitors share its content in their social media behavior) the ability to provide high-quality content that provides real value in terms of the search query and is worth resharing, is something that needs to be taken into account in your content creation strategy.

- **Think visually.** Consider how your title and snippet will look in Google's search. Will they be good enough to entice users to click on the link? Think what images you are going to use to illustrate your article. Image search now brings as much traffic to some websites as conventional link search. This gives the pictures you use on your site a far greater importance than just aids used to alleviate the visual boredom of a page of text. Strive to create or use pictures that fully help your branding, promote your brand or business values and stop the eye of the casual online browser long enough for them to consider clicking on an image to be taken to your website. Images are important because they now act as traffic magnets in their own right. They also play a very prominent role on mobile devices where the smaller screens allow visual elements (such as a picture) to take center stage.

- **Think social.** Search takes place across devices, screen sizes, and verticals and is increasingly personalized. This means no two people see exactly the same first page of Google, for the same search query. You need to make sure your brand and business have a broad enough digital footprint to be able to interrupt your prospects in their journey across the Web.

- **Think apps.** Mobile devices have created an app culture where, frequently, audience attention is captured and a new audience is discovered through the app itself, particularly if it's made available through Google Play or the Apple App Store, both of which help apps find an audience. Apps do two very specific things: A. They deliver targeted and frequently customized content to an audience and B. They capture valuable user data for the app publisher. Both of these are necessary to an online business. Targeted content delivery is a great way to generate direct engagement with your audience and grow your brand reach. Within your app you should work to liberate the content you share with your target audience by allowing those who access it to socialize it by sharing it across the Web.

- **Think influencers.** Identify those in your industry you can most benefit from. Influencers help amplify the reach of your content. A wider audience brings more traffic to a website and increases its social footprint through mentions and content sharing in a social media network environment. Work to create win-win situations, engaging influencers through content they feel they can share and leverage their influence to gain greater exposure.

- **Think authority.** If you cannot be regarded as an authority within your industry from the content you share and the interactions you have, perhaps you should not be in business. Communicate your passion, drive, knowledge, and expertise in an open, direct, accessible way.

The First Page of Google Preparation Checklist

While there is no longer a single first page of Google, the increased personalization of search allows you the opportunity to create a lot more "first page" opportunities.

The following list is designed to help you assess whether your content creation and marketing strategy is helping you or hindering you.

Go through each point and test how prepared you really are.

- Detail how you decide on the type of content you prepare, its frequency, and subject matter.

- Explain in detail your strategy for generating engagement in social media networks.

- Explain in detail your strategy for generating greater depth of interaction with your social media followers. How will you make sure that they engage and stay on topic?

- Explain how you plan to implement the new tools of SEO in your current setup and marketing.

- Explain how you will implement an update strategy on existing content on your website to keep it current and fresh.

- Detail how you will integrate mobile marketing in your current content creation plans.

- Explain how you will achieve amplification of your social media signal to drive awareness of your brand and help improve traffic to your website.

- List all the different ways you could integrate local listings and local content in your current business setup.

- Describe how you think you could make use of the opportunities created by structured data to display rich snippets in search.

- Detail how you will make sure that title and description tags created for each item of content your business or brand generates will be made to reflect a concise marketing message or brand value.

9

The Spread of Influence and Semantic Search

The idea of reputation, influence, and influencers in the offline world is as old as the hills. It's not new on the Web either, but semantic search is creating a portable sense of identity, reputation, and influence that in the days before it simply did not exist. And this is changing everything.

In this chapter we see exactly how identity, reputation, and influence are key to semantic search and crucial for ranking a website. We discuss what you can do to make sure that your business can gain the maximum benefit from the reputation and influence of your marketing team and audience.

The Building Blocks of the Web

At the core of the semantic web lies the frequently mentioned transition from websites to people. This is the true "secret" of semantic search and the hardest part to wrap one's head around. After all, content is still placed on websites. Marketing and branding initiatives still start from websites. The Web is still made up of web-sites, so it is difficult at first glance to understand how it is even possible for the Web to transition from websites to people. This also makes it difficult to see how search ranking can be influenced by people if websites are still the building mate-rial of the Web.

The truth is that websites are not really the building blocks of the Web. Websites are portals through which data enters the Web. Data is the real building block of the Web, and data can come in from many different points. When the Web first came into being there was a lot of data floating across it from web-based email accounts, forums, bulletin boards, chat rooms, and those old plain-vanilla HTML websites of old, complete with flashing starry backgrounds.

The Web of then compared with the Web of now may have gotten a little snazzier, more interactive and responsive, but in terms of data all that has happened is that it has grown by several orders of magnitude. We experience it as different because the technology that rides on top of it has changed.

If we visualize the Web as a sea, then the technology is ships and the websites are islands. The early days of the Web were the age of sail when the technology we had was fairly inert and websites were static concerns that put all their energy just into being. Today the technology is modern ships and the websites have become expensive resorts. The analogy is more than accidental. Just like modern ships the technology we use offers a trade-off between what it costs us to set up and use and what it gives us back. Just like modern resorts, websites try hard to attract you, work at marketing themselves, and once you have visited them they try to hook you somehow so that you can visit again.

While all these changes have been taking place under the name of progress the sea of data beneath it all has simply grown in volume. It has grown *a lot.*

The rate of that growth was driven home by former Google CEO Eric Schmidt who at the Techonomy conference in Lake Tahoe, California, in 2010 rattled off a statis-tic that stunned his audience. According to Schmidt, who presumably was basing his information on Google's monitoring of data on the Web, every two days now we collectively create as much information as we did from the dawn of civilization up until 2003. That's something like five Exabytes of data, he says.

One Exabyte is 10 followed by 18 zeros, which means that it is one quintillion bytes. The primary source of Schmidt's information has never been made clear. While the exact rate of growth has come under some scrutiny since with some sources suggesting it's higher and some lower, there is no denying that we are putting more information online than at any other time in history and the rate at which we are doing it is accelerating. "The real issue is user-generated content," Schmidt is quoted saying at the Techonomy conference. He noted that pictures, instant messages, and tweets all add to this massive flow of data. This is the "us" as data nodes concept, again. The way technology, in the connected economy, makes us all publishers of information, data that enters the Web needs to be indexed, classified, and understood in order to acquire real meaning and greater value.

Had nothing changed on the Web beyond the technology and the slick design, the growth in volume of data flowing under it all would have gone largely unnoticed of course. But things on the Web did not remain the same. Data is essentially chaotic. Even when the direction of its flow is linear and restricted just between point A and point B, this simplicity, scaled many thousands of millions of times, creates a tangled web with data flowing from all directions toward all directions.

It becomes, in short, a place where nothing makes much sense and not much sense can be made out of anything unless you factor in search. From the beginning of the Web search engines became the tools through which it acquired dimensions, depth and width, and some kind of shape. The thing is that the Web took shape and size not according to how big its flow of data grew but according to how much of it we could see, and sight on the Web stands for transparency to search.

While Google's search engine may have been able to index much of the Web it faced two critical issues: Part of the Web it could not index at all because it was closed off to it, and parts of the Web it could index but did not know how to assess the information it had indexed. The former was more problematic than the latter. From a search engine's point of view there is not a lot you can do about content that's hidden behind password protected walls, but content that you can index and just hangs there is being underused.

The reason it is being underused is because there is no easy way to quantify it when you cannot understand its relational value. Imagine, for instance, a forum of expert chefs. They get together and discuss some fantastic ways to cook côte de bæuf and entrecote providing just the kind of tips and tricks of the trade you and I, looking for ways to cook beef chop and rib-eye steak, would give our eyeteeth for. Unfortunately there was no way to easily ferret that information out of the Web unless we happened to know the French words for beef chop and rib-eye steak and then were lucky enough to spot the particular forum in the search results.

That kind of difficulty undercuts the value of information, creates massively underused stacks of data, and makes it harder to find anything of value when carrying out a search. If you imagine the "old" web as being made up of websites that contained information and each website was a dot, then the map of the Web created by search consisted of a great many dots with relatively few connections in between.

Those connections, back then, consisted of links that one website gave to another and clusters of websites that happened to be part of some brand family of sites. But those connections were imprecise at best. Google used links to gauge authority and trust. When a website with a lot of content, high traffic, and original information linked to another website that was smaller and newer, Google considered it a vote of confidence and took a closer look at the website that was being linked to and increased its PageRank (PR).

Understandably the practice was open to abuse and provided a far from equitable result in search, and it did not solve the problem of understanding the relational value of data that was similar in nature but being described using different vocabulary. Without relational data mapping and the entity extraction programming we saw in Chapter 8 Google has no way of knowing that côte de bœuf and entrecote are fancy French names for beef chop and rib-eye steak, respectively, and we, using Google search for the perfect recipe for our BBQ, will simply not find it.

This is where semantic search truly comes in. Within its semantic search index Google indexes the exact same data as before, except this time it also builds a database of personal profiles. Because semantic search uses attributes in a way that is portable, a personal profile under the name of "steaklover" that joined the French Chef's forum can now be linked to the real name profile that has been used to create a Google+ profile and the name used on Twitter. "Steaklover" then begins to acquire importance because search begins to understand who he is.

From there it is only one short step to next look at the type of content that is being shared or discussed and the context within which the interaction takes place to begin to form an idea of what the French Chef's forum really is about. More than that Google also begins to form an idea of what you are about. So next time when you weigh in on a cooking discussion regarding steak and share a link to a website where you can buy good steak from, it will pay attention to your action more than it does to someone else's who usually talks about tennis and shares sports content.

If you also happen to have 10,000 Twitter followers who regularly go gaga over the steak recipes you find and share, then Google is going to pay even more attention to your profile and the content you share and link to. Conceptually this is a fundamental change. A website used to be able to tell Google that it was authoritative and brand-heavy through content that appeared on it that was original, properly laid out, and of a certain length. It verified that authority and brand power through a link-building strategy that accumulated links from a number of equally authoritative websites over a period of time.

Now Google judges all that from the link sharing and commenting behavior of people. Although it still listens to what the website has to say through its content and link profile it further refines it through the interaction of those who are associated with it and applies a similar assessment logic to them, in turn.

The net result of all this is that the Web has stopped being a top-down led affair where companies and brands took their offline power, converted it into online clout, and produced slick presentations, online ad campaigns, and interactive websites. It has now become a much more equitable place where a company that uses its website to "play nice" with its target audience is also more likely to find that it is rewarded through audience-led publicity and greater audience participation that helps it amplify its online marketing.

All this people-led activity forms what we have been looking at and calling the "social signal," and it forms part of the digital footprint of a company's or brand's marketing. The strength of the social signal of each company or brand depends on:

- The number of people its content can reach who will interact with it in some way
- The frequency with which its name and products are mentioned on the Web (called co-citation)
- The freshness of the signal itself
- The depth of the signal (measured in deep interaction on the content itself by way of comments and the accumulation of Likes, +1s and Twitter mentions)
- The breadth of the signal (measured in overall reach and spread through the social media network space)
- The sentiment expressed in the signal (Google employs text analytics to identify and extract subjective information in user-generated content, like comments, for instance)

These are new concerns that have really surfaced only since semantic search came into play, and it's worth spending a little time understanding them.

Interaction between a person and a website's content is important because it signifies user intent to a search engine. As such it can be used to work out the real meaning of the website and the importance of its content and, further along the process of social signal analysis, assess the importance of the website and use it as a ranking signal in search.

The number of people a website can reach is determined by a combination of its online and offline marketing efforts. Its presence and activities on various social media platforms, the number of times links to it are privately shared via email or chat, even its emailing list activities—each of these become part of a website's digital footprint and offers the potential for further interaction by way of commenting, resharing, mentioning, and the far more common and, incidentally, less valuable Likes and +1s.

In the semantic web the mention of a website in a comment or an article, even when there is no link leading back to it, in relation to what the website does and the comment is about becomes important. This is called co-citation in technical SEO terms, and it is a purely semantic search ranking signal that Google now takes into account.

The need to constantly produce content to ensure continued ranking in search is one that is frequently complained about and the one that makes the most sense. In the real world a business always produces content of some kind to attract customers and communicate with them. Advertising, billboards, window displays, special offer labels, competitions, leaflets, and in-store demos are all content. Because we do not really see them as such we frequently overlook the obvious fact that a business that does not engage in such an activity is, essentially, a dead business.

When we take the concept of business and marketing online we are, frequently again, restricted in our thinking in considering that a website needs some "pages" and that's its content. We need perhaps to send out a newsletter, create the occasional blog entry, and that's it; the job's done as long as all the keywords have been used and all the relative headings of value are there. Yet when we think about that with some degree of honesty, it makes little real sense. We wouldn't expect anyone to want to come in and shop in a department store that's cobweb-ridden, has out-of-date stock, and its marketing dates back to the 1960s. Why would we expect someone online to behave differently with a moribund website?

Content online becomes even more important than offline. In the absence of physical contact the content we produce has to work harder to project the identity of the business, its character, the way it works, and the values it stands for. It has to work hard to answer the simple question: "Why should I do business with you?" which means it has to be able to adequately project a sense of authority in what it does and generate that much-needed quality: trust.

Fresh content, even if it is "old" content that has been substantially updated, is how you do all of this.

A properly run online business has to be able to engage its target audience both in terms of how many choose to somehow keep track of its activities through its social media profiles and in terms of how many interact with it at a much deeper level in the ongoing social media "conversation." This is exactly where the sense of breadth and depth of the social signal comes in.

These days, there is an inevitable overlap in many of the activities that would traditionally be classified as pure marketing and the ones that are intended to help a website increase its visibility in search. The defining characteristic of semantic search is that an online business that somehow manages to achieve wide reach in its online marketing through a combination of paid promotion and "bought" online fans is next to useless if it cannot meaningfully engage them, so ideally there should be very little difference between what a business does and the actions it performs to help people find it. Engagement is key because inert followers or fans are as good as nonexistent ones in terms of the good it does a business. They generate few sales, they fail to amplify the appeal of the brand, and they do not amplify the social signal of the brand.

There is, also, one more development that comes from all of this that marks the real sea change semantic search has brought. Traditionally SEO was brought in to "do something." It was the call that went out to the pro or the agency to come in and fix whatever was "wrong" so that a website could show up in search again and online trading could go back to "business as usual." These days an SEO pro is more likely to come in to actually help you understand better what it is you must be doing. As such SEO, as a discipline, is undergoing a radical change in its general approach that's best quantified as a shift from pure tactics to tactics and strategy.

If you are in the business of hiring an SEO agency you really need to find one that is capable of

- Understanding your business and its challenges (as opposed to just knowing SEO).
- Aligning its knowledge of SEO with your targets as a business (using actionables that take into account what you are already doing and explaining how they can be better incorporated into an SEO strategy).
- Leveraging its experience to help you achieve more with your online marketing without increasing operational costs (helping you work smarter rather than harder by connecting the dots between your everyday business activities and their online impact).
- Help your own knowledge and experience grow in the process (education, training and awareness of best SEO practices should be part of the relationship with your agency).

In the semantic web a good SEO agency is more of a business partner than a technical help brought in to perform some SEO "magic" and then go away.

There are two notable things in this semantic web, or rather three, though one is self-evident. The first of these is that the "social signal" that is the direct result of sharing links, commenting on social media platforms about shared links, and commenting directly on websites has a signature that makes it hard to counterfeit. It takes so much time and effort to create a meaningful social signal that will have any kind of impact that to create a fake one provides no benefits in terms of time or cost savings, so it may as well be genuine.

The second is that Google looks for freshness in this signal as a measure of current validity. A website that was well received a year ago and now suddenly finds its content being ignored is a clear signal to Google's search engine that the website is no longer producing content worth sharing. The website will, as a result, naturally drop from Google's rankings, and its content will only appear in search when there are no better, fresher alternatives.

The self-evident, and third thing, that's notable about the semantic web is that it makes for a much fairer web. Quality content will surface, provided it has value. The real effort then goes not so much into marketing your website (something that could only be properly afforded by commercial concerns with deep pockets) but in helping it be discovered in an organic way through the social sharing of its content.

You could say that the real work is done when you're thinking about what your business is really about and how to then get your online audience to totally understand this.

Trust and Influence

What if search became a global vetting mechanism for websites? Would that not beneficially impact all sorts of businesses? Would it not change the nature of search entirely when it came to fostering exchange relationships involving money or personal information? Would it not turn Google into, essentially, a trust engine?

The question is far from theoretical. Any kind of online transaction is an exchange of something for something else. Whether the item that is exchanged is physical (in which case it is acquired, the old fashioned way, in exchange for cash) or digital (in which case it could be "free" but it is given in exchange for increased status and authority) it involves a relationship exchange between two parties (called a bilateral relationship exchange). Trust is the critical ingredient for successfully engaging in relationship exchanges that involve money or personal information. If you are running a website that asks people to buy something in the full expectation that you will deliver what they bought, as agreed, your success depends on your ability to gain their trust in the fulfillment of the transaction. The same applies when you ask someone to part with personal information. Survey results published in a research paper in the *Communications for the Association of Computing Machinery* magazine showed that more than 72% of web users said they would give websites their demographic information if the sites would only provide a statement regarding how the information collected would be used.

The survey, published at the turn of the century, is significant because it highlights an awareness in web surfers of the need to establish parameters in which any bilateral exchange, whether it is one of cash for goods or services, or personal information for something else, takes place within an environment of trust.

So, really, how do you build trust online? For a start it pays to establish that trust online is closely linked to whatever reputation ranking system is in place as opposed to reputation itself. The difference between reputation and a reputation ranking system is that the latter without the former is little more than a license for potential abuse. A well thought-through reputation ranking system addresses the balance of power in any bilateral exchange and provides peace of mind for both parties involved.

For that peace of mind to occur it requires two distinct elements to somehow be in place:

- Environmental control
- Secondary use of information control

Environmental control requires the web surfer to be able to control the actions of a web vendor, and secondary use of information control requires web surfers to be able to control the way their personal information is used subsequent to the transaction in which the information was originally collected.

Immediately you see the magnitude of the problem. Given the fact that relatively few online vendors, even today, go to any length of trouble to allay the concerns of their visitors in either of these two areas, trust, in most cases, relies on the feedback mechanism present that contributes to the ranking of reputation.

In a semantic search web, where all the different points of data associated with an online merchant, for example, are indexed and cataloged and the relationship between them is mapped, reputation becomes synonymous with trust the same way an offline merchant with a good reputation is deemed to be trustworthy.

In that context, in our example, the consumer also has exactly that environmental and secondary use of information control that ensures his peace of mind. How? Because he has access to both rating systems and social media platforms. These allow him to input information that is amplified, in most cases, and linked back to the original vendor. So, if I bought a box of matches from someone who has a website and the website owner fails to deliver I can now not only rate the experience through a system like eBay's, but even if that is not in place I can mention the fact that I was ripped off in a social media platform like Twitter, Facebook, and Google+. Friends of mine, who take my word a lot more seriously than strangers, will also be easily convinced of the validity of my review and further help amplify it by re-sharing it perhaps with their friends.

Bad experiences shared in a social media environment are amplified quickly. Those present can easily see themselves in a similar transaction, and the perception motivates them to step in and somehow contribute by resharing it and even further commenting on it. In that environment a "bad" vendor would find it difficult to do business.

Now in the past that might have been a hardship, but it was far from catastrophic. A website that had managed to accrue damaging comments that hurt its reputation could easily close down and reappear under a different trading name. If the website had been doing its web marketing right and had paid attention to its SEO needs, it would have built up a number of backlinks that linked directly to it and had helped build up its PageRank (PR). Rather than lose all that the knowledgeable vendor would make sure that all those links were redirected (sans the negative ones, of course), and presto you would end up with a shiny new web presence, all white-washed and ready to do business again.

In a semantic search web that cannot happen so easily. When all the data about you is mapped in relation to who you are and what you do, changing your website name and stating you are someone else no longer works. Google can see through that. Not only that, but it can also see the change and its link profile. And it could then decide whether to trust your website through a potential trust rank filter and display it in the search results pages.

The great leveler here is that Google and those carrying out a search query want the same thing: quick, accurate results that deliver a great end-user experience. Google and the website vendor also want the same thing: targeted traffic and a satisfactory outcome through ranking in search. It is this alignment of values between Google, the web vendor, and the person using search that allows the next conceptual leap, which is that, eventually, results that appear in search will come with a high perception of trust placed in them as standard.

This is increasingly critical as search is fragmenting and moving away from the desktop experience to a more direct question and answer type of environment where asking for the "best restaurant for seafood" on Google voice delivers distinctly different results in your locale from asking for "the nearest seafood restaurant."

While this is exactly where semantic search is heading, at its current level today it still has some way to go, primarily because the depth of data and the wealth of mapped connections between it is insufficient. This serves to give all the greater prominence to influencers and influence.

Within any social network there are some power users who gather around them a lot of followers. Power user profiles follow the same pattern. They typically have a high number of followers or they have deep engagement. Some actually do both. Typically the "engagers" also have a pretty high number of followers.

Within any social network power users act either as gate keepers, holding the key to accessing a large group of people (typically their followers) or as connectors (allowing you to connect to people who matter and whose followers will significantly amplify your message).

They also act as trust agents. Their word comes with an implied seal of approval. Their endorsement instantly lowers the resistance threshold of their followers that is the normal expected response when you consider the perceived lack of trust and it then makes it more likely that they will want to deal with you or, in the more rarefied description of semantic search, "enter into an exchange relationship."

The ability of a social network influencer to tip the balance, each time, comes down to a set of factors that are also evident throughout the discussion in Gladwell's book, *The Tipping Point* and that is that you do not get to reach a wide audience and recruit the aid of influencers by doing exactly what everyone else is doing.

For your content to resonate and go viral you really need to do the exceptional. And because you are probably thinking right now that by exceptional I mean outlandish and weird, I will hasten to set you straight by saying that what you need to do is be honest and straightforward.

This is the Ernest Hemingway trick for writing "one honest sentence." When asked what he did when he was stuck and couldn't write the great writer said he simply wrote "one honest sentence and then, another." What he meant of course was that instead of creating writing that showcased his virtuosity he hunkered down and wrote the kind of sentence he could totally defend with his intellect and experience as being true.

The trick works for content creators as well. You need to find your "honest content." If you manage to create the kind of content that captures the passion you have for your business and what it does you cannot help but produce content that is fresh, engaging, and hits a chord deep within the heart of its target audience. And it is that kind of content that is easy to reshare and which has a good chance at going viral. A classic example of this we see in Figure 9.1.

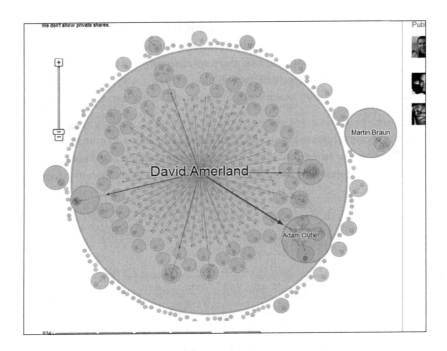

Figure 9.1   *The "gatekeeper" effect in a social network can be seen in a post of mine that went viral in Google's Google+ social network. My profile within it became key for discovery of the article after I had posted it. Each of the circles represents the influence the poster possessed by way of reshares.*

The large number of people highlighted within my "circle" of sharing indicates the reach of my influence on that particular topic. The moment I posted it, it caused many other people who follow my profile to pick it up and reshare it. This made the post go viral which then caused it to be "discovered" by people outside my own social network and influence (the smaller circles on the periphery of mine) who, however, added to the overall post's reach through their own resharing of it.

Engaging influencers in a social network is a standard tactic for anyone who wants to help promote their website and help its content reach a wider audience. It also helps, significantly, to amplify the website's "social signal," which makes it easier to index and rank in Google's search. The ability of influencers to act as connectors, helping content be discovered by other influential people who then share it with their followers, is seen in the example in Figure 9.2.

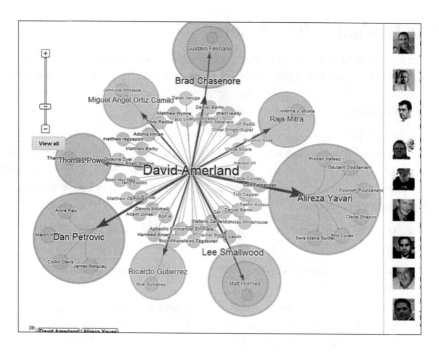

Figure 9.2   *The "connector" effect in a social media network can be seen in a different post of mine on a different topic. In this diagram we can see that although the post still reached a fair number of people through my direct efforts, what really helped it spread were larger circles around it. Because I am connected to influencers with large followings of their own, (i.e. they are "gatekeepers") I was able to "push" the content to them and they then promoted it through their own considerable network of connections, helping it spread and go viral.*

The two examples cover the two classic cases of influencer behavior in a social network: either the influencer you reach has a large following that is interested in the content you have created or they are connected to influencers who have a following that is interested in the content you are creating.

This makes it critical for you to be able to first identify what type of influencers you have in your network and second what their area of interest is. It is quite possible that, depending on the subject matter, influencers can be either gatekeepers or connectors. Engaging with them requires that you understand what they are and what they do.

How to Identify Influencers

The biggest hurdle when you're starting out is that you're never sure where to start from. Despite there being just a handful of massive social networks the task is not made any easier. Each one has a specific feel and audience and type of interaction, and what works in one may not work in another.

You need to be able, for a start, to identify where your influencers are, which means you need to find out what they are talking about. To achieve this, you need to use social media monitoring tools that will help you find them either by subject or by score (as some of them grade them). To help you out here I have added a list of the most popular ones:

- SocialMention (http://socialmention.com)—Monitors all social media platforms.
- SocialBlade (http://socialblade.com)—Specializes in specific social media channels.
- Klout (http://klout.com)—Measures social media influence using a number of social media network platforms and ascribing a score from 1—100 to the influencer's profile.
- Peerindex (http://peerindex.com)—A social media influence measuring website not unlike Klout's.
- PlusClout (http://plusclout.com)—Measures influence on Google+ based on the person's profile and ascribes a score between 1—100.
- Topsy (http://topsy.com)—A social media monitoring site that can help you keep track of mentions of your company, find influencers on specific subjects and discover which social media channels deliver the most activity for your subject.
- Followerwonk (http://followerwonk.com)—A Twitter analytics tool that can provide some very granular analysis of your Twitter account and its activity and followers helping you identify the influencers in your Twitter network.
- Socialbro (http://socialbro.com)—A Twitter and social media analytics tool that helps you keep track of mentions, tweets, and social media activity.

Your first task is to draw up a list of criteria to guide you:

- Decide which social media channels you want to find influencers in.
- Decide the minimum size of following your influencers need to have.
- Decide whether you want your influencers to have more reach or more depth.

Once you have your short list of social media influencers criteria and the channel in which they should be active, the next step is to decide who is suitable for what you need to do. You should always aim to have a number of influencers on your target list. Some of these will be true specialists in their field while others will simply be popular with a wide following but only tangential to the core audience you are trying to target. Each will have their use.

To be truly useful your list of influencers needs to be refined further by assessing the profile of each one you have found and pigeonholing him. To do this successfully you need to create a second list.

Your task here is to help filter the influencers you have through a number of steps:

- Define the topic your business covers either by keyword or by theme.
- Use the social media tools discussed previously and input your keyword or theme.
- Make a list of the influencers that come up with each search.
- Use your previously drawn up criteria to filter your list of influencers to one that's most relevant to you.

Once you have your list of influencers there is one more set of steps to go through to refine it a little further.

The steps associated with this process involve

- Identify the influencers from your list who are consistently posting information or content relevant to your business. They are the ones who will have the greatest affinity with what you want to share and are most likely to respond to it.
- Go through your short list and, in turn, mark against each name the number of mentions of each that come up online. You will probably have to use SocialMention or Topsy for that. Check to see if the mentions are relevant to the keywords or theme you want to promote. The ones most relevant to your requirements you want to keep. The rest can be discarded.
- As one more step of refining, look up each of your social network influencers' individual profiles in each of the major social networks and get an idea of who is a specialist within a particular social network and who has a more general presence on each one.
- Next, for each name on your list place their Klout scores (if they have one), their total follower number (it gives you an idea of the size of the audience you can reach through them), their average number of posts per day (it gives you an idea of their level of activity and perhaps response time).

- Finally it is a good idea to have an idea of the format of content they post. Some influencers have built up a large following in some social networks sharing nothing but pictures and quotes, for instance. They are then unlikely to be of much use in helping you promote your text-driven message regardless of how relevant it might be.

This exercise, incidentally, is a rather crude grading of social media profiles that mirrors the much more sophisticated weighing and assessment that takes place within Google's semantic search index.

Influencers are not automatic gateways to total social media network success for whoever approaches them. Their reputations have been built up slowly and can be lost easily. As a result they are careful in what they share. For them to share your content there has to be a close alignment of values, and, obviously, you have to create some top-notch content. Even then that's not enough. An influencer who has built up his reputation and power in a social network, over time, is a celebrity within it. He is very careful how he interacts with those who ask him to reshare stuff and no matter how good your content may be or how it may resonate an influencer will be unlikely to become involved with it on the basis of a single request.

Everything in the semantic web is about relationships. You will need to allocate time and energy in the development of your relationships with those you hope to use in your social network marketing this way, and you will also have to clearly establish the reciprocal value to them, if they are to help you out. This is yet another relational exchange and it will involve both parties getting something. If you have no clear idea of how the exchange will work for those you approach as well as for you, the chances are that it won't work at all and you will find a closed door.

Owned, Paid, Earned, and Shared Media

Owned media is your website, the platform where you completely control your content and brand message. You are solely responsible for its content.

Paid media is advertising. It takes place offsite. The branding and brand message are also controlled. You are solely responsible for setting this up.

Earned media is made up of mentions, shares, "weak" interactions like Likes or +1s, and user-generated content. This is media you do not control.

By now you have gathered just how important relationship building is. Visibility on the semantic web hinges on a website being able to leverage its presence and create a strong digital footprint.

Traditional online marketing takes place within the triangle whose three points are your owned, paid, and earned media. This is what agencies and corporate marketing teams frequently call the golden triangle of marketing.

In the traditional online marketing world of the pre-semantic search web, each point of the triangle of marketing worked in relative isolation. What happened at each point stayed at each point, and search visibility required search engine optimization to take place, primarily, at the point called owned media.

With semantic search each of the points of the marketing triangle is drawn into an activity of sharing. An advertisement about your website can be shared and commented on just as easily as content. User-generated content can lead to further sharing that also increases the shareability of your website's other content. This creates a much greater synchronization between your marketing and SEO activities as Figure 9.3 shows.

Figure 9.3   *The three points of the marketing triangle now take place against the backdrop of semantic search that unites them all under the label of Shared Media. It is important to note here that social media networks like Facebook, Twitter, Pinterest and LinkedIn can be as much a part of your "Paid Media" efforts as your "Earned Media." They all have the option of using sponsored content within their respective networks. Google, of course, has the hugely successful Google Adwords program that serves contextual ads right on search. The implication here is that every point of the marketing triangle now informs search and contributes to the creation of a semantic identity, called Entity for the website.*

At this point it may seem that unless you are in the business of selling something really popular using search to actually do it is an impossible task. Nothing could be further from the truth.

Consider how difficult a proposition it is to try and use search to sell more onions. Yet that was exactly the challenge faced by the Vidalia Onion Committee when dropping sales due to consumers being faced with ever-increasing choices led them to consider using search as the dominant marketing option.

In a classic case of social media outreach, the committee guided its marketing team to identify likely bloggers and influencers active across the major social media platforms. Having carefully selected who they were going to reach, they then launched a strong content marketing campaign.

In an interview feature in *Advertising Age*, the executive director of the Vidalia Onion Committee, Wendy Brannen, explained the strategy they decided to adopt: "There's been a learning curve with marketers, bloggers, and consumers like a triangle. The consumer had to figure out who's credible. We had to figure out where the credible bloggers are; where we can put out trust. Now, the consumers and marketers are getting a grasp on the cream of the crop that have risen from the blogosphere, but it's about narrowing down how much of this is worth my time."

Their blogosphere and social media outreach approach has increased the visibility of Vidalia onions in search across many of the current search verticals and has led to an increase in sales, much stronger brand equity, and a revival of the fortunes of the produce.

This is classic case of being able to capture online user attention made possible only through the ability of semantic search to discover the relationship between different types of content and assign a specific meaning to what a website does, as opposed to just what type of content it contains.

Search engine optimization in the semantic web is all about aiding entity extraction as opposed to just using keywords to help a website appear in search in response to search queries, and that's exactly what we discuss in the next chapter.

Influence Marketing Preparation Checklist

Leveraging the presence of influencers in social media network platforms is not just smart marketing, it is also cost-effective marketing because it helps amplify your website's social signal at next to zero cost.

To succeed the practice requires the same degree of relevancy and context in the content that is being shared as that exhibited by semantic search when it ranks content in response to specific search queries. This is no coincidence. Semantic search maps meaning and intent.

Your preparation checklist is designed to help you maintain focus on your influence marketing so that both the meaning and intent of your website begin to surface through its social media content marketing activities.

- Explain how you will maintain the freshness of your company website's content signal.

- Detail all the different subject areas you think your content addresses and which can then impact your website's digital footprint.

- List all the social media platforms you think you can use that will enhance your company's or brand's social signal.

- Explain how you propose to approach influencers in your business vertical and engage them so that they can then be used to help with the spread of your content in their social media networks. It is a good idea to also work up, here, a detailed timeline that will show the stages you will go through as you build up your relationship with your online influencers. Like in most relationships trust takes time to build up; there is no shortcut you can take.

- Detail how you intend to manage your social media outreach program.

- Detail how you will ensure alignment of your brand or company values with those of the influencers and bloggers you reach out to.

- Detail all the ways you will use to establish trust between your company or brand website and your potential online audience.

- Detail your strategy for sustaining engagement with your website's content across social media platforms.

- Detail your company's or brand's current allocation of resources between owned, paid, and earned media.

- Explain how you plan to foster greater sharing of your owned and paid content.

10

Entity Extraction and the Semantic Web

Entity extraction is key to the semantic web, and it is exactly what powers semantic search. The Web, in its current state, is made up largely of unstructured data. Search engine optimization techniques are designed to help websites that have unstructured data get indexed properly in the semantic web graph.

In this chapter we see how this can be achieved. We discuss exactly what entities are and how Google extracts them. We learn what search engines look for and what you can do to provide them with exactly what they need in order to help your ranking in search.

Entities and Your Website

It has frequently been argued that in a perfect world we would not have the need for SEO. Search engines would find a website, index it, and then rank it exactly the way it should be ranked so that it can be found by those who are looking for it.

You hardly need me to tell you that the world is not perfect. In the days before semantic search, search engine optimization was necessary because websites were not always easy to index. Myriad obstacles could stand in the way between a website's content and its proper ranking in search. These could range from a website's architecture to excessive use of iFrames or JavaScript and even poor linking that hid content behind tabs.

Search engine optimization, at its best, amounted to no more than a detailed analysis of a website designed to discover all the flaws that prevented proper ranking and then work to fix them. In the semantic web the task is compounded by the fact that a large extent of semantic SEO involves ways of extracting content from a website so that Google can form a better idea of what the website is intended to do. This applies pressure on the traditional role of the search engine optimizer to evolve into something akin to content marketer with as detailed an idea of your business and its target audience as you have.

This usually begs the question: Why?

We have seen that semantic search, to work correctly, requires relevance and context. These are the two elements that determine the value and meaning of a particular piece of data. Relevance and context can then be used to infer the meaning of a set of data and display it in search in response to a search query. It's a simple enough notion that's underpinned by complex mathematics that uses a formal language to explain concepts that go by the name of "data types," "strings," "alphabet set," "array." These are terms that stand for something specific. The abstractions they represent have real form in terms of data and allow the meaningful harvesting and classification of information to take place. Their manipulation and use leads to the formation of the topology of the semantic graph. Its undulations, structural density, and growth are utterly dependent upon the Web's ability to be indexed this way, and it is this indexing that changes everything, transforms the meaningless and chaotic into a meaningful and organized structure. The language of semantic search is of importance but here we will look only at those terms that are of practical value to us in terms of SEO and we'll gloss over the rest that are of use, primarily, to computer scientists.

In this context "text strings" is the name given to the abstract representation of specific word sequences. What we'd popularly call keywords. Keywords, in the Boolean world of search we've left behind, acquire meaning according to placement and frequency and co-occurrence.

To use an example, suppose your website is about apples. The word "apple" will probably appear a number of times in your content because you know that keyword frequency (the "keyword density" that used to feature so prominently in the past) is an important element of SEO. The problem with keywords is that differentiating between synonyms is difficult. Apple, the fruit is the same as Apple, the computer. Google does have ways of doing this but the differentiation is moot when it cannot understand what you are looking for (i.e. the intent of your search query).

Google's goal is to actually infer that your website is about apples, the fruit, as opposed to about Apple, the computer company, and serve it in direct answer to queries that need that answer. Actually Google wants to do more than that. It wants to, in relation to a specific text query, also be able to bring up any customer reviews it has found of your website and its apples, photographs that customers who have bought your apples may have uploaded to a publicly available folder in a social media network, and the feedback they may have left.

To do all this Google needs to understand that "apples" is a specific entity (a fruit), and the moment it does that it has to be able to relate it to an entirely different set of associated entities (customers, photographs, jam). It is this relational association that lies behind the idea of an entity in a semantic web that is capable of constant refinement and improvement, and it's totally scalable across the Web.

If you were the marketing director of the apple jam selling website then you would have to consider that the words "apple jam" are no longer a text string (a "keyword") that have to be used together and achieve a specific keyword density for the website to show up in search.

From an SEO point of view this has several benefits. First of all it significantly broadens the keyword list, changing it from a restrictive list of words that had to be repeated to a specified frequency and placement in text, to a more natural way of writing that closely matches how we speak. So here "apple jam" will be interchangeable with "apple preserve," for instance, and the focus will be more on the questions the content tries to address rather than an intention to build up keyword repetition.

"Apple jam" instead can now also become "apple preserve" or "fruit preserve" that can be produced in a variety of ways. It may be sold in a number of different outlets, a number of different locations may be associated with its sale, and there will be product reviews associated with it.

The context that Google uses to create all these associations is the direct result of a public collaboration with Microsoft and Yahoo, and it is documented at Schema.org (http://www.schema.org). Schema.org details the technical language necessary to create a structured web of data that's easily readable to semantic indexing and although it is not a requirement in any grand sense of the word, it should definitely be on your radar in terms of implementing, where possible, on your website. There is a small problem with this, at the moment, in that no Content Management System (CMS) allows for semantic markup. It has to be input manually which means that unless you are able to work with the code on your website a little bit, you will have to ask your developer to assist.

Of course, HTML has included the ability to add semantic markup to a website, since its inception. In an HTML document, the author may, among other things, add a title; add headings and paragraphs; add emphasis to the text (through italicized content); add images (with proper alt tags); add links to other pages; and use various kinds of lists in a way that more fully enriches the informational value of the page. Some of these practices rose to greater prominence in pre-semantic web SEO while others (italicized text that's important to the page's content, for example) were used less frequently.

Even though their data may be largely unstructured, website pages that have been set up properly, using a Content Management System (CMS) that allows the page author to fill in all the relevant metadata fields, including, where possible, tags that describe the page, are easier to crawl by Google and incorporate in the semantic web.

Acknowledging the increasing importance of structured data and structured markup on a website Google has provided a Data Highlighter tool that can be accessed through your Webmaster Tools panel (http://goo.gl/dhdZp). There you tell Google just what information on your website can be taken into a structured data format. Google does this on the fly so no code on your website is changed, the search engine "understands" the data you highlight better and, even more importantly, it understands how to treat similar pages it encounters, so this is also a training tool that allows webmasters to train search.

At the moment the Data Highlighter is limited to Events and Reviews so its benefits are only to websites that carry one of these, at least. It is likely it will be expanded to include other parameters in the near future, however.

In our example, the rich web of relationships then that Google associates with the term "apple jam" means that when a search query for apple jam is actually typed in search there would appear a result that would be based on the exact state of the entity in Google's semantic index, relative to your location. What I mean by that is if there is a local, annual apple festival associated with your apple jam it would appear to those who looked for "apple jam" and whose location was near it. It would also appear to them in relation to its date, so that if the search query took place in, let's say August, while the apple season is in the fall, the apple festival would appear as a deprecated result of academic more than practical value. It would be visible in desktop search, perhaps, but not in mobile search where location awareness is a stronger signal and the results are graded differently.

This suggests a couple of important things. First, semantic search creates a fluidity of content that is relevant only when it is truly relevant. The search for "apple jam" in October, for instance, provides different results from the same search carried out in August. Second, the search vertical the query is placed in draws results from a different index and informs it through a different understanding of the search query intent (i.e. why you're actually looking for "apple jam"). Google voice search for "apple jam" for instance would present different results from a Google desktop search. Figure 10.1 shows the results delivered for the exact same search term carried out on A. my laptop (desktop search) and B. my smartphone (using voice search).

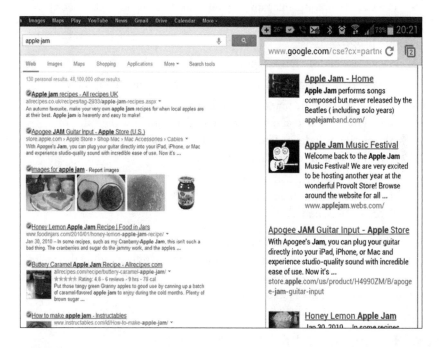

Figure 10.1   *The search query "apple jam" has been carried out here from the exact same location using two different devices.*

The first is desktop search, which makes some obvious assumptions given my IP address and past search history (for the record this is the first time I have ever searched for "apple jam" online). The second, on the right is the result returned by my Android voice search, informed by a different index plus the geolocation supplied by the GPS signal of my phone. As you can see the results are entirely different. Given the fact that I have never searched for "apple jam" before on my phone either the assumption Google made was that I was after downloadable music (for which I frequently search) or an apple jam recipe.

All this suggests that the results to the query for "apple jam" are there to beautifully serve the needs of both the apple jam seller and the apple jam buyer, equally. The whole edifice collapses when there is insufficient data to form the kind of relationship mapping that produces results. Then the search results are supplied conventionally, the gaps in Google's knowledge filled by what it has indexed and graded using the normal search index.

The action plan for the "apple jam" website of our example would then include

- Sufficient spread of the information in the social web, to allow the extraction of semantic meaning
- The use of semantic markup on your website using the Schema.org vocabulary (http://goo.gl/HLJzl) to allow Google to index the information properly
- Proper use of descriptive tags on the website itself
- The use of hashtags when sharing the website's content on the Web
- The use of semantic markup on your website, using Google's Data Highlighter Tool, to allow Google to understand how the value of information it indexes changes, as in the case of specific events held on certain dates and in certain places, for instance
- A social media outreach program that would allow extensive mapping of your website's content in association with other entities, such as places, outlets, and so on

Seeing how important the idea of an entity is, it would help at this stage to look a little more closely at how exactly it is constructed. Understanding that helps develop really granular, customized SEO activities designed to help Google index an entity better and understand it more completely.

How a Semantic Entity Is Extracted

If the entire world lived in an ideal scenario every piece of online data would be tagged using the Schema.org semantic tagging that explains exactly what any piece of data placed on the Web is, without cheating, and semantic search would be a reality, providing fast 100% accurate results. We know this doesn't happen. What's more, it is unlikely to ever happen, though things will certainly improve.

This then leaves us with the current option: the need to extract structured data from the masses of unstructured data that are on the Web already. Entity extraction is the process of automatically extracting document metadata (i.e. data about data that explains the purpose of a web document) from unstructured text documents. Most of the content on the Web contains information that is hard for search engines to understand properly. These pages consist mostly of text (i.e. articles, blog posts, and even comments to these). Making it easier to extract key entities such as person names, locations, dates, specialized terms, and product terminology from free-form text can help any company or brand to not only improve its standing in keyword search but also open the door to true semantic search, faceted search, and document repurposing.

Faceted search allows us to ascribe multiple attributes to an item and then classify it in different ways so a book, for instance, may be a "hardback," "classic," and "science fiction" and it can come up in faceted search (like Amazon's for example) when the end-user applies a number of filters to look for products. Faceted search is useful because it increases the options for discovery of a product, or page.

Document repurposing involves taking the different visual cues present in a document that make it readable to humans (spatial intervals, contrast in font families, colors in font, sizes, and weights) and rendering it in a way that preserves it but, at the same time makes the document machine readable.

If you can understand how a semantic entity is formed out of nothing but the raw text that is found on pages on the Web, you can then understand what you have to do every time to help the process along and implement a content creation and marketing strategy that will allow your website to rank high in search.

How entity extraction is achieved, using mathematics, is a true marvel of mathematical analysis, governed by logic rules that simulate intelligence and technology, and governed by the hardware that are Google's data centers. For our purposes we are only really interested in the first part of this process, as a piece of raw text that has no particular meaning to a machine at one end begins on a journey that at the other end can produce answers to questions such as "What is the capital of Greece?" right there, on search, or show all the relevant results that apply to a local set of circumstances for the search query "apple jam."

This is achieved through a two-step, largely parallel process where step 1 could be called entity detection and step 2 relation detection. A successful entity entry in Google's database then requires those two steps to come seamlessly together.

Entity detection begins with nothing but raw text that is referred to as strings (the data strings we saw at the beginning of this chapter). Unfortunately, a little bit of jargon is necessary here, but it's fairly accessible. Strings are specific pieces of text found on a web page that, at that stage, are nothing more than raw material that holds potential but little real meaning. Like any raw material, for usefulness to come out of it, it needs to be processed.

Text that's indexed in semantic search undergoes a filtering process that begins with sentence analysis and segmentation and a comparison of its value in relation to similar text found elsewhere on the Web. This is when issues of duplicate content crop up, or text that's written with enough keywords to attract the attention of a search engine in the first instance, but insufficient value to then pass on to the next stage and get indexed in semantic search.

The segmentation of text is formalized through a process called *tokenization*. Tokenization is the chopping up of a sentence into individual words. In the process also any redundant characters such as punctuation or unnecessary repetition are discarded. Tokenization is a little like filtering, but it would be wrong to think of it as reductive. As a matter of fact it is quite the opposite because it takes the segmented list of strings (also known as the sentence) and enriches it with meaningful variations.

As an example consider that the tokenization for the simple word "aren't" includes the variations "aren't," "aren t," "arent," and "are nt," all of which are necessary to be able to make sense of a future search query and provide an answer in relation to it. To make matters even more complicated consider that tokenization is always language specific so the semantic search rules you write for, let's say, the English search index, are going to be somewhat different from the ones for the French index, and one could argue that even within the same language a US and UK difference in usage needs to be accounted for in search.

Tokenization then produces a list of lists of strings (a metadata of sorts). The next step is to take these lists into a part of speech tagging filter that actually begins to understand what the words are so that "make" is identified as a verb, "apple" and "pie" as nouns.

At the same time that Google carries out all this detailed analysis in its entity detection, it also indexes linked data across the Web. Because step 1 is parallel and, in most cases, predates step 2, when it encounters the words "apple pie" in linked data sets Google knows that it is a noun and that it can be "made." It now begins to associate the words "apple pie" with apple, the fruit, apple jam, fruit conserves, the apple picking season, apple cider, and apple cider festivals.

To make sense of all this associated data Google puts it together in ordered sets called *tuples*. In mathematics and computer science, a tuple is just an ordered list of elements.

In the next step the precise understanding of what the words "make apple pie" mean is brought together along with all the associated linked data to create the entity "apple" that is a fruit that can be made into jam, a pie, or cider and that can be bought in a shop, celebrated at a festival, and picked at a particular time of the year. And all this is adjusted depending on when you carry out the search and where you are as shown in the diagrams in Figure 10.2.

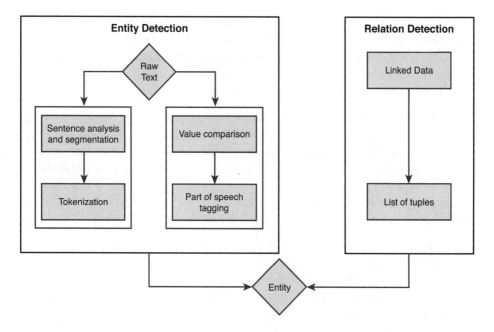

Figure 10.2   *Through entity detection and relation detection raw text extracted from web pages in unstructured data format at one end becomes a responsive, refined entity that can provide an intelligent answer in semantic search at the other.*

Now that you know the process through which the raw text on your website is turned into semantic search entities you understand that for a website to rank in the semantic search web requires

- Content that is original, timely, and of high informational quality
- Clear linking strategies on the pages of your website (I return to this a little later in the chapter)
- Content that reflects the unique identity of your company or brand
- Content that clearly reflects the value proposition of your products or services
- Content that is constructed in a way that can invite further engagement

The one item I need to draw attention to here is on-page linking strategies. Seeing how all content begins its indexing journey the same way (that is, as raw text) and Google looks for relation detection (i.e. where else that content appears and in what context), this provides an opportunity to create link clusters (or groups of links) on your website that have specific themes, enrich a specific subject, and, in themselves, provide greater informational value because they are linked than if they had been standalone pages.

Imagine, from our example, that a page that features a recipe for apple pie makes use of the link cluster idea to link to specific types of apples that make extraordinarily good apple pie. The page might also provide links to outlets where these apples can be bought and might conceivably link to an external site where homemade apple pies can be ordered, completing the value of that particular link cluster.

This kind of link signature has two distinct effects: First within your own company or brand site it creates a knowledge base that increases the value of your website, can contribute to how authoritative Google considers it to be, and can help increase its ranking in search. Second by including in this link signature external websites that have further information that provides greater depth, your website increases its informational value and becomes further elevated in terms of its value to a search query.

Ranking in semantic search is all about delivering value. Value, whether informational (for example, a piece of news or an item of information) or transactional (such as in being able to buy something) is a ranking signal that can help elevate your website even higher in Google search and significantly increase its visibility across many of the search verticals consumers use to look for answers on the Web.

Semantic Search Is Personalized

Just like there is no real "first page of Google" any more that can be exactly the same for someone carrying out the same search query in California and in Cambria, in the UK, there is no single Google search index.

Today search takes place across all screen sizes and devices, and it is as important and ubiquitous when the individual is on the go as it is when she sits behind a desk staring at a large desktop monitor. Semantic search is unique in that it collects data and classifies it in ways that permit high levels of adaptability and relevance to the user profile.

In other words, semantic search is capable of being highly personalized, with a classic example being Google Now that uses location aware services to preload information you may want to look up, such as weather, flight schedules, and even local restaurants. This is done automatically in the background of your daily activities and based on either information you have provided voluntarily or what Google knows about your search patterns and profile preferences.

One excellent example of just how much personalization is possible to carry out in search and how valuable this feature has become is a search experiment that Google is carrying out on a limited basis. For those who choose to take part in it, Google securely links their Gmail data to search and, when logged into their Google Account, searchers are able to see on Google.com, emails, files uploaded to Google Drive, and Calendar Events that contain the information they seek. At the same time, the search feature within Gmail, itself, benefits from the shared data of the person's search pattern that is brought in from Google.com and searches within Gmail begin to feature the same, fast, predictive text and pre-loading of results that we are familiar with on the Google.com page.

The seamlessness of Google Now and the positive way it has been received highlight two things in search. First, it now works invisibly. In his 2012 "Update from the CEO" Google CEO, Larry Page, outlined his vision of search describing just that: "I have always believed that technology should do the hard work—discovery, organization, communication—so users can do what makes them happiest: living and loving, not messing with annoying computers!...People shouldn't have to navigate Google to get stuff done. It should just happen."

Second, Google+ plays a pivotal role in identifying connections between people. This means that it is also central to the relation detection part of the process of semantic search. Google will always work hard to discover relationships between people and websites, intention, and outcome in search, but having a Google+ profile with a sizeable amount of data to work with is always an advantage.

Again, this is something Larry Page talked about in his "Update from the CEO":

> If you're searching for a particular person, you want the results for that person—not everyone else with the same name. These are hard problems to solve without knowing your identity, your interests, or the people you care about.... Google+ helps solve this problem for us because it enables Google to understand people and their connections.... This kind of next-generation search in which Google understands real-world entities—things, not strings—will help improve our results in exciting new ways. It's about building genuine knowledge into our search engine.

Having an active presence in Google+ is, inevitably, part of the new search engine optimization techniques. Businesses can have pages with significant ability to connect and interact that is similar to those of personal profiles. This is no coincidence. The interaction provides a rich tapestry of connections that then directly inform semantic search.

Google's search engine associates attributes and facts with named entities, and when it comes to local search, it associates addresses and websites as well. Much of the basic SEO activity at semantic search level involves having sufficient data in social media profiles and linking everything so that Google understands the associations.

Your Google+ page, for instance, should be linked to your company website, as we discussed in Chapters 4 and 5, and the rel=publisher tag should be used. Your company's staff who have personal profiles and blog on your company website should be linked to the blog posts using the rel=author tag. Your various social media network profiles like LinkedIn should point to both your website and your other social network profiles. In short you should be building an indexable map of your connections as a professional.

For brick–and-mortar businesses there should be a listing in Google Places for Business (www.google.com/placesforbusiness/). The "connecting of the dots" that semantic search has begun to do so well should be done first by yourself, your SEO agency, or your in-house SEO team.

The habitual "six degrees of separation" we cite as an example of the shrinking of the world, in a semantic search web becomes ever smaller. The connections that unite us then increase exponentially. Being able to pierce the personal search bubble that semantic search can generate so easily and increase the visibility of your digital properties requires a content marketing net that has to be cast far and wide.

Widening the digital footprint cast by your company or brand does not just make good marketing sense, it also makes perfect SEO sense.

The reason I went into such depth in this chapter regarding how semantic search works to index unstructured data is not just because it helps us understand how Google works, which then makes it clearer how to provide unstructured data in a Google-friendly way, but because it also helps us understand what Google is likely to do next.

The subject of where semantic search is heading and how to best take advantage of the knowledge to improve your website ranking in Google search is something we address in detail in the next chapter. The bridge to it is provided, however, by the next section where we look at how the content we create matches up to end-user intentions in search and Google's understanding of the search query.

Content, Intentions, and Search Queries

When Google looks at a search query typed in by a user, today it tries to understand the intention behind the query. As such it favors presenting content that has been crafted with user intent in mind. Considering the nebulous thread of connections Google maps to create entities and deliver results in search, asking for a focus on user intent at this stage seems like wishing for a crystal ball.

Far from it. Search is governed by analytics, and even the craziest intent behind a search query can be mapped and classified. All it takes is sufficient volume. The method behind the madness becomes apparent when I say that there are two types of content and just four types of search query, and content can be segregated into four subcategories—one each for each type of query.

With that approach in mind there is no end-user intent that cannot be successfully answered, and that also means that there should be no reason for a website with the proper type of content not to rank in search.

The two types of content are evergreen and seasonal.

The four types of query intent are navigational, informational, commercial, and transactional. Each of these poses a specific type of search query (a question) and has a specific type of content providing the answer. Figure 10.3 shows examples of informational search queries.

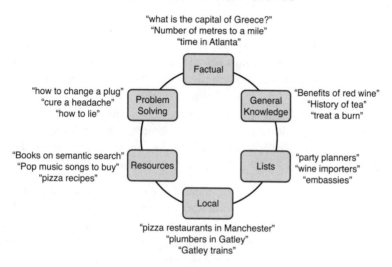

Informational Search Queries

Figure 10.3   *You can see how an informational search query can generate a huge number of subsets of queries based on specific user intent and needs.*

Evergreen content, as the name suggests, is content that is always going to be in demand. In that category fall "How-to" type articles that answer specific questions (for example, "How to start a business," "How to get my website to the first page of Google," "How to prepare for a job interview").

Seasonal content is pretty self-explanatory. It is content that has a seasonal or mainly seasonal appeal (for example, Christmas pudding recipes, suntan lotion advice, when to plant for a winter garden). Seasonal content is characterized by peaks and troughs, and unlike evergreen content it may well need updating before it can become current again.

Having seen the type of content that can be produced, we now also need to look at the different types of queries.

Navigational queries are probably the lowest value of query you can get. They are queries that ask for a particular website, so the opportunity to market anything to the end-user there is pretty slim, unless of course it is your website that is being looked for. Examples of the navigational type of query include "Facebook login," "Coca Cola," "Honda.com."

Informational queries are queries that can be best satisfied through articles, images, videos, infographics, podcasts, and any combination of these. Informational queries offer great opportunities for capturing attention, creating virality in your content, inspiring your audience, turning potential customers into brand evangelists, and educating the end-user. Examples of informational queries include "How do I nail a job interview?"; "How do I make my site rank high on Google search?"; "What's the capital of Greece?"

Commercial queries are queries that have a commercial intent. They are best seen as leads that come in through search but are not yet ready to be converted. They are a great way to initially establish a relationship with your target audience and then work to improve it. A good way to do this is by offering free information through email subscriptions, polls, surveys, feed subscriptions, or a series of specialized articles pertinent to your business expertise. Examples of commercial queries include "the price of second-hand BMW convertibles," "the specifications of Galaxy S4 smartphone," "the hidden cost of advertising online."

Transactional queries are the most valuable and competitive, and deliver the most targeted traffic. They are also the easiest to lose if you don't provide a simple and easy way to do business with you. The success of transactional queries depends on the overall user experience, the layout and setup of your website and its programming, and the number of steps the end-user needs to complete as he goes from first time visit to complete transaction. Here the elements of authority, reputation, and trust really come into their own. Typical examples of a transactional query include "Where can I buy a laptop," "Galaxy tab special offer," "used cars."

The reason we looked at all this is because search query types pose a question, and content provides an answer. At a certain level of detachment it is easy to see that success in semantic search requires you to have content on your website that provides answers to posed questions.

It sounds simple. It isn't. Predicting possible search queries and accurately answering the intent behind them by providing detailed content that does just that takes time, effort, and money. It can be done, however, and "doing it" here demands a plan that looks at your business as a whole, takes into consideration your content creation strategy and your content creation plan, and then aligns your company's or brand's content creation with search query intent.

Accurate search query intent research follows specific steps:

- **Search query intent behind the keywords.** Keyword research still has a place, but now it must take part within the broader context of search queries and search query intent.

- **Social mention of search queries.** Use your own digital assets plus online social media profiles, online surveys, questionnaires, and onsite polls to help mine search query intent within a social media context.

- **Owned assets log query.** If your website has a search function (and most websites do) querying the log files of that function will give you a wealth of information on what your site visitors are looking for exactly when they search your website, what pages they found, how long they spent there, and where they went next.

- **Focus groups and brainstorming.** Don't discount the ability of small, informal, offline "blue sky thinking" sessions to deliver the kind of value you need in terms of real search insights. Away from the constraining space of a search box, offline sessions can frequently provide helpful search query intent insights.

The moment you are able to use your website content creatively to answer search query intent you will find that you receive steady traffic to your website, across all of Google's search verticals.

Search Query Intent Preparation Checklist

It takes a lot of planning and organization to succeed in the semantic web. Typically all of this takes place long before we get to the execution. At times it feels like you are having to second guess those who look for your products and services, but this is not the case.

Semantic search is heading toward the point where a search engine is more than just a search engine. It is a prediction engine and a trust engine all rolled into one. It can predict with accuracy what the searcher wants before she knows she wants it, and then it can deliver content that can be trusted.

The preparation checklist builds on what you have learned to date to help you create a web presence that is totally relevant, ranks high on Google search, and continues to rank high with time.

- Detail all the ways you have at your disposal that allow you to research keywords, search queries, and query intent.

- Explain how you will map the query intent that your research uncovers to your company or brand values and your content creation activities.

- Describe the current division between evergreen and seasonal content in your content creation plan.

- Explain what reporting mechanism you have in place that allows you to capture search query intent and end-user sentiment on your website and in the social media network platforms where you maintain a presence.

- Detail all the digital assets you have networked (your website, your presence on Facebook, LinkedIn and Google+ etc.).

- Explain how you propose to help Google search create a clear understanding of what your business is about, where it's at, and what it does exactly.

- Explain if you use any of the approved semantic search marking on your owned digital assets. If not, why not? How do you intend to compensate for not using it? If yes, where and how do you measure effectiveness?

- Explain the process through which an entity is formed and assess whether critical omissions in your content creation strategy provide unintentional blind spots.

- Explain how you propose to monitor success in semantic search marketing and what contingency plans you have in place if the metrics do not provide the picture you expect.

- List the four types of search query and then ascribe a percentage value to each one that reflects your target audience. Explain how you came by your conclusion.

11

The Four Vs of Semantic Search

The secret to semantic search can be summarized in four words: volume, velocity, variety, and veracity. These are Big Data components, and semantic search is a Big Data manifestation. Unsurprisingly, it is governed by various combinations of these four Big Data components that hold as true for SEOs promoting a website as they do for a business or a brand promoting specific content.

In this chapter you learn exactly how the four components of semantic search impact the tools you use and the SEO practices you implement.

Volume

We talk about semantic search without much considering what it really is. The fact that there is a "search" function of some description that's designed to find and present results to queries stops us thinking too deeply about the entire process of asking questions and finding answers.

The Web is data. Search is data. Search queries are data. And at the point of asking a question and looking for some answer our search behavior also becomes data. What's more, at that point the Web, search, and search queries all interact, producing fresh data that also must be taken into account when delivering a question.

When the Evil Queen gets online and asks the question "Google, Google, on the Web, who is the fairest of them all?" the answer relies not just on the data that exists but also on the behavior of everyone else who has asked this question.

Google search, in a way, is a mirror of what we search for. Its autosuggest feature, with some minor adjustments, reflects what people across the Web are typing into Google search in relation to specific questions. Its results are informed, in part by the Click Through Rate (CTR) of the people who asked the same or a similar question and then clicked on the suggested results that came up as an answer.

Those results are filtered, in turn, by the behavior of those who clicked on them and left within a few seconds, considering them as either the wrong answer or a poor quality answer.

Semantic search makes "sense" of all this because sufficient indexing, classifying, and processing power has been assigned to the task. Semantic search is Big Data or at least an application of Big Data heuristics applied on a truly massive scale. As such it is bound by the same four dimensions of volume, velocity, variety, and veracity as any other Big Data application.

Volume is about taking massive amounts of raw data and doing something meaningful with it. Turn 12 terabytes of tweets created each day into improved product sentiment analysis. Convert 100 billion monthly searches on Google into autosuggestions and search results that provide clearer answers.

Volume helps Google become smarter because it helps the search engine understand how we search, what we search for, and what we do once we carry out a search and have the results displayed for us. Google voice search, to use only one example, has been "fed" over 230 billion words, drawn from direct queries, to teach it how to better recognize spoken speech.

Volume also helps at a much smaller scale with semantic search SEO techniques. You need volume, for instance, in your Google+ responses to help boost the social signal generated by your posts in that environment. You need volume in the sharing of your content to increase your website's reach and authority ranking. You need volume in your content creation to be able to generate the right level of subject-specific depth and expertise that Google search loves. Volume is also present as a requirement in the number of followers in your social media profiles and in the visitors who come to your website each month, if either of these two is to be taken seriously.

As a matter of fact, volume appears to be a requirement right across the board of activities you need to engage in to be noticed in the new, semantic web. Much of this chapter is a slightly more formalized statement of what we have been covering in detail until now. By restating it here through the perspective of the four Big Data components it helps in the creation of better strategy and planning when it comes to achieving greater visibility on the Web through improved rankings in search.

Here's how volume translates across the tangibles in your digital properties:

In Content   Volume is necessary both in the length of posts and the frequency of publishing content. Google now looks at a post's length as a measure of how "serious" the publisher is about the content provided. Tainted by the 300-400 word length of the past that produced millions of spam pages and websites, length is now something you need to definitely keep in mind. Similarly, Google's freshness algorithm prioritizes fresh content over content that's been there for a long time as being more timely and of greater relevance. This is not to say that content that's either short in length or "old" is now totally worthless. The guiding principle is, always, value to the end user as determined by relevance to a search query. If something can be said succinctly in 250 words, working it up to a post double that size is unlikely to win you any favors either with Google or online visitors.

In Social Media Profiles   Volume in the number of followers of social media network profiles is used as a rough-and-ready signal to gauge trust and influence. A large number of followers becomes a persuasive perceptual signal of the profile's validity and apparent trust by those who see it. The caveat here is that quality continues to be a strong determinant. Acquiring half a million followers in a social media network who are inert is practically of the same value as if you had none. Engagement continues to be a vital metric for success in social media.

In Social Interaction   Volume is necessary in creating a strong social signature. It is definitely needed where weak social signals such as +1s in the Google+ social network, or Likes in Facebook are concerned. It is also needed to boost stronger social signals such as reshares and social media network comments. Interaction is different than engagement. When someone engages with you on a social media network they initiate an online discussion which can go on for some time and may even involve others who take part in it. Interaction, usually, does not require any such discussion. Content is usually "approved" by way of Liking it or adding a +1 to it, or it is re-shared because it fits in with the re-sharer's subject expertise. The more interaction you get by way of +1s, Likes, re-tweets and reshares, the better, particularly if you can consistently deliver high numbers on all these.

In Social Media Engagement   Engagement has become just about the only metric that matters when it comes to social media interaction, and volume is present in that as well. A high number of engagers from a particular subject matter or interest denotes depth of engagement while a high number of engagers from across the board denotes breadth of engagement. Either way volume is required in both cases. A social media profile that has breadth and depth is considered to be both trustworthy and highly influential. It's worth remembering that engagement is measured by the number of comments, their length and persistence, whether they are one-off or the beginning of an online dialogue and so on.

In Website Traffic   Volume of traffic to a website is, of course, one of the aims of SEO. It is also a ranking signal in Google search, particularly when the volume of traffic is further refined by the behavior of those who constitute it. Put more plainly, 10,000 people who visit your website in one day and stay for a few seconds each are not the same as 3,000 who stay for over eight minutes, access more than one page, leave comments, and reshare your content in their social media network following.

In Mentions Across the Web   Frequently referred to as co-citation, mentions of a website, service, or product in direct relation to a website are noted and can trigger the ranking of the website for relevant search queries even when there is no apparent link-related or keyword activity associated with that search query on the website. Volume in the instances of co-citation is a signal that Google uses increasingly in the semantic web.

In Links   Volume in links leading to your website is not new of course. What is new is that Google now looks closely at the link signature in an attempt to stump out the gaming of its algorithm through link farms, bought links, and links that have been acquired in a nonorganic way. A large number of high-quality links from websites that are trusted and directly relevant to your sector increases the confidence that Google has in your website.

In User-Generated Content   Comments made on a blog post on your site provide greater weight in terms of keywords, interest, and, depending on your choice of commenting system, social media exposure and extra traffic. The more user-generated content you have on each page of your website, the more likely it is to rank high for those pages on related search queries. User-generated content, by way of comments on blog posts, adds to the depth of content of a particular web page and helps increase its authority and value. Although user-generated comment is similar to engagement in a social media network environment, it takes place on your own website and is not considered to be part of your website's "social signal," unless there are permalinks in the comments that can be reshared.

I hope I made the point here on the importance of volume across every SEO-related activity. Figure 11.1 creates a visual representation of the principle. If we consider that data across the Web is signified as individual dots, each of which is a data point, volume is signified by a proliferation of data points, all of which are visible to semantic search indexing.

Volume

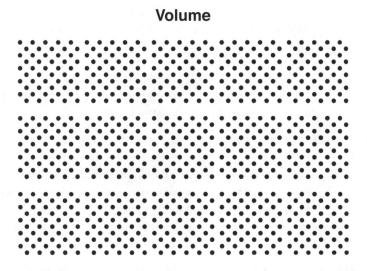

Figure 11.1   *Volume requires a proliferation of our data nodes (or data points) across the Web.*

Velocity

The need for speed is not just something felt by Maverick in the 1986 blockbuster movie, *Top Gun*. It is also something that is felt right across the Web. As a matter of fact the concept of speed, or rather, velocity and the Web were made for each other. Digital just makes everything faster, and faster, and faster. And then it keeps making it faster. Being able to crawl terabytes of data as it happens and display results of a sports event right on search, or an earthquake, is what velocity in search is all about.

The problem of velocity in data is not that it has to be caught in time to be of use but that it also has to be classified quickly so that it can be indexed and served in search. Any public relations executive who has had to deal with a breaking social media disaster for his company or brand will tell you that velocity is a nightmare. It compounds every possible issue you can imagine by several orders of magnitude and Google is developing a fresh suite of tools to help cope with it.

In a Big Data setting velocity refers to the speed at which critical data comes in and has to be dealt with. Semantic search is particularly challenged by velocity and, like volume, it is present in each one of the tangibles in your digital properties that is used to determine ranking:

In Content   Velocity looks at the speed at which content is produced. Most companies and brands, of course, do not have a dedicated newsroom given over to producing content for the Web. Nevertheless, even at the much more sedate pace of production that most companies and brands can manage, velocity is a factor that shows whether there are peaks and troughs, what drives them, how they fit in with the nature of your business and your website, and the search queries that they are designed to answer. Seasonal business or specialist business can find themselves propelled to the first page of Google for content designed to answer an increasing volume of similar search queries. A piece of content that's gone viral and suddenly gets spread fast across the Web displays velocity in its reach that begins to be taken into account when it is being ranked in Google's search.

In Social Media Profiles   Velocity in the growth of a social media profile, that suddenly gets a massive influx of followers, leads to a sudden amplification of its social signal and influence. Velocity can also be applied to the spread of interaction of posts within that profile (the familiar accumulation of +1s, Likes, and re-tweets). A post that produces a lot of reshares and other interactions acquires its own velocity, which then impacts the content being reshared and the status of the social media profile it came from.

In Social Interaction   Interaction with the content shared from social media network profiles can be of a slow-burning, cumulative sort that gradually gets you a number of Likes, +1s, and reshares, or it can explode into a wildly growing instance of a social media network post that's gone viral. The moment velocity is applied to a social media profile its reach and influence grow and so does the strength of the social signal it generates, the same social signal that is considered as a ranking factor when it comes to content and your website showing up in Google's search.

In Social Media Engagement   Velocity, when applied to engagement, is an incredibly strong signal because it shows specific intent that frequently produces content that can be indexed in its own right and therefore can be assessed. A social media network post that elicits 4,000 comments within a short space of time, some of which are pretty wordy, is a clear signal of something important happening on the Web.

In Website Traffic   Velocity in website traffic refers to the rate at which traffic to a website grows. This is a clear indication of the popularity of a website, or a sudden rise in popularity. It can signal a sudden topicality to a website's content in relation to a peak in specific search queries.

In Mentions Across the Web   The rate at which co-citations arise across the Web can also play a significant role in ranking. Velocity here is also important as it can become part of the signal that a website is now topical thanks to specific content.

A good example of this are websites that cater to recurring sports events like the World Series in baseball or the FIFA World Cup in football.

In Links   Velocity in links signals a jump in the number of websites linking to yours. This is usually a negative signal that Google looks at closely as it is usually the mark of an intensive link-building campaign and can signify the creation of many low-quality links with the intent to game search. Google knows what an organic link signature looks like. A surge in links here can be potentially damaging if it falls foul of Google's filters.

In User-Generated Content   Velocity in user-generated content is a surge in content created by users on a website. This is a clear signal of engagement with the content of the website, and it can significantly help the particular page where the interaction is taking place rank higher due to increased attention and, arguably, increased value generated by the comments. It can also help the website raise its profile.

Just as a sudden acceleration in incoming links to a website can send up a lot of red flags for Google so does an increase in any of these dimensions present a problem of verifying whether the boost is artificial (and therefore potentially spammy) or real. The social elements are a lot easier to verify for Google than links so although alarm bells may ring it is usually an acceleration of link building that presents real issues.

Velocity in data nodes, figuratively shown in Figure 11.2, makes the data-mapping a lot more challenging.

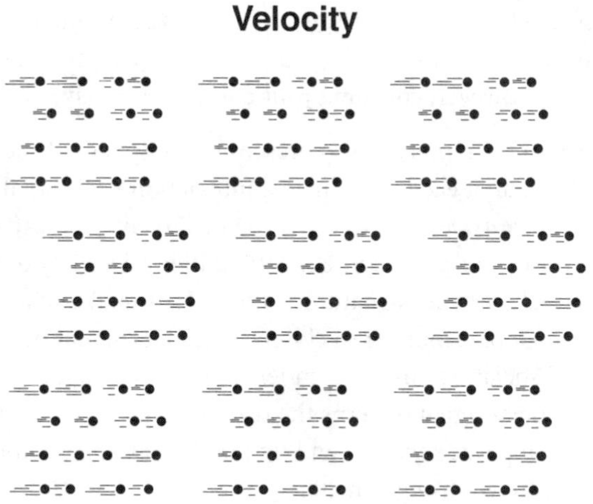

Figure 11.2   *Velocity across the semantic web is marked by an acceleration in the increase and spread of data. The data points of our example suddenly become much more mobile and energetic.*

Variety

Variety is not just the spice of life, but also of data. Just like Big Data is any kind of data, both structured and unstructured, so does semantic search have to take into account every type of data. As a matter of fact one of the biggest challenges lies in pulling together structured and unstructured data such as text, sensor data, audio, video, click streams, log files, and more. New insights are found when analyzing these data types together, examining their relational aspects so that entities can be created.

Variety is a constant in search regardless of whether you are a search engine indexing the Web at large or a marketing manager charged with creating content for your website.

In Content   Variety in content means that content is created in many different formats, including audio files created for podcasts, video, images and infographics, PDF documents, and text files. Structured and unstructured data are all part of what a website that is being run properly should have in its content output. It also means that a certain level of uniqueness in the content itself or, at the very least, in its synthesis is required.

In Social Media Profiles   When it comes to the output of a social media profile, there are a number of options to choose from. Pictures, video, and text come into it here. The appeal of each type of content that constitutes the variety factor in this area depends primarily on the targeted audience, the type of social media platform, and the kind of message being broadcast in the medium. The degree to which you use variety in the content shared in social media profiles determines whether your profile achieves depth (becomes a relatively specialized profile with great engagement on certain subjects) or breadth (you reach a large number of people, the majority of whom, however, consume your content passively).

In Social Interaction   Variety is also present in the sphere of social interactions. While the social signal of each social media interaction is different in its strength, with +1s, Likes and re-tweets, for instance, being largely deprecated by Google because it is hard to work out the intent behind them, a variety of social interactions creates a largely organic signature to the social signal that aids in the ranking of a website. With Google looking so closely at the link signature of websites and since it collects all social signals it can index, it would be logical to assume that there are natural social signal patterns the search engine is aware of. By the same token any unnatural pattern would send up red flags as an attempt to game search, and that is likely to have strong penalties.

In Social Media Engagement   No matter how good your social media engagement is there is bound to be a large variety in the nature, length, and type of responses that are generated as a result. Again, in search, this is probably a desirable thing with variety across engagement signaling authenticity in the engagement.

In Website Traffic   Even the biggest websites have traffic profiles that dip and rise unexpectedly. Variety in traffic profiles in all likelihood contributes to an organic signature in a website's overall profile. It is probably hard to ascribe a value to website traffic variations, though, again, since Google is aware of traffic profiles across the Web, it is highly unlikely the search engine has not found a way to correlate them to websites that work organically and are of high quality and those that are not.

In Mentions Across the Web   When it comes to co-citation, variety is used as a means of verification of authenticity. If suddenly a website's name is mentioned across the Web with the exact same sentence describing what it does and what it sells, it is, in all likelihood, an attempt to game search. Something similar happened with the British website of Interflora over Valentine's Day, with hundreds of paid advertisements appearing in regional newspaper sites in the United Kingdom. Each of these had a similar phrasing and heading, all pointing to Interflora. Google not only delisted Interflora over the infraction, but it also penalized each of the regional newspaper websites by dropping their PageRank (PR) to zero. Considering that some of them had PR8 (i.e. a highly trusted score) at the time, this was a major loss to their online credibility.

In Links   Variety is probably nowhere more important than in the link signature it creates of links pointing to a website. In the past links became one of the easiest areas of search to game. An entire link economy grew around the buying and selling of links, and entire businesses were set up as link farms or link networks designed to help a website rise in search by acquiring high quality links. Google clamped down on all of this. Its successive Penguin updates have targeted websites and networks that display an unnatural link signature. Variety in the way your links are growing is then a desirable characteristic as it safeguards your website from being unfairly penalized.

In User-Generated Content   Just like social media engagement, user-generated content on your website also inevitably displays variety. Again this is a necessary quality with repercussions likely to occur if, for whatever reason, a page on your site suddenly receives hundreds of user-generated comments of about the same average length and syntax.

Variety is probably the hardest of the four Big Data attributes to measure. It is safe to say, however, that Google is actively looking at the variety patterns of online activity, and semantic search takes them into account. An indication of how variety looks across the data nodes on the Web is given in Figure 11.3.

Variety

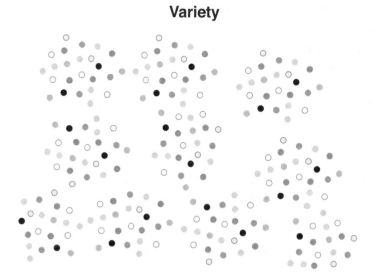

Figure 11.3 *Variety across the Web means that the data points that are indexed by semantic search that are relevant to you display variety in their makeup, emergence, and even speed of distribution.*

Veracity

Information, as it stands at the moment, is easy to fake and hard to verify. If you or I are looking up something on the Web and want to be sure of its authenticity we have one of two choices: A) Only consume information from sources we trust (and there is no real guarantee that at some point we will not make a mistake), or B) Undertake the burden of verifying the information, doing our own due diligence, as required.

The problem with A is that the Web then becomes a limiting and limited space for us, just as it is exponentially expanding, and the problem with B is that we hardly have enough time to consume the information we need to consume, as it is. If we are forced to verify information each time, as well, we may as well opt for choice A and only consume it from the same handful of sources we have always used.

Semantic search, with its capability to gaze at the entire Web and hunt up relational associations no matter how tenuous, can act as a verification engine. It can do this because it can actually become very detailed, very fast in a totally machine-scalable way.

For instance Google can use its knowledge of websites and their history to see how a website got where it is now, whether it was something else before, and who is associated with it in the social media network spectrum. Who are they really? Who associates with them? What is their activity? What is the website's activity? What is the website's reputation score (based on real reviews)? What is the authority and trust score of the people whose profiles are associated with the website?

It can do that quickly and return results of trusted or verified websites. The moment Google search does that it will have made the transition from search to verification engine with an implied vote of trust in each of the 10 results it gives on its top page.

As the variety and number of sources of information grow, establishing trust in the results returned by search becomes paramount. Google is aware of the need for just such a verification process. When Google+ first got under way one of the issues that first cropped up was the need for real names that were to be used on the network. Former CEO of Google and current president, Eric Schmidt, has publicly said on a number of occasions that Google+ is an "identity service." What he most probably meant by that is that Google initially used the network and its insistence on real names to kick-start the verification process of websites, information, people, and sources through links based on real people with real profiles.

In Content   Veracity in content is always necessary. How you show it is another matter. Wherever research or figures are cited it is good to be able to link back to the source. This helps Google's semantic search verify the information you are citing by crawling the link and accessing the source. The real value of your content lies in its original point of view and its practical value, so linking to sources of information that complete the content of a website page you have created helps to increase the usefulness of your own page. It also helps mark it as being trustworthy and verifiable, and this tends to give a little boost when it comes to ranking in search.

In Social Media Profiles   Social media profiles that are fake, have fake names, or, even worse, are used only for marketing purposes and therefore have fake usage patterns are mapped and can adversely affect any website they are associated with. Veracity in social media profiles is a requirement that's only become necessary with semantic search and its ability to map relational connections across the Web. Certainly, within the Google+ network authorship should be taken advantage of with the rel=author tag, for people, and the rel=publisher tag, for businesses and brands, being used to verify real interaction and claim ownership of content.

In Social Interaction   There is a real, inherent difficulty in determining intent behind social media interaction. A Like or a +1 could mean any number of things that range from merely acknowledging a piece of content to bookmarking it for a later time to actually liking it. The uncertainty that exists over this kind of interaction naturally makes it hard to take into account as a strong signal. The same cannot be said for more active and genuine forms of interaction such as reshares and commenting, both of which require a lot more thinking before the action takes place. Veracity in social media interactions generates a readable social signal that Google can use when it determines the ranking of a website.

In Social Media Engagement   Engagement in a social media environment is probably one of the most difficult things to fake, not least because the time and effort required to do it is so intensive that it produces no savings in time and effort and therefore makes no economic sense. There is no saving in cost. As a result it is relatively easy for Google's search engine to verify the veracity of engagement (i.e. comments and mentions) in a social media platform, particularly if that platform is YouTube or Google+, both of which are its properties. The admonition here is against creating marketing personas in a social media network in the belief that they will somehow help by creating a sense of engagement with your posts. You shouldn't do it, and they won't help if you do.

In Website Traffic   An old SEO technique was to use a bot to artificially drive up the number of visits and traffic to a website making it look popular with search engines. This approach has not worked for some time now. I mention it here to stress how important it is that your website's traffic signature be a natural one. These days, those who try to fake it are caught fast.

In Mentions Across the Web   Co-citation (the mentioning of brand or business in relation to a particular service or product) is one SEO activity that is prone to some abuse. In a transparent web where semantic search sees everything and is busy constantly enriching its mapping of data points across the Web, fake co-citations are going to be uncovered before too long. The obvious solution here is to work to create the kind of content and the kind of online presence that absolutely amazes anyone who sees it and makes it more likely that they will mention your website in their comments or, even better, link to it.

In Links   Real links is what Google wants. There is such a thing as an organic link signature that refers to the average pattern of link generation that a normal website should expect to have. Anything that falls outside the average will most likely raise red flags with Google. Veracity in your link creation requires some care on who you link to and who links back to you.

In User-Generated Content   In the days before commenting systems were embedded on websites, websites had their own native systems (and some still do). It was standard practice for website owners to kick-start the conversation by putting a few fake comments on their site. Needless to say this is a self-defeating practice. It is preferable to have a handful of comments or none at all than to try to fake user-generated content. It will be discovered.

Veracity and trust are major concerns on the semantic web. As search becomes more hidden in its mechanics we rely more and more on its results, and having confidence in how those results are derived is crucial.

Google knows that. There is a vision, as we see in the next chapter, of search acting as our own personal trust engine. Whether we get to that outcome any time soon is not certain, but at least you know that semantic search looks at verifying data, and when it finds it lacking it demotes that website in ranking.

This should also guide your activities when it comes to marketing the content of your website and its promotion on the Web. The need to transparently link back to original sources and provide proof of data is shown, conceptually, in Figure 11.4.

Veracity

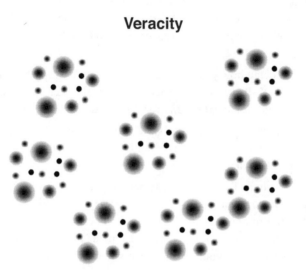

Figure 11.4 *Data points that are verifiable are clearly defined. Those where the data is uncertain are much fuzzier. Semantic search has the potential to eventually act as a verification engine.*

The Four Vs Preparation Checklist

The four Vs of semantic search truly constitute the "secret sauce" to what makes a search engine optimization strategy successful. The thing to remember with semantic search and the new SEO is that it is not just difficult to game results, it is also unwise.

The transparency of connections that is happening at an ever more refined rate only means that eventually any unnatural promotion of a website that has ranked in search will be discovered. Google has a vested interest in algorithmically verifying results. That means that the refinements and improvements are unlikely to ever let up.

The following checklist helps you take advantage of the momentum created by the volume, velocity, variety, and veracity as you craft your search engine optimization strategy and content creation plans.

- Explain how you plan to have a sustainable flow of content across all your digital properties and how you will ensure that there is sustainable activity across all your social media platforms.

- List all the means you have in place that monitor traffic to your website and activity across your social media platforms and then explain all the activities you can engage in the moment you see a social media post has gone viral or a particular page on your website has become popular.

- Explain in detail how you think each of the four Vs impacts your current set of website promotional activities. List all potentially problematic areas and explain what can or should be done to fix them.

- Detail how you plan to monitor variety in your content production, what impact you expect it to have, and how you think it best reflects your audience reach aims.

- Detail how you will ensure veracity across all your social media connections. In particular, list all the different ways you will use to help establish the authenticity of the content you post on your website. Then detail how you will use your social media profiles to establish a depth of expertise in your business that will then help your content socialization aims.

- List all the challenges that are in operation across your business or brand setup that prevent you from using any of the four Vs properly. Pay special attention to insurmountable limitations, such as human resources, budgets, hierarchical approval, lack of skilled content creators, anything in short that will compromise your ability to promote your digital properties properly in the semantic web. This list is also the first step to outlining your own strengths, weaknesses, and potential problems in digital marketing.

- Explain how you plan to kick-start social interaction and foster greater engagement across your digital properties when engagement levels are low or nonexistent.

- Detail all the different types of content that you create under variety, and explain how each of these reflects your online identity and company or brand values. Then explain how it meets target audience expectations and how you assess that.

- List all the tools you use to monitor social media interactions. Then list all the social media network and website platforms you use to create a digital presence. Use a dot map with each of your online presences representing a distinct data point. Around them list the tools you use for each one and then link the data points that connect to each other. See if there is any part of the picture forming that is unclear.

- Explain how you will keep an eye on link growth to make sure you avoid creating any unnatural link pattern that raises any of Google's flags.

How Search Became Invisible

From its inception to the present, search has been getting smarter and smarter. One effect of this inexorable march to intelligence is that as it grows in complexity search becomes less and less obtrusive, less and less visible. What is great for users who simply get to discover what they want without much apparent effort makes it harder for marketers who want to optimize their website to rank high in search.

In this chapter you learn how the implications of a smarter search affect your marketing and what you can do to make sure your website ranks well not just now but also in any future incarnation of semantic search.

The Disappearing Search

All technology follows a predictable development arc. First it appears. It's a little bit clunky. Its form is obvious and obtrusive. Its performance less than sterling. Yet, it is used because it's new, does something useful, and enables us to do more with less. Then it gets more complicated. The simplicity of the past tends to disappear. We have to learn to use it in more complicated ways to get from it the usefulness of what it could do. Then it gets more refined. It begins to improve to the point that we cannot consider being without it. Then it "disappears."

The final stage of course is a sleight of hand. Technology at that point does not really disappear, but it becomes ubiquitous and therefore it is largely invisible. If you think about computers, for example, you will see what I mean. We carry, today, in our pockets, more computing power than was used to put a man on the moon in the 1960s. We use it to send and receive emails, check bank accounts, make payments, make the odd voice call, check the news, keep abreast of specific developments (through alerts), write notes, record ideas, take pictures, shoot videos, and connect to the wider world we are part of.

Yet we hardly think about it. We do not stop and marvel any longer at the power of computers. At the fact that we possess one. At the ability of what we have to do an incredible number of calculations per second. Computers and computing power have become so easy to use that we only become aware of them when things go wrong—we become aware of the fact that we have a computer when the motherboard dies and suddenly our window into the digital world, the conduit through which we lived our digital life, is closed. We become aware of the form and shape of our phone when the connection fails or the service is out. We become aware of it only when the impact of its failure makes itself felt on our lives. We miss appointments, can no longer receive emails on the go, and cannot get updates from our favorite social network. And then we realize how complicated it all actually has become.

Search is no different. When search was synonymous with a little text box on Google.com it was easy to understand that there was some kind of index, somewhere, and results needed to be placed in it, somehow, and then assessed and ranked to show up in response to search queries.

That made both the act of searching and the act of search engine optimizing different, if not necessarily easier. End-users were prepared to spend a little time delving into the results. Search engine optimizers knew what would work in terms of promoting a website. More importantly, however, both parties knew where their two respective domains—that of those looking for something and the one of those who were offering an answer to that search—came together.

It was on Google search and its "ten blue links."

The convergence of intent both from those who sought to discover something on the Web and those who had something to offer to be discovered created a common interface both parties could understand. A website had to somehow be "placed" in search (or Google's index more precisely) in order to appear and when it was placed there it had to be classified according to the content it had. This is no longer quite the case.

The busy businessman on the go talking to his Android phone and asking for best restaurant locations is hardly aware that in the intervening microseconds before he gets an answer back Google has checked his location, looked at its store of local knowledge, checked his Google account profile and his social connections, looked at reviews of local restaurants any social connections of his may have made, and looked at independent reviews of local restaurants on independent review sites. It has assessed the restaurants it has found based on its knowledge of the quality of their websites and the behavior of those who visit them, and it has drawn up a short list to show on search, based on distance from where the businessman is.

That kind of complexity boggles the mind. Yet the interface has become incredibly easy to use. The speed at which the results are delivered is hardly possible with the old, statistically driven search where Google's algorithm would have had to run text analysis on the keywords (recognized, probably imprecisely through speech) and then delivered restaurants in downtown Philadelphia that had been optimized for the words "best restaurant" when our businessman happened to be in London, UK.

To deliver speed in search Google now needs to be able to understand the search query "best restaurants" the same way a person would. The answer will be different depending on the location and time. A search made at midnight, for instance, when most restaurants are closed is no good if you are looking for one that is actually open.

This kind of detail, which is the strength of semantic search, also shows the issues currently associated with it from a search engine optimization point of view. Instead of focusing on a first page of Google listing for a keyword that will certainly stroke the ego but may not really deliver much value in terms of real business, optimization now is a challenge that addresses the question: "How can I get all the relevant information about my business indexed by Google?"

And Google search is now diversified into

- Google desktop search
- Google mobile search
- Google Voice search
- Google Now
- Google Local search
- Google personalized search (Google search + Your World)

- Google incognito search
- YouTube
- Google universal search
- Google Maps

As a matter of fact "search" these days is a complex blend between so called "horizontal" and "vertical" search results. Horizontal search results are pulled from across the entire web (as the name suggests) while vertical search results are pulled from a much more narrow, specialized index and Google has a few of them:

- Google Maps with Google+ Local
- Google Flight Search
- Google Shopping
- Google Videos
- Google Images

All of these now become the interface through which a business needs to meet its customers by supplying an answer to their queries. I realize that suddenly the task of search engine optimization no longer appears to be "easy" nor can it be said that it will be cost-effective.

A business chasing search in all those verticals is probably burning up so much money doing so that it makes it difficult to get a decent return on investment (ROI) from those it reaches. And all this is before we get into the tricky part of conversion where those who do end up on your landing page or do come across your business now need to be convinced to become your customers.

Search technology is changing at an incredible pace. Keeping up with it so that it can be "helped" to promote a website is an incredibly time-consuming and, for a business, a frequently disruptive task. It is also unnecessary. Search engine optimization, to really work for you in a semantic search world, now has to do what it was advised to do in the past: "Help you identify the values your business stands for and then promote them."

This affects the way you will have to deal with an SEO agency (if you outsource your SEO) where the changes in its work will include

- Transitioning from purely technical SEO to strategic SEO
- Understanding what your business tries to achieve as opposed to what it says it wants to do
- Aligning its work with your other promotional efforts
- Aligning its work with all in-house marketing efforts
- Informing and training your marketing team

- Closely communicating with sales
- Helping increase your brand equity
- Being part of your social media outreach
- Being part of your wider content creation strategy
- Being part of your wider content marketing strategy

If you change the words "SEO agency" to "in-house SEO team" you get the same resulting list. Search engine optimization now has to be part of a company's DNA. Because it affects so much of a company's success it can no longer be the sole responsibility of a single person or even a single department working in isolation.

Every time I have seen this happen I have also seen a looming crisis in search marketing that will have to be addressed in the near future as sales dip, brand equity takes a hit, and a company's or brand's market share nosedives.

Each search vertical now requires its own, distinct search engine optimization methodology, and just looking at a handful of them helps you understand the commonalities involved.

Google desktop search requires you to

- Target keywords.
- Target search queries.
- Target local customers.
- Create specialized, high-quality content.
- Make it more likely your content is linked to.
- Make your website easier to index through its structure and programming.
- Make sure your website offers a great end-user experience through the studied use of layouts and interface.
- Ensure that you adhere to all the detailed SEO principles regarding spam and duplicate content.
- Claim content authorship of content through the use of rel=author and rel=publisher tags.
- Have a strong social signal.
- Make use of structured data markup wherever possible.
- Work across different types of content.
- Work with different content channels.

Google mobile search requires you to

- Have a responsive website that can work on mobile devices (or have a mobile site).

- Provide local details and data where appropriate.
- Focus on the end-user experience. (Design, styling, visual impact, ease of navigation, and load times are all critical on mobile devices.)
- Create strong brand recognition that converts to sales.
- Create solution-oriented content that users on the go need to access.
- Use mobile keywords that are usually slightly different from desktop search ones.
- Have an app or two to capture mobile audience attention.

Google Voice search requires you to

- Be aware of content that matches natural language usage as opposed to keywords.
- Have location settings and data on your website.
- Work to link up all the data points of your digital presence and include as much relational information as possible to inform Google's semantic search index better.

To illustrate the magnitude of the problem consider that Google's Voice search index for American English gets over 230 billion words drawn from direct, real-life search queries used by searchers. A Voice search index now needs to be built for each language and each spoken version of a language. Figure 12.1 shows some examples.

Example Query

images of the grand canyon

what's the average weight of a rhinoceros

map of san francisco

what time is it in bangalore

weather scarsdale new york

bank of america dot com

A T and T

eighty on walker road

videos of obama state of the union address

genetics of color blindness

Figure 12.1   *This is a list of popular, real Voice queries sent to Google's Voice search. Google's Voice search is a location-aware service producing different answers to the same search query performed from different locales. It is worth noting here that in this sample of popular search queries natural language patterns predominate rather than keywords.*

Google Now is Google's predictive search engine. It preloads information on the mobile device of the user in the background based on

- Location
- User preferences
- Available data

It is designed to give you the information you need through a narrow understanding of your current needs.

There never has been much value in withholding information from Google search that could help your business be found. By the same token it has not always been easy to provide all the relevant information Google needs. The main reason for that is usually the way search engine optimization has been handled in the past where the person (or agency) responsible for it has been either compartmentalized or kept at arm's length and has been given very little to work with beyond the immediate needs of marketing.

Something I cannot stress enough is that the fundamental change in the transition from good old-fashioned Boolean search to semantic search lies in creating transparency in your company or brand data to Google's search. Rather than "telling" search what you think it needs to get you in front of those looking for your services, show it who you are and what you do.

This is a change in mindset that transforms Google from an "adversary" of sorts that had to be managed, coerced, and somehow convinced to rank your website and serve it in search to an ally interested in the same things you are: giving the right answer to those who ask a question through search.

As search "disappears" and becomes a ubiquitous service that people use, it becomes all the more critical to be conscious of the need to provide everything about a business or a brand that will help Google "connect all the dots."

Trust Agents in Semantic Search

It was the father of the Web, Sir Tim Berners-Lee, who at the first World Wide Web Conference in 1994 articulated the semantic web as a vision where the Web was no longer just a place consisting of documents for humans to read but one that included data and information for computers to manipulate. The semantic web was described back then as a Web that would be capable of actionable information. A place where the logical connection of terms established interoperability between systems.

The search that Tim Berners-Lee envisioned back then was one composed of individual search agents that could work seamlessly in the background getting you what you wanted as answers rather than web pages that you would need to trawl through yourself.

Anyone using Google Voice and getting the answer to the question "Who is the fastest man in the world?" or "Get me pictures of whales" will think that we are just about there. Those who have experienced the predictive magic of Google Now will think that we probably have even exceeded that original vision of search. Both these views would be wrong.

One thing that Tim Berners-Lee visualized in that context was a search intelligent enough not just to retrieve the answers to our questions but also to verify the sources and practically guarantee the results. Veracity, the fourth of the four Vs around which Big Data and semantic search revolve, is also the trickiest one to get right and, computationally speaking, the most complicated.

Verifying any kind of source is predicated on search being able to correctly determine its history. Provenance, the when, where, who, and the conditions under which data originated, has now become a key requirement to a range of applications, search included.

The pay-off here is that the moment semantic search succeeds in its capability to provide verification of the content it serves automatically on request, we will reach an entirely new metric for conversions and an entirely new level for competition on Google search.

The understanding is that, in this instance, to show up at all is a win because the website and by inference the business behind that website have been vetted. Their reputation has already been checked and the verification process itself transparent. What that is worth to a business can only be left to speculation.

The direction is clear enough to suggest that you should already be taking measures to ensure that there is a hierarchical progression in search that goes from social media visibility to reputation building to search engine content marketing to high visibility in search.

Semantic search goes through incremental leaps where it uses the information it discovers to "calculate" fresh values for the websites that contain new information, as shown in Figure 12.2.

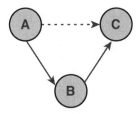

Figure 12.2   *The way trust in results is calculated in the semantic web is predicated on the ability of search to uncover relational connections and measure the authority of each one. In the example above, for instance, an inference as to the veracity of data point A through data point C, which is unknown to it, can be made via data point B.*

Semantic search implies that a reputation algorithm will always be on, and it will work roughly the same way that real-life reputation systems work. If, for instance, you wanted to know if you could trust someone to do business with, you would, most probably, ask your professional network of contacts.

The chances that someone among them will know or have heard about the person you are suggesting to do business with is pretty high. The reason it's high lies in context and relevance. If you are in the business of breeding horses, for example, most of your business network connections will be relevant to your business. Similarly most of the people you will want to do any kind of business with will come from a background that is at least tangential to what you do. There is simply no way someone totally unknown to you and your network of business contacts will pick you out of the blue.

This real world vetting mechanism is based on the Small World theory where connections from any point to any other point are no more than a few degrees of separation away. This also has a direct correlation to the online world because it's based on the idea that you can vet reputation by inferring it from sources. Because semantic reputation networks are essentially social networks, they have the Small World properties of connection with the added ability to cache values that have been worked out before and make the calculating process even faster.

Facebook's Graph Search is based upon the very same principle. The expectation behind it is that the social connections generated by Facebook's one billion strong membership base will enable Facebook to put in place a search that unearths relevant information with a high trust value.

In each case trust is treated as a measure of uncertainty in a person or a resource. Specifically, given an ambiguous path where the outcome of a relational transaction such as the purchase of an object can have either a positive or a negative outcome, having trust in a person is defined as a measure of the confidence that the person will take the action that leads to the positive result. Reputation is what you call the measure of that trust.

The point is that in the semantic web trust and reputation are machine-driven and scalable and governed by the Small World theory. The incremental steps that govern this calculation are shown in Figure 12.3.

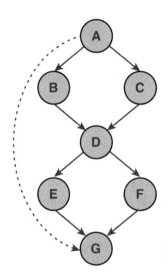

Figure 12.3   *In the semantic web trust and reputation can be inferred algorithmically with previously calculated values being cached to speed up the process where a large number of jumps are required before data point A can assess the reputation of data point G.*

For a business or brand building reputation online, the "plan" begins to become clear:

- Form as many relevant social connections as possible.
- Leverage your staff to become connection points in the social network marketing of your business through the establishment of authorship.
- Create transparency that will allow the establishment of trust and reputation parameters quickly.
- Establish a multilateral web presence that makes full use of the social dimension.

There are a couple of things of deep value to take away from the approach Google has taken on the assessment of trust, authority, and reputation. First, the assessment itself in semantic search is capable of nearly infinite segmentation. It allows for the establishment of trust in specific subjects, for instance, which means that just as in real life a personal profile that is trusted for recommendations in coffee brands will not enjoy the same level of trust if it switches to, let's say, cars. The same holds true for websites, companies, and brands. Second, trust and reputation are not forever. They hold true as long as there is a freshness in activity. Again, just like real life, the moment a personal profile stops being active or a company or brand stops producing content, their hard-earned trust and reputation begin to evaporate.

In the semantic web what ultimately works for a company or brand is "mindshare." The moment you have managed to create a strong enough brand equity and a powerful enough presence in search and a widespread enough presence in social media networks you have succeeded in gaining the minds of your target audience.

When it comes to creating online profiles that will benefit you in semantic search, a long-term plan that is sustainable always works better than a short-term one that produces only temporary results, and for that you need to have the kind of online marketing and search engine optimization activity that produces continuity, flow, context, and relevance.

Continuity and Flow, Context and Relevance

Over the writing of this book I also engaged in a fair amount of travel as I had speaking engagements with corporate staff across Europe. As so often happens in these circumstances, questions that get asked as we talk about search and social media begin to worm their way into my writing.

Semantic search is different enough to actually warrant a different mindset to successfully deal with. The practical side of SEO, however, is not that far removed from what has always happened. You still need to create content. You still need to have social media profiles. You still need to get linked to. You still need to have your content reshared. You still need to have your brand or website talked about. You still need to pay attention to all those details that in the past made up SEO.

So what is really different? The difference lies in thinking. Whereas in the past you worked from a single digital presence (usually your company or brand website) and established authority through it with SEO methods designed exclusively to promote it, now you are using the same methods to help Google's search engine understand what your business is really about, who you are, who your staff are, and what you all do.

It's a little scary, right? It involves giving up control of your content, identity, and reputation and working hard to make sure that as it travels across the Web from the "owned" digital space that you control to the "shared" one that you don't it does not morph into something other than you intended.

Control of your content, now, has to be done differently. Just because the sharing of your message and the interaction on your posts do not happen in your own digital space does not mean that there is no mechanism for maintaining control.

To understand this and the impact of semantic search we need a definition for reputation. Cambridge University researcher Wilson Roberts in a 1985 paper defined reputation as a "characteristic or attribute ascribed to one person by another. Operationally, this is usually represented as a prediction about likely future behavior. It is, however, primarily an empirical statement. Its predictive power depends on the supposition that past behavior is indicative of future behavior."

Leaving aside the "past cannot accurately predict the future" aspect of this, which at any rate, we cannot do anything about, what is cogent to us in the semantic search world is the fact that reputation is an attribute that can be ascribed, read, and transferred to environments other than the one it occurs in.

Reputation is the aggregation of sophisticated social opinion that is implicitly applied to the notion of trust as a means of complexity reduction in any kind of relational exchange. Reputation can be ascribed to a person, a community, or even a company or brand. The important thing to bear in mind about reputation is that although reputation owners are directly affected by the reputation score that accumulates, they have no control over how the reputation values are accredited. This, however, does not mean that the ascription process cannot be influenced.

If your company develops a highly valued reputation, for instance, of delivering high-quality goods at reasonable prices, it is valued because reputation is seen as something totally independent of you. You cannot buy it or coerce it in any way, and it therefore has real value because it is considered to be an independent metric of whether you can be trusted to deliver high quality at a reasonable price.

The way this reputation can be developed further and protected from any future tarnishing that could impact on your company's business is through the studied application of four elements that directly impact the building of your identity. These are

- Continuity
- Flow
- Context
- Relevance

Examining the relation of each of these to identity gives you the controls you need to safeguard your reputation in a semantic web.

Continuity

Continuity states that since the reputation value of a person, brand, or business is based on the perception of who they are, any change of identity or any departure from the value system that informs that identity then risks damaging their reputation. When GAP spent $5 million revamping its logo in 2010 the social media firestorm that blew up was directly linked to the implication that it was also changing its values.

By failing to involve all stakeholders in its decision GAP sent a message that created mistrust, cost the company a lot of money, and forced it to U-turn.

The impact of reputation through shared stakeholder values for a company or brand affects

- The efficiency of your marketing
- Consumers' desire to buy your products or services
- The credibility of your communications
- The morale of your employees
- The confidence of investors in your company
- Journalists' disposition to report positively or negatively about you
- People's willingness to hear your side of the story

It is obvious then why any change of identity, even a perceived one, can have such a serious impact on the reputation of a business.

Continuity in who you are, your identity, is established through consistently projected values and ideas in

- Your website
- Your social media network content
- Your social media network commenting
- The various formats of content that you produce
- Your advertising

Flow

Flow is the halo effect that allows you to use reputation values you have established in one area, to gain trust and have an impact on another. Gucci, to name but one example, has used that successfully to incrementally transfer the company's reputation for styling to a wide variety of products that now includes perfumes, dress accessories, and footwear. We can see a similar effect with the Porsche Design label that also applies its unique approach to design across a wide variety of products that include automobile engines and watches.

Flow succeeds only when the move to leverage gained reputation is

- Incremental
- Tangential
- Delivering on its promise

Context

Context is key. All reputation is contextual. It is accrued through the establishment of nine key elements that define the context of any kind of interaction in a specific environment (whether that is the Web at large, a community, a social network, or a forum). They are the same whether you are a person, company, or brand, and they are

- Role fulfillment (what you are expected to do within that context). Here we see the need for defining the role of a person marketing in a social media network. We also see the necessity for defining exactly what a company or brand does, which then helps us understand how to best communicate this.

- Relationship (how do you interact with the other participants in the community). The way a person, company, or brand interacts with the other members of the community the interaction takes place in defines areas of commonality and shared values.

- Knowledge (how knowledgeable are you in your interactions and how do you show that knowledge in a way that helps establish trust in you). Fairly self-explanatory.

- Experience (how experienced you are in the subjects you discuss or promote and how you prove that). This is linked to all of the previous points.

- Credentials (what are the credentials that make you an authority in your subject, be that SEO or styling). Porsche Design, to use an example, enjoys an instant advantage on perceived quality because of its credentials.

- Competence (how capable are you at accomplishing a task). This is a perceptual value that accrues over time, with consistency.

- Honesty (how you establish that you can be trusted to deal with).

- Favorability (an element of reputation that hinges on popularity, perceived status, or charisma). Within a social network, for example, a person with a large number of followers has a better chance at enjoying a good reputation than someone who has just two. Similarly, Porsche Design (because of its association with the iconic sports car) is more likely to be trusted than, say, XYZ Design despite the fact that both companies might be equally talented in design.

- Faith (refers to the likelihood to accept as true, something that one has been told by someone who is believed to be trustworthy). Individuals, companies, or brands that have worked on establishing the previous eight points find that they can then make the transition to other areas and enjoy the halo effect, because people are more inclined to have faith in them.

To quantify just how different semantic search's effect is on marketing, consider that in the pre-semantic web all of the above had nothing to do with the SEO team and, maybe even, marketing. They were perhaps the domain of PR or whoever was responsible for branding. In the semantic web, however, there is a transparency of connections, which also leads to the transfer of attributes like reputation that then informs ranking in search.

Relevance

Relevance, the final aspect of the equation, refers directly to the connecting point between all of the activities that are behind the elements detailed in this section the moment that they result in a website showing up in search as the answer to a relevant search query.

There is a truism about search in that Google has, from the get-go, said that successful search engine optimization is not about analyzing the changes in Google search and repositioning to meet them, but about delivering a consistency in real value in as authentic a way as possible.

That admonition was easy to ignore in the past. Creating consistency in value or trying to understand just what was meant by "authenticity" and deliver it was a lot harder than engaging in keyword-filled content creation, link-building strategies, and the buying of social network followers.

It's no longer the case. Success in dominating the search of tomorrow, actually starts today. And there are no shortcuts you can take.

The Search of Tomorrow

Writing a book is a funny business. As much as I, as a writer, want to inform and get across some of the enthusiasm I feel for the subject, I am also aware that what readers really want are the insights, the "secrets," the takeaways they can't find elsewhere that will give them a competitive advantage over everyone who has not yet read the book.

That's fair enough, and in this last section we look at what those secrets just might be. Like in most industries the "secret sauce" is not actually that secret. Most of the time, it's fairly obvious but poorly understood, yet its application can truly make a difference.

Although there are no shortcuts in semantic search, some activities will not only give you greater return for the effort than others but also keep on providing greater return for as long as you engage in them.

The list is short. The actions associated with it, unfortunately, aren't.

- **Get into Google+.** Don't just create a profile there and spam the stream with one post after another with your content. Think about what you really want to say and say it. Use a company or brand page and, again, post content that in its totality actually has a meaning that goes beyond a series of links posted there for Google to index. We frequently talk about the online "conversation." Unlike a real conversation that forces us to listen to the person we are conversing with, and respond in a way that allows us to establish our identity and authority, the online conversation is fragmented and asynchronous. Yet, in its totality it is exactly that: a conversation. It has to "listen" and "respond" in a way that addresses conversation subjects and helps establish a sense of identity, trust, and reputation. If your "conversations" on the Web do not fit into an overall picture, then you may want to rethink your approach a little.

- **Connect all of your online activities.** Your company or brand is not just a Google+ profile, a Facebook page, or a LinkedIn account. Interconnect everything, where you can by cross-linking profiles and establishing the same contact details. This is part of you casting a wide net. If, for instance, I came across a single tweet from you, I would then be able to follow the trail, understand who you are, get what you do, and land on your website.

- **Authenticate everything.** Link up your Google+ profile to content you produce through the rel=author tag, attributing authorship to you. Use the rel=publisher tag for multiblogger blogs. Use the Google+ sign-in for pages on your company website that have comments enabled so that Google+ members can use that to log in and leave comments. Work, in short, on an ever-expanding basis, to help Google access as much information about your website, your services, and who you are as possible. This is a question of trust and reputation, and in the Web of the future it is going to be even more critical than it is right now.

- **Be authoritative.** You did not go into business to be a copycat. Whatever business you happen to be in, whatever you may be doing, you are fired up each morning by the singular desire to do it differently and better than anybody else. To back it up you have ideas, experience, skills, knowledge, and passion. Work, at every single opportunity you get, to get this across in the online and offline world. This, more than anything else, will help you gain the kind of traction that semantic search is built for.

When the semantic web was first visualized everyone thought that it would be highly structured in the way it held information and totally machine-readable.

They thought it would be maintained by people who have a vested interest in the Web being transparent and readable.

People only have a vested interest in their part of the Web being more transparent and readable than any other, so a people-maintained semantic web is not a reasonable expectation any longer. What's more, given the amount of information that is being created every second through interaction, whether this may be in the resharing of information, comments left on blogs or made on social media network platforms, photographs and videos being uploaded to the Web, or the repurposing of existing content into something else, there will always be more unstructured data on the Web than structured data.

This totally transforms the problem of semantic search from simply how to index an ever-expanding lode of data to how to accurately classify data that is being indexed and is unstructured.

The four activities mentioned previously address this very issue. By following them, thinking about them, constantly improving on them, and working to optimize them, you are essentially future-proofing your business or brand from any change in the way ranking is calculated in semantic search.

Success in search really depends on having your content in front of what is increasingly a totally customized first page of Google. The only certain way of doing that is to create fantastic content that is widely talked about, linked to, and reshared across social networks. The only way to consistently do that is to mine your passion and transfer it into the digital image you create, on the Web.

The Final Semantic Search Checklist

This is the end of the book, though far from the end of the road. Semantic search is just beginning to take hold. The web technologies we use are only now beginning to have direct impact on our everyday lives at a really deep level. The Web is becoming, again, a much more exciting place, buzzing with the kind of energy that I have not seen since the closing years of the last century.

Future-proofing your website against the rapid onslaught of changes in semantic search depends upon your willingness to put everything you have learned into use. The predominant idea here is that the Web is, again, the great equalizer. A website with just a few pages of strong content and a great drive behind it, powered by hot passion and cool ideas, has as much chance of succeeding as a multinational corporation that throws its teams of marketers at the Web and produces slick content that costs tens of thousands of dollars.

The final checklist here is to make sure you are that website, irrespective of your marketing budget and company size.

- Examine how you project the image and values of your company or brand across all your digital properties and list all the different ways that help build authenticity. Remember that being authentic is part of your online identity-building efforts. It helps in terms of veracity, which is a primary driver of semantic search indexing. It goes a long way toward establishing reputation and trust.

- Detail what else you could do that would help your company or brand develop a unique voice in the online space. Include in this all your social media channels as well as the digital media that you own and control (such as your company website, social media profiles and blogs).

- Explain all the different ways you use to create stakeholders out of your staff and customers so that they more fully participate in the online dialogue with your business.

- List all the different digital properties you own, from websites to online profiles in social media networks, video broadcast channels, and sites where you release press releases or guest blog. Check to see that each is as interlinked to the others as much as possible.

- Detail your mobile content marketing strategy. Explain how you link that up to your desktop content marketing strategy, paying close attention to the connecting points that help your audience transition between the two.

- Detail how you create transparency for search in every aspect of your business. Explain how you will scale this as your business activities grow and your business interests expand.

- Detail how the concepts of identity and flow, context and relevance are expressed in each of the online activities your company or brand undertakes. Explain how you assess the effectiveness of that and what measures you can take to fix potential issues that come to light.

- Explain how you measure trust and reputation in your business. What processes do you have in place that allow you to continually monitor progress here, and what measures can you take if you discover that things are going wrong and you now need to rectify them?

- List all of the Google services where you have a presence. This should include Google Maps, Google Local, YouTube, Gmail, and Google+ as well as any monitoring services like Google Alerts, Google Webmaster Tools, and so on.

- Explain exactly how you plan to make the passion that drives your business the primary motivation behind the development of its marketing, services, and online presence. List all the challenges that you face in achieving this and explain how you plan to overcome them.

Bibliography

Much of the research on semantic search derives from academia, where the need to index closed sets of data (that is, university files) and retrieve information from them quickly and accurately has always provided rich ground in which to experiment. This book is based on this research, which now, thanks to Google's move to semantic search, is finding its way into the mainstream. Paradoxically, while putting together a practical book about search, I had to spend months studying academic research papers about information retrieval. Google, which is central to so many practical things we do on the Web today, started out as a Stanford University information-retrieval project organized in 1996 by two students: Larry Page and Sergey Brin. The rest, as they say, is history.

Chapter 1

Brandy E. King, "Boolean vs. Semantic Search Interfaces: Which Work Better?" Paper presented at: Special Libraries Association, Baltimore, MD, http://www.sla.org/PDFs/2006CPKing. pdf (2005).

Duygu Tümer, Mohammad Ahmed Shah, and Yıltan Bitirim, "An Empirical Evaluation on Semantic Search Performance of Keyword-Based and Semantic Search Engines: Google, Yahoo, Msn and Hakia," in ICIMP '09 Proceedings of the 2009 Fourth International Conference on Internet Monitoring and Protection (2009).

B. J. Jansen and A. Spink, "Sponsored Search: Is Money a Motivator for Providing Relevant Results?" *IEEE Computer* 40(8) (2007): 52–57.

Wordtracker, "The Top 200 Long-Term Keyword Report," *The Wordtracker Report* (February 5, 2008).

Y. Y. Yao, "Measuring Retrieval Effectiveness Based on User Preference of Documents," *Journal of the American Society for Information Science* 46(2) (1995): 133–145.

Maria Teresa Pazienza, Noemi Scarpato, and Armando Stellato, "Application of a Semantic Search Algorithm to Semi-Automatic GUI Generation," in Proceedings of the Eight International Conference on Language Resources and Evaluation (2012).

Miranda Miller, "53% of Organic Search Clicks Go to First Link," Study, http://searchenginewatch.com/article/2215868/53-of-Organic-Search-Clicks-Go-to-First-Link-Study (2012).

T. Berners-Lee, J. Hendler, and O. Lassila, "The Semantic Web," *Scientific American* (May 17, 2001): 34–43

A. Deitel, C. Faron, and R. Dieng, "Learning Ontologies from RDF Annotations," Workshop in Ontology Learning, Seventeenth International Joint Conference on Artificial Intelligence, Seattle, CEUR-WS (2001).

Nesrine Ben Mustapha, Hajer Baazaoui Zghal, Marie-Aude Aufaure, and Henda Ben Ghezala, Combining Semantic Search and Ontology Learning for Incremental Web Ontology Engineering, International Workshop on Web Information Systems Modeling (WISM 2009) (Held in conjunction with CAiSE 2009), Amsterdam (2009).

Chapter 2

N. Stojanovic, L. Stojanovic, and R. Volz, "A Reverse Engineering Approach for Migrating Data-intensive Web Sites to the Semantic Web," 17th World Computer Congress, Kluwer Academic Publishers (2002): 141–154.

Khadija Elbedweihy, Stuart N. Wrigley, and Fabio Ciravegna, Evaluating Semantic Search Query Approaches with Expert and Casual Users, The Semantic Web – ISWC 2012, Lecture Notes in Computer Science 7650 (2012): 274–286.

Markus Holi, "Crisp, Fuzzy and Probablistic, Faceted Semantic Search," Dissertation, Aalto University School of Science and Technology Faculty of Information and Natural Sciences (2010).

Devis Bianchini, Valeria De Antonellis, and Michele Melchiori, "Service-Based Semantic Search in P2P Systems," ECOWS '09, Seventh IEEE European Conference on Web Services (2009).

Vera Hollink, Theodora Tsikrika, and Arjen de Vries, "The Semantics of Query Modification," in Proceedings from RIAO '10 Adaptivity, Personalization and Fusion of Heterogeneous Information (2010).

B. J. Jansen, D. L. Booth, and A. Spink, "Patterns of Query Reformulation During Web Searching," *Journal of the American Society for Information Scienceand Technology* 60(7) (2009): 1358–1371.

C. Bizer, T. Heath, and T. Berners-Lee, "Linked Data - The Story So Far," *International Journal on Semantic Web and Information Systems*, Special Issue on Linked Data (2008).

Chapter 3

Kevin Kelly, "1000 True Fans," http://www.kk.org/thetechnium/archives/2008/03/1000_true_fans.php (2008).

Miriam Fernandez, Vanessa Lopez, Marta Sabou, Victoria Uren, David Vallet, Enrico Motta, Pablo Castells, "Semantic Search meets the Web," 2008 IEEE International Conference on Semantic Computing (2008).

R. Renuga, G. Sudhasadasivam, V. Sakthivel, C. Kathiravan, S. Arun Kumar and R. Shanmugam (2009), Semantic Search Using Content Based Search Technique with Spread Activation Technique, *International Journal of Recent Trends in Engineering* 1(2) (May 2009).

Christoph Mangold, *A Survey and Classification of Semantic Search Approaches, International Journal of Metadata, Semantics and Ontology* 2(1) (2007).

E. Motta and M. Sabou, "Next Generation Semantic Web Applications," 1st Asian Semantic Web Conference, Beijing (2006).

P. Cimiano, P. Haase, and J. Heizmann, "Porting Natural Language Interfaces Between Domains—An Experimental User Study with the ORAKEL System," in Proceedings of the International Conference on Intelligent User Interfaces (2007).

C. Rocha, D. Schwabe, and M. P. de Aragão, "A Hybrid Approach for Searching in the Semantic Web," in Proceedings of the 13th International World Wide Web Conference 2004 (2004).

Chapter 4

Eric Schmidt, "Transcript on G+ as Identity Service," https://plus.google.com/+AndyCarvin/posts/CjM2MPKocQP and https://plus.google.com/+AndyCarvin/posts/2y7vqXBtLny (2011).

Jon Brodkin, "Google+ Says Truman Capote, Dead 28 Years, Now Writes for the NYT," http://arstechnica.com/business/2012/12/google-says-truman-capote-dead-28-years-now-writes-for-the-nyt/ (2012).

A. J. Kohn, "Incorrect Authorship," https://plus.google.com/115106448444522478339/posts/2LARVL1MoLD (2012).

Tim Berners-Lee, *Weaving the Web: The Original Design and Ultimate Destiny of the World Wide Web*, HarperBusiness (2000).

Rehab Alnemr, Stefan Koenig, Torsten Eymann, and Christoph Meinel, "Reputation and the Web," *Journal of Theoretical and Applied Electronic Commerce Research* (2010)

Mark Sweney, "Facebook Quarterly Report Reveals 83m Profiles Are Fake, *The Guardian*, http://www.guardian.co.uk/technology/2012/aug/02/facebook-83m-profiles-bogus-fake (2012).

U. Shardanand and P. Maes, "Social Information Filtering: Algorithms for Automating "Word Of Mouth," in Proceedings of the Conference on Human Factors in Computing Systems (CHI95), Denver, CO (1995): 210–217.

R. Schmalensee, "Advertising and Product Quality," *Journal of Political Economy* 86 (1978): 485–503.

P. Kollock, "The Production of Trust in Online Markets," in *Advances in Group Processes* 16, eds. E. J. Lawler, M. Macy, S. Thyne, and H. A. Walker, Greenwich, CT: JAI Press (1999).

John Dunn, "The concept of 'trust' in the politics of John Locke," in *Philosophy in History*, eds. Richard Rorty, J. B. Schneewind, and Quentin Skinner, Cambridge University Press (1984).

Susan D Boon and John G. Holmes, "The Dynamics of Interpersonal Trust: Resolving Uncertainty in the Face of Risk," in *Cooperation and Prosocial Behaviour*, eds. Robert A. Hinde and Jo Groebel, Cambridge University Press (1991).

Y. Bakos, "Reducing Buyer Search Costs: Implications for Electronic Marketplaces," *Management Science* 43(12) (December 1997).

Chapter 5

G. Zacharia, A. Moukas, and P. Maes, "Collaborative Reputation Mechanisms in Online Marketplaces," in Proceedings of 32nd Hawaii International Conference on System Sciences (HICSS-32), Maui, Hawaii (January 1999).

Robert Wilson, "Reputations in Games and Markets," in *Game-Theoretic Models of Bargaining*, ed. Alvin Roth, Cambridge University Press (1985).

Zoltan Gyongyi, Hector Garcia-Molina, and Jan Pedersen, "Combating Web Spam with TrustRank," in VLDB '04 Proceedings of the Thirtieth international conference on Very large data bases - Volume 30 (2004).

J. M. Kleinberg, Authoritative Sources in a Hyper-Linked Environment," *Journal of the ACM* 46(5), Stanford University Computer Science Department (1999): 604–632.

R. Guha and Ravi Kumar, Propagation of Trust and Distrust, IBM (2004).

P. Kollock, "The Production of Trust in Online Markets," in *Advances in Group Processes* 16, eds. E .J. Lawler, M. Macy. S. Thyne, and H. A. Walker, JAI Press (1999).

Thanh Tran, Philipp Cimiano, Sebastian Rudolph, and Rudi Studer, "Ontology-Based Interpretation of Keywords for Semantic Search," Institute AIFB, Universität Karlsruhe, Germany (2007).

P. Cimiano, P. Haase, and J. Heizmann, "Porting Natural Language Interfaces Between domains—A Case Study with the ORAKEL System," in Proceedings of the International Conference on Intelligent User Interfaces (IUI) (2007): 180–189.

A. Popescu, O. Etzioni, and H. Kautz, "Towards a Theory of Natural Language Interfaces to Databases," in Proceedings of the International Conference on Intelligent User Interfaces (2003): 149–157.

Y. Lei, V. Uren, and E. Motta, "Semsearch: A Search Engine for the Semantic Web," in EKAW 2006, LNCS (LNAI) 4248, eds. S. Staab and V. Svátek, Springer (2006).

A. Bernstein and E. Kaufmann, "GINO—A Guided Input Natural Language Ontology Editor," in ISWC2006. LNCS 4273, eds. I. Cruz, S. Decker, D. Allemang, C. Preist, D. Schwabe, P. Mika, M. Uschold, and L. Aroyo, Springer (2006).

Malcom Gladwell, *The Tipping Point: How Little Things Can Make a Big Difference*, Black Bay Books (2002).

Chapter 6

I. Poggi and F. Dérrico, "Cognitive Modeling of Human Social Signals," in Proceedings of the 2nd International Workshop on Social Signal Processing, (2010).

D. Sánchez, "Domain Ontology Learning from the Web," Thesis in Artificial Intelligence, 2007.

M. A. Aufaure, R. Soussi, H. Baazaoui Zghal, and H. Ben Ghezala, "SIRO (2003) On-Line Semantic Information Retrieval Using Ontologies," in 2nd International Conference on Digital Information Management, IEEE Computer Society Press: 321–326.

N. Ben Mustapha, R. Soussi, H. Baazaoui Zghal, and M. A. Aufaure, "A Metaontology for Domain Ontology Enriching in an Information Retrieval System," in *Second Francophone Day of Ontologies*, ACM Press (2008).

N. Ben Mustapha, H. Baazaoui Zghal, and M. A. Aufaure, "A Prototype for Knowledge Extraction from Semantic Web Based on Ontological Components Construction," in 3rd International Conference on Web Information Systems and Technologies, Barcelona, Spain (2007).

K. S. Esmaili, H. Abolhassani, "A Categorization Scheme for Semantic Web Search Engines," in 4th International Conference on Computer Systems and Applications, IEEE Computer Society, UAE (2006)

D. Rose and D. Levinson, "Understanding User Goals in Web Search," in 13th International Conference on World Wide Web, ACM Press (2004).

Dimoklis Despotakis, Dhavalkumar Thakker, Lydia Lau, and Vania Dimitrova, "Capturing the Semantics of Individual Viewpoints on Social Signals in Interpersonal Communication," http://www.semantic-web-journal.net (2011).

Chapter 7

D. Sanchez and A. "Moreno, Creating Ontologies from Web Documents," *Recent Advances in Artificial Intelligence Research and Development* 113, IOS Press (2004): 11–18.

H. Baazaoui Zghal, M. A. Aufaure, and N. Ben Mustapha, "A Model-Driven Approach of Ontological Components for On-line Semantic Web Information Retrieval," *Journal on Web Engineering* 6(4), Special Issue on Engineering the Semantic Web, Rinton Press (2007): 309–336.

M. A. Hearst, "Automated Discovery of WordNet Relations," in WordNet: An Electronic Lexical Database, MIT Press (1998).

D. Faure and C. Nedellec, "A Corpus-Based Conceptual Clustering Method for Verb Frames and Ontology Acquisition," in Workshop on Adapting Lexical and Corpus Resources to Sublanguages and Applications, 1st International Conference on Language Resources and Evaluation, Granada, Spain (1998).

Google, Official Blog, "Giving You Fresher, More Recent Search Results," http://googleblog.blogspot.gr/2011/11/giving-you-fresher-more-recent-search.html (2011).

Ali Khalili and Sören Auer, "User Interfaces for Semantic Content Authoring: A Systematic Literature Review," University at Leipzig, Institut fur Informatik, AKSW, Leipzig, Germany. (2011).

V. Lopez, V. Uren, M. Sabou, and E. Motta, "Is Question Answering Fit for the Semantic Web?" Semantic Web — Interoperability, Usability, Applicability 2(2) (2011): 125.

Rehab Alnemr, Stefan Koenig, Torsten Eymann, and Christoph Meinel, "Enabling Usage Control Through Reputation Objects: A Discussion on E-Commerce and the Internet of Services Environments," *Journal of Theoretical and Applied Electronic Commerce Research, ISSN 0718-1876*, Electronic Version 5(2) (August 2010): 59–76.

Chapter 8

J. Sabater, "Trust and Reputation for Agent Societies," Ph.D. thesis, Institut d'Investigació en Intelligéncia Artificial (IIIA), CSIC, Barcelona, Spain (2003),

J. Sabater and C. Sierra, "Review on Computational Trust and Reputation Models," *Artificial Intelligence Review* 24(1) (2005): 33–60.

R. Sandhu, "Lattice-Based Access Control Models," *IEEE Computer* 26(11) (1993): 9–19.

G. Silverman, *The Secrets of Word-of-Mouth Marketing: How to Trigger Exponential Sales Through Runaway Word of Mouth*, AMACOM (2001).

W. Streitberger, S. Hudert, T. Eymann, B. Schnizler, F. Zini, and M. Catalano, "On the Simulation of Grid Market Coordination Approaches," *Journal of Grid Computing* 6(3) (2008): 349–366.

O. Tafreschi, "Trust Building and Usage Control for Electronic Business Processes," PhD thesis, Technische Unversität, Darmstadt, Germany (2009),.

X. Zhang, F. Parisi-Presicce, R. Sandhu, and J. Park, "Formal Model and Policy Specification of Usage Control," *ACM Transactions on Information and System Security* 8(4) (2005), 351–387.

E. Maximilien and M. Singh, "Conceptual Model of Web Service Reputation," *ACM SIGMOD Record* 31(4) (2002): 36–41.

E. Maximilien and M. Singh, "Toward Autonomic Web Services Trust and Selection," in Proceedings of the 2nd International Conference on Service Oriented Computing, New York, 2004.

Chapter 9

Wang Wei, Payam M.Barnaghi, and Andrzej Bargiela, "The Anatomy and Design of a Semantic Search Engine," Research paper, School of Computer Science University of Nottingham (Malaysia Campus) (2009).

C. J. van Rijsbergen, "A New Theoretical Framework for Information, in *SIGIR*, ACM (1986).

W. Wang, P. M. Barnaghi, and A. Bargiela, "Semantic-Enhanced Information Search and Retrieval," in Proceedings of the 6th International Conference on Advanced Language Processing and Web Information Technology (2007).

S. Wasserman and K. Faust, *Social Network Analysis: Methods and Applications*, Cambridge University Press (1997).

H. H. Wu, G. Cheng, and Y. Z. Qu, Falcon-s: A Ontology-Based Approach To Searching Objects and Images in the Soccer Domain," in Proceedings of the International Semantic Web Conference (2006).

Chapter 10

Robert K. Merton and Elinor Barber, *The Travels and Adventures of Serendipity: A Study in Sociological Semantics and the Sociology of Science*, Princeton University Press (2004).

G. Madhu and Dr. A. Govardhan, and Dr. T. V. Rajinikanth, "Intelligent Semantic Web Search Engines: A Brief Survey," *International Journal of Web & Semantic Technology* 2(1) (January 2011).

S. A. Inamdar and G. N. Shinde, "An Agent Based Intelligent Search Engine System for Web Mining, Research," *Reflections and Innovations in Integrating ICT in Education* (2008).

T. Berner-Lee and M. Fishetti, *Weaving the Web*, Harper Collins Publishers (1999).

T. Berners-Lee, J. Hendler, and O. Lassila, "The Semantic Web," *Scientific American* (May 2001).

Adam Souzis, "Building a Semantic Wiki," *IEEE Intelligent Systems* 20(5) (September/October 2005).

Dieter Fensel, James A. Hendler, Henry Lieberman, and Wolfgang Wahlster, eds., *Spinning the Semantic Web*, MIT Press (2003). Foreword by Tim Berners-Lee.

Sebastian Schaffert, François Bry, Joachim Baumeister, and Malte Kiesel, "Semantic Wikis," *IEEE Software* (2008).

Chapter 11

Mohammed Kayed and Chia-Hui Chang, "FiVaTech: Page-Level Web Data Extraction from Template Pages," *IEEE Transactions on Knowledge and Data Engineering* 22(2) (2009): 249–263.

Amal Zouaq and Roger Nkambou, "Evaluating the Generation of Domain Ontologies in the Knowledge Puzzle Project," *IEEE Transactions on Knowledge and Data Engineering* 21(11) (2008): 1559–1572.

P. Pabitha, K. R. Vignesh Nandha Kumar, N. Pandurangan, R. Vijayakumar and M. Rajaram, "Semantic Search in Wiki Using HTML5 Microdata for Semantic Annotation," *IJCSI International Journal of Computer Science Issues* 8(3) No. 1, May 2011 ISSN (Online): 1694-0814 (2011).

L. Obrst, "Ontology and Ontologies: Why It and They Matter to the Intelligence Community," in Proceedings of the Second International Ontology for the Intelligence Community Conference, OIC-2007, Columbia, MD (November 28-29, 2007).

V. Raskin, *Towards a Theory of Language Subsystems*, Moscow State University Press (1971).

V. Raskin, "Script-Based Semantic Theory," in Contemporary Issues in Language and Discourse Processes, eds. D. G. Ellis and W. A. Donahue, Erlbaum (1986).

V. Raskin, C. F. Hempelmann, and K. E. Triezenberg, "Ontological Semantic Forensics: Meaning-Based Deception Detection," Paper submitted to the 23rd International Information Security Conference (SEC 2008), Milan, Italy (September 8–10, 2008).

Christian F. Hempelmann and Victor Raskin, "Semantic Search: Content vs. Formalism," Research paper, Purdue University (2009).

Chapter 12

Li Ding, Tim Finin, Anupam Joshi, Yun Peng, Rong Pan, and Pavan Reddivari, "Search on the Semantic Web," Paper, University of Maryland, Baltimore County (2005).

Youyong Zou, Tim Finin, Li Ding, Harry Chen, and Rong Pan, "Using Semantic Web Technology in Multi-Agent Systems: A Case Study in the TAGA Trading Agent Environment," in Proceeding of the 5th International Conference on Electronic Commerce (2003).

Amit Sheth, Boanerges Aleman Meza, I. Budak Arpinar, Chris Halaschek, Cartic Ramakrishnan, Clemens Bertram, Yashodhan Warke, David Avant, F. Sena Arpinar, Kemafor Anyanwu, and Krys Kochut, "Semantic Association Identification and Knowledge Discovery for National Security Applications," *Journal of Database Management on Database Technology for Enhancing National Security*, Special Issue (2005).

Index

S

FREE
Online Edition

Safari
Books Online

Your purchase of **Google™ Semantic Search** includes access to a free online edition for 45 days through the **Safari Books Online** subscription service. Nearly every Que book is available online through **Safari Books Online**, along with thousands of books and videos from publishers such as Addison-Wesley Professional, Cisco Press, Exam Cram, IBM Press, O'Reilly Media, Prentice Hall, and Sams.

Safari Books Online is a digital library providing searchable, on-demand access to thousands of technology, digital media, and professional development books and videos from leading publishers. With one monthly or yearly subscription price, you get unlimited access to learning tools and information on topics including mobile app and software development, tips and tricks on using your favorite gadgets, networking, project management, graphic design, and much more.

Activate your FREE Online Edition at
informit.com/safarifree

STEP 1:   Enter the coupon code: AVZWNGA.

STEP 2:   New Safari users, complete the brief registration form. Safari subscribers, just log in.

If you have difficulty registering on Safari or accessing the online edition, please e-mail customer-service@safaribooksonline.com